Television

Celebrities have come to increasingly dominate the media and its study in contemporary culture. Although acknowledged as part of this general rise in the importance of celebrity culture, television's specific forms of stardom have until now remained largely under-theorised. *Television Personalities: Stardom and the Small Screen* examines how television personalities function as commodities, and also function ideologically, thus relating them to issues of class, national identity, sexuality, gender and social history.

Television Personalities sets out a new way of considering televisual fame, arguing that it must be understood on its own terms, and thus establishing the television personality as a particular set of performers whose celebrity is constructed through discourses of ordinariness, authenticity and intimacy. The book is divided into three sections that trace the historical development of televisual fame from the 1950s through to the emergence of 'DIY' celebrity in the digital era. It examines the economics, aesthetics, production, histories, futures and ideological functions of the television personality across a range of examples, including:

- Benny Hill, Oprah Winfrey, Cilla Black, Simon Cowell, Ricky Gervais, Alan Titchmarsh, Jamie Oliver
- the stars of YouTube and television's smaller screens
- *Extras, Top Gear, The Naked Chef, The Weakest Link.*

Television Personalities is an original, indispensable guide for undergraduate and postgraduate students of media, television and celebrity studies, as well as those interested in digital culture more widely.

James Bennett is Head of Area for Media, Information and Communications at London Metropolitan University, UK. His work focuses upon digital, interactive television and television fame in the United Kingdom. He has published articles in *Screen, Cinema Journal, New Review of Film and Television Studies, Convergence* and *Celebrity Studies Journal*. He is co-editor of *Film and Television After DVD* (with Tom Brown, 2008) and *Television as Digital Media* (with Niki Strange, forthcoming, 2011).

Television Personalities is a wonderfully researched and critically invigorating exploration of fame as it variously plays out on the box, in the home, and through the hearts and minds of viewers that it reaches and affects. Bennett's intervention here is a major one: he recalibrates our understanding of the television personality, offers us new insights on television history and the television industry, and he finds skill, intimacy, and ideological complexity in what are the key sites and moments of broadcasting through the years. *Television Personalities* is going to be one of the defining texts in the fields of television, and celebrity studies. It is an outstanding piece of scholarship that is beautifully, accessibly written.

Sean Redmond, Editor of *Celebrity Studies* journal

In this useful, thoughtful book, Bennett investigates a crucial element that has gone missing from our current understanding of television: precisely how it participates in the production and consumption of celebrity. He explores the longstanding assumptions about how television stardom works, making the book essential reading for anyone interested in contemporary television.

Graeme Turner, Professor of Critical and Cultural Studies,
University of Queensland, Australia

Television Personalities

Stardom and the small screen

James Bennett

Routledge
Taylor & Francis Group

LONDON AND NEW YORK

First published 2011
by Routledge
2 Park Square, Milton Park, Abingdon, Oxon OX14 4RN

Simultaneously published in the USA and Canada
by Routledge
270 Madison Ave, New York, NY 10016

Routledge is an imprint of the Taylor & Francis Group, an informa business

Typeset in Galliard by
Book Now Ltd, London
Printed and bound in Great Britain by CPI Antony Rowe, Chippenham, Wiltshire

British Library Cataloguing in Publication Data
A catalogue record for this book is available from the British Library

Library of Congress Cataloging in Publication Data
Bennett, James.
Television personalities : stardom and the small screen / James Bennett.
    p. cm.
Includes bibliographical references and index.
1. Television broadcasting—Social aspects—Great Britain. 2. Television personalities—Great Britain. 3. Television broadcasting—Social aspects—United States. 4. Television personalities—United States. 5. Fame. I. Title.

PN1992.3.G7B37 2010

791.450'280922—dc22   2010012030

ISBN13: 978-0-415-48188-5 (hbk)
ISBN13: 978-0-415-48189-2 (pbk)
ISBN13: 978-0-203-84268-3 (ebk)

To my wife

Contents

PART III
The television personality system revisited:
Ordinariness and DIY fame   141

Illustrations

Table

Figures

Acknowledgements

This has been a book some years in the writing; my research on television personalities and television fame having commenced in 2001. Via some lengthy detours into work on digital culture – much of which informs Chapter 7 here – I have continued to work on this project for much of the last decade. Many friends, colleagues and family have endured me babbling and ranting about the topic, as well as prolonged absences from their company whilst I've completed the book. In various ways they've all contributed to my knowledge about television and television fame, offering clippings (thanks Eva!), programmes and personalities for exploration. I'm very grateful to you all.

Routledge has been a great publisher to work with and I would like to thank Natalie Foster for commissioning this work and guiding it through to completion, and Emily Laughton who was a fantastic source of support in gathering together the final manuscript and mastering the hoops to be jumped through. In the researching of the book, particular thanks should go to Els Boonen at the BBC Written Archives Centre for her invaluable support in exploring the historical background of this project. Also to Lauren Hayward-Gaynor who acted as an enthusiastic and inquisitive research assistant on the project: and for whom I hope feminism is no longer such a dull topic! Staff at the British Library were also a key source of information and support for this work. My thanks to Elizabeth Evans, Paul Grainge and Roberta Pearson at the University of Nottingham and James Walters at the University of Birmingham for the opportunity to trial run some of the material herein in a receptive and positive atmosphere. London Metropolitan's Communication Cultures and Media Research Capability Fund, and its able handling by Paul Cobley and Bill Osgerby in particular, generously supported this project in its early stages and provided useful feedback and advice on the archival research. The university's film and television group, particularly Paul Kerr and Mike Chopra-Gant, offered an excellent sounding board and a range of collegial criticisms that helped shape my ideas (including why bring together digital culture and television personalities!). I have also been extremely fortunate to receive thoughtful feedback from Karen Lury and Lynn Spigel in working on this material for different publications. Given the long period of time that this book has been written over, invariably small parts have appeared in previous publications, though substantially reworked in the context of this book. A version of Chapter 1 appeared as 'The television personality system: Televisual stardom revisited after film theory', *Screen*, 49(1): 32–50; and an iteration of Chapter 7 will appear in 2011 (although written long before I completed the work for this book) as 'Architectures of participation: Fame, television and Web2.0', in J. Bennett and N. Strange (eds) *Television as Digital Media*, Durham, NC: Duke University Press.

I owe a large debt of gratitude to Rachel Moseley for her support and encouragement during the early stages of this project. During the later stages of this work Su Holmes has been a fantastic source of support, knowledge and encouragement: thank you.

Finally, my thanks to Niki for her unfailing love, support and generosity in sharing her ideas: I promise you get your husband back now!

James Bennett
Brighton, 2010

Permissions

Chapter 1
A version of this chapter first appeared as 'The television personality system: Televisual stardom revisited after film theory', by James Bennett, in *Screen*, Vol. 49, No. 1, pp. 32–50 © 2008, Oxford Journals, Oxford University Press.

Figure 3.2
Image from *The Best of Times* by Alison Pressley, reproduced by kind permission of the publishers © 1999 Michael O'Mara Books Limited.

Figure 4.6
Front cover of Ant & Dec, Garfield, P. (2002) 'How Ant and Dec conquered primetime TV', *Observer Magazine*, May 12, 2002 © Guardian News & Media Ltd.

Figure 6.1
Gillian Wearing cover for G2 supplement of *The Guardian*, January 7, 2003 © Guardian News & Media Ltd.

Chapter 7
A version of this chapter will be published as 'Architectures of participation: Fame, television and Web2.0', by James Bennett, in Bennett, J. and Strange, N. (eds) *Television as Digital Media* (forthcoming, 2011, Durham, NC: Duke University Press).

Introduction

> If one puzzle remains it is in the minds of those who are bewildered by
> television fame. So-and-so's name has become a household name – but
> why? What do they *do*? The answer is that television fame must be judged
> by television standards, all others forgotten. When we make friends we do
> not stop to ask: What do they do? We like them for their personality
> alone. The medium of the small screen has brought new friends to every
> household. And that, for sure, *is* television.
>
> (Editorial, *TV Mirror Annual*, 1956: 5)[1]

The above editorial neatly encapsulates some of the prevailing assumptions
and norms that have governed our understanding of television fame: namely,
that personalities must appear to be 'just-as-they-are', to be ordinary, authentic and to come intimately into the viewer's home without the appearance of
performance. As early as 1956, therefore, television has been understood as a
purveyor of 'personalities'; a term the academy has subsequently gone on to
understand in contradistinction to stars: ordinary rather than extraordinary,
an authentic rather than an unattainable image. It is not my intention in this
book to refute this dichotomy or to suggest that television personalities
should be recognised as conforming to the same regime of fame as film, pop,
or sports stars. Quite the converse indeed: television fame should be judged
by 'television standards'. Whilst it may prove impossible to follow the editorial's suggestion to forget all other definitions or standards of fame – particularly because television's hybridity is central to its formation of celebrity – I
do want to suggest that we should take television's own regime of fame seriously and on its own terms.

In this book I therefore aim to critically evaluate television personalities.
More particularly, I aim to do so in a way that takes the hallmarks of television
fame as worthy of such study – its ordinariness, its authenticity, its intimacy, its
ephemerality and its pervasiveness. Within television, film, media and the more
recent field of 'celebrity studies', the study of television personalities has largely
been informed by two tendencies. The first, from the 'founding fathers' of
studies of television fame, sees television personalities as different, and inferior
to cinema's star system. The use of the term 'television personality' within such

studies has come to signify a 'lack', a quality absent, from the television apparatus. Indeed the contrast between the 'silver' screen and television's 'small
screen' expressly enunciates this relationship of superiority/inferiority. This
body of work comes from, or is largely informed by, television studies' emergence from film studies as characterised by John Langer's (1997[1981]) and
John Ellis's (1992[1982]) work on television's personality system in the early
1980s. The second body of work comes from both media studies and celebrity
studies. As Su Holmes and I have argued elsewhere, here the scholarly trend
has been to take less interest in the specificity of media forms and boundaries
and instead concentrate on the pervasiveness and increasing importance of
celebrity in society. Television, via the rise of reality TV and its production of
celebrity, has figured prominently in such debates. However, as a result of this
movement away from the specific to the general, the real complexities of television fame have fallen somewhat between the analytic cracks (Bennett and
Holmes, 2010). In this second body of work, mirroring a trend established in
the first, there is a failure to account for the various *forms* of fame that television produces: not all of which can be usefully subsumed within the term
'television personality', itself a category distinct from the 'TV star' and the
wider milieu of television celebrity.

   This book treats television personalities as one distinct category within the
kinds of fame circulated by television. And although television personalities
might be a large part of everyday discussion of television – from evaluative
judgements regarding how much we might like Ant and Dec or John Stewart,
through to their use in simply describing our television experience ('did you
see the new Jamie Oliver series last night'), and of course their place in celebrity gossip ('I heard Simon Cowell was going to stop doing *American Idol*
next year') – it is not always clear what we mean and to whom we are referring
when we use this term. The popular press might refer to anyone, from a leading player in a soap opera to a reality TV contestant through to a light entertainment host or actor in an American quality drama series, as a 'television
personality' or 'TV star'. In this book I make a fundamental distinction
between the two. Following Karen Lury's work (1995), I want to suggest
that we need to disentangle the categories of television personality and television actor, whereby it is only the latter that can be understood in relation to
the paradigm of stardom. That is, if the work that looms largest over any
discussion of fame is Richard Dyer's inescapable *Stars* (2001), then we must
pay attention to the way his analysis is predicated on the basis that stars play
characters, understood as constructed representations of persons; a distinction
that goes towards understanding the extraordinary/ordinary paradox of stardom (Dyer, 2001: 89). In contrast, television personalities only ever play
themselves, emphasising the continuousness and authenticity of their *ordinary* persona: Jamie Oliver as 'Jamie Oliver', etc.

   To treat this set of performers as a distinct category allows us to understand
televisual fame on its own terms and move beyond the presupposition that

television's regime of celebrity should neatly conform to that of film stardom, defending or attacking television personalities against this measure. This is not to say that television stardom might not exist: a number of scholars, such as Susan Murray (2005), Alexander Doty (1990), Mary Desjardins (2002), Christine Becker (2009) and Deborah Jermyn (2006) have made important contributions to developing our understanding of how this regime might be applied to television. However, we must not conflate these two kinds of performers – for there is little to be gained in comparing Oprah Winfrey with Sarah Jessica Parker, Jade Goody with Delia Smith, or subsuming Lucille Ball and Gilbert Harding within the same category, when their modes of performance, their relationship between on- and off-screen selves and, in turn, their economic and cultural value remain so distinct. Television's regime of fame is clearly too multifarious to be dealt with, or dismissed, within one undifferentiated conglomerate. In turn, therefore, I pay attention to the 'television personality' as part of television's wider production of fame: from TV stars – such as Ricky Gervais discussed in Part II – through to do-it-yourself (DIY) and multiplatform forms of televisual fame – such as Stephen Fry and Kevin Rose discussed in Chapter 7. Television's personality system, as I discuss in Chapter 1, is informed by its relationship to other types of performer and celebrities.

However, by taking television personalities as a central locus of study, rather than a subsidiary or undifferentiated form of fame, I hope to unpick the construction of ordinariness, intimacy and authenticity of such performers, the various forms of skill and labour that go into making up these persona and performances, and the economic, cultural and ideological functions and values they serve. Whilst the case studies in the book predominantly come from UK television, my aim in this mapping is primarily conceptual, and throughout the book I point to shorter exemplars from other contexts that indicate the transferability of the ideas I set out here. Although the role of public service broadcasting in the British context provides a particular inflection to some of the readings of performance, political economy, history and ideological meanings I undertake, my aim is to take the television personality system as intrinsically international. I am thus concerned to understand the place of television personalities in celebrity culture, the meanings and role they play in relation to both television and our everyday life, as well as why they continue to be a source of pleasure and interest for us. I do this across a range of sites and historical instances, ranging from the invention of the television personality in Britain during the 1950s, through to the construction of multiplatform and DIY forms of television personality in an era where reality TV and social media forms increasingly provide opportunities for fame amongst 'ordinary people'. In so doing I examine television personalities in relation to issues of national identity, gender, political economy, aesthetics and cultural value. It is this question of cultural value that I suggest has been instrumental in the neglect of television personalities and the specificities of their celebrity form. I want to turn to this issue in the remainder of this introduction as it underpins the investigation across all the remaining chapters.

The cultural value of television fame

It's all television's fault. Not just celebrity, but all the vast and radical changes that have afflicted our culture in the last two or three decades .... It is the primary force in the breaking down of the barriers that formerly existed between the well-known and the unknown. This ... has something to do with the way it brings famous folk into our living room in psychically manageable size ... not from ... very large screens, as they are in the movies, where scale helps to keep us humble before the image.

(Schickel, 1985: 9–10)

What television does present is the 'personality'. The personality is someone who is famous for being famous, and is famous only in so far as he or she makes frequent television appearances .... In some ways [television personalities] are the opposite of stars, agreeable voids rather than sites of conflicting meanings.

(Ellis, 1982: 107)

On April 4, 2009 over 2,000 people crowded around large screens outside St John the Baptist Church in Buckhurst Hill, Essex, whilst an estimated further 3,000 had watched a hearse wind its long route through the streets of London. Inevitably described as a 'Princess Diana-style funeral' by the *Daily Mail*,[2] the hysteria and sheer scale of the media coverage that surrounded Jade Goody's death seemed to those who have questioned the worth of television celebrity – a mere purveyor of personalities – to epitomise the devaluation of contemporary fame. The funeral was what Daniel Boorstin would describe as a pseudo-event in and of itself: constructed as a media circus that was designed primarily as a promotional vehicle for the culture industries' commercial interests (Boorstin, 1961). Moreover, it celebrated (or calculatedly promoted) the fame of a manufactured celebrity who emerged from the archetypal pseudo-event, *Big Brother* (Endemol for Channel 4, 2000–2010), and via comparisons with Royalty proceeded to break down the barriers between the known and unknown. The media coverage of Goody's funeral therefore appeared to confirm an irretrievable divorce of fame from achievement, merit or talent: with television to blame.

As P. David Marshall explains, such a view of celebrity understands fame as 'success without the requisite association with work' (Marshall, 1997: ix). Marshall's examination of celebrity culture establishes how such a perspective, informed by the mass culture analyses of the Frankfurt school, works by positioning contemporary celebrity as an anathema to earlier cultures of authentic fame that rewarded work, talent and achievement. In contrast, in contemporary society the 'sign of the celebrity is ridiculed and derided because it represents the centre of false value …. It articulates the individual as commodity' (ibid.: xi). In turn, this 'democratisation' of celebrity is perceived to have negative effects on society. For example, commenting on the British Home Secretary's decision to allow Goody's fiancée to vary the conditions of his parole in order for the pair to wed before Goody's death, David Hughes of *The Telegraph* argued:

> Goody is a wholly-owned subsidiary of the red tops [British tabloids] and everything she does, including dying of cancer, is commodified for the tabloids …. Ministers seem to cleave to the pitiful notion that by associating themselves with tabloid obsessions, they somehow seem 'closer to the people' or more attuned to popular culture …. What sort of precedent does Straw think he's setting?[3]

In a similar vein, a Facebook group was set up that asked 'Who thinks Jade Goody is milking it?', in which posters vilified her for a lack of dignity, whilst another site called 'When will Jade Goody die?' offered an Apple iPod as a prize for the person who predicted the date of her death. Such a viewpoint is therefore informed by a cultural pessimism that links the extension of celebrity to 'ordinary people', such as reality TV contestants, with wider ills in society.

However, this is not the only view of Goody's celebrity available. As *The Observer* newspaper noted earlier that year in surveying the coverage that accompanied the news that Goody had terminal cancer, Jade's story was a 'tale for our times … straight from a soap opera script'. Jade emerged as the fourth place contestant in the 2002 series of *Big Brother* and succeeded in maintaining her media profile between 2002 and 2007. The narrative of her fame then 'lurched between making money … to becoming a figure of notoriety' after she fell from public grace during the 2007 *Celebrity Big Brother* (Endemol for Channel 4, 2001–2010) 'race' row, in which she was accused of racist bullying in her behaviour towards fellow celebrity housemate, Bollywood star Shilpa Shetty. The parable of Jade's story ended, however, with a final chapter of 'Goody and cancer', which saw her rehabilitated into the media spotlight as bravely battling and raising awareness about cancer.[4] A great deal of press that detailed Goody's battle with cancer therefore revealed a counter discourse to those more pessimistic understandings of contemporary celebrity discussed above. In these accounts a 400,000 rise in women screened for cervical cancer in 2009 was attributed to Goody's celebrity and the coverage that therefore accompanied her diagnosis.[5]

As Marshall and others such as Jessica Evans and David Hesmondhalgh have noted, the expansion of celebrity to such 'ordinary' people as Goody has also been understood as a democratising process, extending fame to an ever more diverse collective that provides for pluralism in the range of identities it gives voice to (Evans and Hesmondhalgh, 2005). In this second perspective the plethora of celebrities in the public eye may not necessarily be positioned as inherently 'good' for society, but as Joshua Gamson has suggested, their presence and the increasing acknowledgement of their manufacture speaks to a 'long-standing pull between the democratic and the aristocratic in fame discourse', which raises 'important questions about the dynamics of public visibility in democratic, consumer-capitalist society' (Gamson, 2001: 277). Reality TV has been a prime staging ground for these debates, with theorists such as Graeme Turner (2004), Mark Andrejevic (2002), Nick Couldry (2002), Su Holmes (2004a, 2004b, 2005a, 2006a, 2008a) and John Hartley (2004a) offering a variety of perspectives that range across the continuum established between these positions. Perhaps one of the most useful is Graeme Turner's conception of this extension of celebrity to ordinary people as a 'demotic turn'. Discussing both reality TV and the DIY forms of celebrity offered by digital media, Turner argues that, far from a democratic turn, such developments are 'demotic', generating 'the performance of endless and unmotivated diversity for its own sake' (Turner, 2004: 83). Ultimately, Turner's position is more easily aligned with the first perspective on celebrity, which perceives this production of diversity as an asset to be mined and harvested by the 'major corporate structures of the traditional media conglomerates' (ibid.: 84). Indeed celebrity studies is largely defined by the extent to which theorists and commentators understand the extension of fame to an increasingly diverse, and ordinary, range of celebrities as good/bad for democracy and/or different from/similar to earlier paradigms of fame.

And yet, despite the emergence of a paradigm of celebrity studies and the subsequent taking seriously of the pleasures they offer, as well as the political, economic and ideological functions celebrities perform, television's regime of fame remains both under-explored and theorised, as well as largely denigrated or dismissed; often on grounds that either explicitly or implicitly draw on the first paradigm's attitude to the extension of fame to those without discernible talent or hard work. As Ellis and Schickel have argued, the television personality is merely 'someone who is famous for being famous', with the extension of fame to such ordinary people as Goody being 'all television's fault'. Embedded within this perspective is the equation of television personalities with an elision of on-/off-screen self, whereby they have been conceptually and culturally understood in terms of authenticity: merely being or playing 'themselves', no 'skill' or talent required. As the 1956 editorial to *TV Mirror Annual* that opens this book suggests, therefore, 'what do they do?' Yet, as Su Holmes and I have argued, such questions are suggestive of a negative evaluation of television's specific regime of fame: 'after all, whilst "ordinariness" and "authenticity" are often qualities which are highly praised in relation to stars and celebrities (Dyer, 1986), being "oneself" is unlikely to be applauded as a skill on TV' (Bennett and Holmes, 2010: 66). As a result, the 'perceived specificities of television celebrity … have therefore simultaneously functioned to "denigrate the stature" of television fame' (Beckes, quoted in ibid.).

This assumption largely comes from the work of John Langer and John Ellis. Langer's 1981 article 'Television's personality system' commences with the question, 'What is the significance of the fact that whereas the cinema established a "star system", television has not?'. Langer goes on to assert that:

> Whereas the star system operates from the realms of the spectacular, the inaccessible ... the personality system is cultivated almost exclusively as 'part of life'; whereas the star system always ... insist[s] on the 'exceptional', the personality system works directly to construct and foreground intimacy and immediacy ... whereas stars emanate as idealisations or archetypal expressions, to be contemplated, revered, desired and even blatantly imitated, stubbornly standing outside the realms of the familiar and the routinized, personalities are distinguished for their representativeness, their typicality, the 'will to ordinariness' to be accepted, normalized, experienced as *familiar*.
>
> (Langer, 1997: 165–167)

This has been termed television's 'personality effect', whereby the medium's rhetoric of familiarity and intimacy, combined with the domestic context of its reception, are said to mitigate against the paradoxical and enigmatic construction of cinematic stardom as understood in film scholarship. That is, following John Ellis, it is through the photo effect that cinema induces a 'present absence' in the cinema experience, in turn, playing a central role in stars' simultaneous extraordinariness and ordinariness. In contrast, television fame is premised on people appearing 'just-as-they-are', without any extraordinary talent, and/or the revelation (and commoditisation) of the authentic self: a dichotomy that the emergence of reality TV has tended to cement by associating television inextricably with what many perceive as a cultural decline in the value of celebrity.

This view continues to inform wider understandings of television's personality system, including personalities who might more demonstrably have achieved their fame. Chris Rojek has suggested that there are broadly three forms of celebrity: ascribed, achieved and attributed. The move away from ascribed celebrity – whereby fame was the preserve of hereditary lines of nobility and royalty – is generally welcomed by both perspectives on contemporary celebrity culture discussed so far. However, there is a clear hierarchical evaluation of achieved and attributed celebrity. Thus Rojek lists film stars such as Brad Pitt amongst those who have '*achieved* celebrity ... from the perceived accomplishments of the individual in open competition', whilst British gardening television personality Charlie Dimmock is listed as an 'ordinary' person whose fame follows 'from mere attribution ... the result of the concentrated representation of an individual as noteworthy or exceptional by cultural intermediaries' (Rojek, 2001: 18).

Indeed, the inferiority of television's personality system – informed by these earlier accounts – has largely been taken as 'given' within media studies generally, and celebrity studies more specifically. For example, after reviewing the different range of 'stars' television produces – from what he terms the 'stars' of soap opera and situation comedy to the 'presenters' of 'news and live or simulated live television' – P. David Marshall concludes:

> With reference to the system of celebrity, television is generally an ancillary system. It is less active in the generation of new celebrities than in the process of substantiating the significance of public personalities that have emerged in other domains. I have called this the familiarization function of the medium.
>
> (Marshall, 1997: 130–131)

Marshall then goes on to analyse Oprah Winfrey, one of the most powerful women in media (let alone television), to demonstrate this function. In so doing, he suggests that televisual fame is therefore always-already subservient to other forms of celebrity, for it 'depends upon the proximity to and powers of explaining other celebrities' (ibid.: 148). Like Ellis, Marshall's account positions television personalities as 'agreeable voids', following Schickel's argument that television has been instrumental in breaking down the barriers between known and unknown, with its personalities functioning as prime sites for this 'familiarisation'.

In so doing, Marshall's work, like so many other analyses of celebrity, fails to accord due weight to the *achievement* and *specificity* of Oprah's television fame; her talent, hard work and skill being at the heart of the economic power he goes on to detail that she wields. That is, in situating her power and fame as dependent on the proximity to other forms of celebrity, he fails to acknowledge that it is *for* Oprah – as a *performer* in her own right – that viewers regularly tune in, become members of her book club and have become such a large, and culturally valuable, audience as to enable her to launch her own television channel. In turn, it is through her image that political, cultural and celebrity meanings are negotiated more widely, from Tom Cruise's meltdown on the programme to her role in facilitating the place of a Black President in US society.[6] Thus the acceptance of earlier paradigms of analysis of television fame leave Marshall in a double bind: at once caught in acknowledging the power Oprah has attained through the development of a successful television persona, but at the same time forced by film studies' dogma to denigrate the value of that persona by situating it as subservient to the fame and stardom of other media forms.

Oprah and Jade provide two polar exemplars of the forms of celebrity that television's personality system generates, not only in terms of relative cultural value, but also the national institutions that structure and inform their fame. In turn, the polarity of their televisual fame also illustrates why a closer examination of the specificities of televisual fame is long overdue. This is not to say that achievement itself is an a priori criterion for the consideration of celebrities as worthy of study – whatever view one takes of the merit of Goody's fame, her role in celebrity culture is certainly an important site of analysis. However, the category of achievement does help us delineate the television personality from wider forms of celebrity: to separate Jade Goody from Oprah Winfrey. And in turn, this helps us understand the way television personalities' apparent familiarity, everyday-ness, ordinariness and authenticity are clearly constructed and function differently to other celebrities.

In this book I therefore want to delineate the category of the television personality more clearly and move beyond an appreciation of television personalities as 'the opposite of stars'. Thus I argue that it is important to understand the television personality's ordinariness, authenticity and intimacy not in terms of a 'lack' in relation to the film star, but precisely as a site of their economic, ideological, textual and cultural importance. In turn, such an approach concentrates our attention on the skill, labour and performance that goes into the construction of the television personality's image. Far from 'agreeable voids', across the rest of the book I demonstrate that television personalities are conflicting sites of meaning that deserve careful attention in order to unpick their role in television's historical, contemporary and future meaning. Finally, I would suggest that to treat television personalities as worthy as a site of such study is not necessarily to align myself irrevocably with the 'celebrity as democracy' viewpoint I outlined above. Whilst I have much sympathy with this view, I want to move beyond this debate here. My overriding concern is therefore to suggest how a closer appreciation of television personalities can help us understand both television and celebrity culture more fully.

Naturally, such a wide-ranging argument raises the question of methodology and the selection of case studies. Across the book I employ a range of methods, using archival, trade, policy, journalistic and secondary sources to 'test' my textual readings of programmings and intertextual personas. I deal with my use of archival and trade sources more explicitly in the introductory remarks to each part of the book where my methodological emphasis changes across chapters – thus whilst Chapters 2 and 3 are primarily concerned with archival work, Chapters 5 and 6 build primarily on textual analysis and Chapters 4 and 7 range across journalistic and industry sources. In dealing with the range of personalities discussed therein there is the question of exemplarity and representativeness of the examples chosen for discussion. Jonathan Bignell has examined this question of how choosing specific moments for analysis in television drama can tend to both canonise particular texts as well as naturalise certain choices, obscuring the range of ideological, methodological and practical questions at stake in their selection (Bignell, 2005a). For an analysis of television personalities who – necessarily from the generic definition of the television personality I have already outlined – deal in what

Frances Bonner (2003) has described as 'ordinary television', there is a vast amount of output from which to select particular moments for discussion; unlike most television drama, the non-fiction programming forms here are often daily and run over many years.

The case studies attempt to avoid some of the pitfalls to which Bignell points – drawing attention to the theoretical approaches that surround them, placing programmes and archival documents in their social and production context – but they are ultimately shaped by some of the practical considerations that he suggests we must be reflexive about. Most prominently here, in pulling out particular programmes and scenes for analysis, these selections are framed by what Lury has described as my 'television memory' (Lury, 1995). But it is also true that the political economy of academic publishing and researching that Bignell draws our attention to inform this work (Bignell, 2005a: 30–31): research funding to access the BBC written archives played an important role in my work on early television fame, whilst my attempts to demonstrate the transferability of the concepts discussed in the book by drawing on international examples is informed by the economies of academic publishing. Whilst I set out the rationale for each case study discussed in part and chapter introductions, it must be acknowledged that my own evaluative judgements are at play in the case studies and selections that follow (which is not to say I enjoy all of the performers discussed within; some viewing has most definitely been *hard* work). But my primary concern is to demonstrate both how television personality fame is *achieved* and what the ideological and cultural implications of this fame are for the role television plays in celebrity culture and social life more widely. As with Dyer's study of stars, television personalities 'articulate what it is to be human in society: that is, they express the particular notion that we hold of the "individual"' (Dyer, 1986: 8), but they do so on a more every day, intimate and domestic scale. In many ways this makes their ideological function more powerful, and the need to understand it more pressing.

I do this over a range of case studies and mapping of the conceptual terrain concerned with celebrity. The book is divided into three parts, with the chapters in each part dealing with congruent questions and periodisations in televisual fame. Whilst this is not intended as a totalising historical account of the development of the television personality system, following a rough chronology does help to map out the contingencies and changing meanings of television personalities more clearly. The divisions between parts roughly follow those John Ellis draws in charting UK television's development from a period of 'scarcity' through to 'availability' and 'plenty' – a periodisation that approximates the delineation of TVI, TVII and TVIII in US network television (see Creeber and Hills, 2007; Pearson, 2011; Rogers *et al.*, 2002). Thus, in Part I, I focus on what John Ellis terms the period of 'scarcity', discussing the emergence of televisual fame during the 1950s in the United Kingdom when television was not yet a mass medium, restricted in terms of the channels available and viewership able to watch them. In Part II, I examine the prevailing characteristics of the television personality system in terms of performance and political economy during the 1980s and 1990s, which are congruent with the stabilisation of television as a mass, broadcast medium in an era of 'availability'. Part III's discussion of the rise of lifestyle television in the late 1990s, together with the emergence of DIY fame in the digital mediascape of the early 2000s, corresponds to Ellis's periodisation of 'plenty' where what television means is 'uncertain' (Ellis, 2000: 400). Part I is preceded by Chapter 1 that reviews a range of literature from film, television, new media, cultural and media studies that help us understand the specificities of the television personality. In particular how, as part of a wider system of television celebrity (discussed as the television personality system), such performers function in relation to key discourses of ordinariness, authenticity, intimacy and skill. In this chapter I set out how the television personality is both distinct from other forms of celebrity as well as a category comprising a range of performers itself. This conceptual discussion of the television personality system sets up key discourses and categories that are used throughout the book.

It is followed by two chapters in Part I that seek to provide a historical excavation of television fame in the British context, examining the invention of the television personality during the 1950s. In Chapter 2, I focus on the emergence of televisual fame and its entwinement with discourses of televisual skill in the genre of light entertainment and variety programming. The development and acquirement of televisual skill, I argue, became pivotal to the successful television personality and their creation of a televisual image. However, the resultant fame had to be negotiated within the confines of the institutional parameters of the BBC's public service ethos and culture of the time, which I suggest led to an emphasis on the ordinariness and authenticity of a personality's persona. In Chapter 3, I further explore the notion of televisual skill in relation to the BBC's in-vision continuity announcers. Away from any palpable vocational validation of their appearance on television – such as vaudeville or music hall routines, cookery or lifestyle expertise – the roster of BBC announcers exemplified the notion of televisual skill by being trained solely in television presentation. However, beyond such discourses of televisual skill, a focus on the female announcers reveals how television fame is capable of conferring a glamorous televisual image. Moreover, I argue that such discourses of glamour did not bring about an extraordinary/ordinary paradox, but actually emphasised ordinariness in order to negotiate the place of the feminine in early British television culture.

In Part II, my focus moves to the cultural, ideological and economic function of contemporary television personalities. In both Chapters 4 and 5 the notion of authenticity is explored in greater detail for the way in which it structures the political economy and aesthetics of performance in televisual fame. In Chapter 4, I set out how the television personality system has developed from the early broadcast era of television, paying attention to a range of personalities to show how the schedule, genre, formats, vehicles and digital distribution structure the economies of televisual fame. Examining the BBC presenter-pay scandal of 2006 to demonstrate the way public service broadcasting inflects these economies, I suggest how both public service broadcasting and the stable economies of the television personality system are challenged in the emerging digital television landscape where an emphasis on entrepreneurial forms of celebrity has emerged. In Chapter 5, I discuss the notion of performance across a range of programming in order to set out how presenting can be understood as a site of pleasure and meaning that is capable of sustaining critical attention. Drawing on film studies' discourses of acting and presenting, I argue that the performance of authenticity differs across genres and can be assessed for its achievement of the programme's goals. Performance, I argue, is a key form of labour in television's personality system that functions at the intersections of its distinction from wider celebrity culture, its political economy and ideological function.

The chapters in Part III turn to this question of the ideological role of the television personality more explicitly, focusing on the way ordinariness serves to promote particular ideological projects of the self in relation to lifestyle programming and television's digitalisation. In Chapter 6 I focus on the way national identity is negotiated by Alan Titchmarsh's intertextual persona as part of lifestyle television's project of 'ordinari-ising' particular forms of knowledge and expertise. Setting out how Titchmarsh's vocational skill as a gardener is central to his ordinariness, I argue that across a range of intertexts his persona promotes a conservative image of 'ordinary Britain' that is capable of reconciling a range of ideological conflicts around community and individuality, self-empowerment and regulation. Finally, in Chapter 7 I return to the television personality system in relation to television's convergence with digital media to suggest how the increasing ordinari-isation of fame draws on televisual discourses of intimacy, authenticity and ordinariness. I argue that taking the television personality seriously can illuminate our understanding of debates about the democratic turn in both digital and celebrity media forms. As I argue there, the ideological implications of such fame are more profound than can be accounted for by the binary debates about contemporary celebrity's apparent evisceration of political debate or its revitalisation of democracy.

Ultimately, this is a book concerned with why we should treat television personalities as a site worthy of study. And in turn, what the rewards and problematics involved in such study might reveal. The television personality remains under-theorised, and this book makes only a small contribution in correcting this neglect. I hope the gaps and problems it opens up become a fecund site for further study from others interested in the way television and its forms of celebrity function in our daily lives.

Chapter 1

The television personality system

Who are these *personalities* who have recently come among us in excessive numbers? How do they differ from the rest of us persons? ... Television personalities ... seem to be persons whose faces are instantly recognizable from exposure on television and in photographs in newspapers, but who have no other obvious talents.

(Philip Howard, *The Times*, 14 July, 1978: np)

Long after *TV Mirror Annual* opined that television fame was a 'puzzle' in 1956, Philip Howard's piece for *The Times* suggested this puzzle remained pertinent in 1978. Equally, published long before the coming of a personality like Jade Goody or the diatribes of Ellis, Langer and Schickel discussed in this book's introduction, his piece – 'the making of a personality' – resonates with the cultural value placed on television personalities' fame: that is, famous for being famous. However, Howard poses two questions that need answering in any sustained study of the television personality: Who are they? And how are they different – to us, to other forms of celebrity? In this chapter I set out the category of the television personality as discussed throughout the book in more depth. In so doing I review a range of work from film, television and celebrity studies that have considered the specificities of television fame. In turn, drawing more widely on cultural, new media and media studies, I set out an understanding of the key discourses of ordinariness, intimacy, authenticity and skill that structure the investigation in the remainder of this book. It is the confluence of these discourses, I argue, that set television personalities apart from both 'ordinary' people and other forms of celebrity. A closer understanding of this challenges the diminished status of television's forms of fame and the notion that television personalities have no 'obvious talents'.

The association of television with the extension of fame to ordinary people such as Jade Goody seems to both exemplify Howard's and others' arguments about the devaluation of contemporary celebrity. But it also provides a fitting example of the difficulty in discussing television fame: variously described as a 'celebrity', a 'TV star', a 'reality TV star' or contestant, as well as a 'television personality',[1] Goody was certainly a celebrity, but we can ask in what way is it useful to understand her celebrity as specifically configured by television? Previous academic studies of television personalities have tended to treat the television celebrity as an undifferentiated conglomerate which, as I have suggested, unhelpfully forces us to treat performers such as Goody and Oprah Winfrey as belonging to the same category. For Langer the term 'television personality' is applied to anyone 'who makes regular appearances' on television: 'newsreaders, moderators, hosts, comperes or characters' (Langer, 1997: 165), whilst Ellis finds that the terms 'personality' or 'star' are applied to 'anybody who appears on its screen: even the weather forecasters' (Ellis, 1991: 313). Arguably Goody's celebrity exemplifies why the term 'TV star' has been resisted within the academy: because television can seemingly confer fame on anyone; because if manufactures what Boorstin has termed 'pseudo-events' (Boorstin, 1961) like *Big Brother* that provide a steady stream of 'wannabes' willing to surrender to the process of celebrity manufacture; and, ultimately, because such fame fails to conform to cinema's 'photo effect', which constructs stars as paradoxical figures – at once present and absent, extraordinary and ordinary. Like so many of the celebrities television produces, Goody is simply ordinary, with no distinction or dialectic between on- and off-screen self.

This failure of television to produce paradoxical 'star' images of its performers has been applied to all forms of celebrity television produces – from reality TV contestants, to presenters, hosts and actors. For example, a common critique of television actors suggests they can never be understood via the parameters of stardom, by virtue of the fact they do not appear to have a separate private persona to the characters they inhabit on screen. Jeremy Butler's analysis of the soap opera actor therefore argues that a star system is incapable of being applied to soap actors on the television screen due to the fact that the soap opera actor's presence is largely 'invisible, repressed by a variety of ideological, economic and aesthetic factors' that ensures such performers are 'practically treated as ciphers' for the character (Butler, 1991: 81). Consequently, television actors are often subsumed within the characters that they play, an illusion reinforced by their intertextual appearances in other media that emphasise a compare/contrast approach to the performer and their character. The elision of on-/off-screen self by television appears further confirmed by both non-fiction programming, in which presenters play themselves with no dramatic role or narrative conceit to mask the authentic self, and reality TV's emphasis on ordinariness and authenticity that requires self-revelation as a prerequisite to celebrity. As a result, all forms of television celebrity have tended to be amalgamated in order to draw a 'well caught distinction' between film and television's mode of celebrity, in which television's emphasis on the continuity of its performers' image, its ordinariness and intimate connection to the audience is underscored (Turner, 2004: 15). However, we cannot simply conflate the range of performers appearing on television within this easy binary between film and television – recognising the different forms of celebrity television circulates helps us understand the way in which key discourses of authenticity, ordinariness, intimacy and skill function very specifically in the construction of television personality fame.

A 'well caught distinction'? Celebrities, stars and television personalities

Television has always constructed its own 'personalities' while simultaneously circulating personae from other domains, and these categories cannot simply be conflated.

(Holmes, 2007a: 429)

Television has often been depicted as a mere relayer of other forms of celebrity, with televisual fame always-already positioned as both facilitating the presence of other 'stars' on the small screen and, in so doing, producing a form of celebrity that is inferior to other realms: from 'hosting' the presence of stars on chat shows (Marshall, 1997), through to mass producing 'celetoids' (Rojek, 2001), through to reality TV programming whose fame is ephemeral (Turner, 2004). However, a growing body of work has emerged that attempts to pay greater attention to the specificities of televisual fame. Su Holmes's work is crucial here, particularly in a British context, where her analysis of a range of contemporary and historical examples has done much to unpick the way in which ordinariness and authenticity functions in relationship to a range of performers on television. Whilst Holmes offers compelling arguments in relationship to the way these concepts function in the construction of television fame that I shall return to below, she also points to the way in which television produces its own form of celebrity as well as circulates personas from other media. In so doing, she has questioned the way terminology has constructed television fame, suggesting it is within the relationship between popular and academic discourse that the cultural value and interpretations of 'different forms of media fame are fought out' (Bennett and Holmes, 2010: 67). Whilst Holmes has demonstrated the term 'television star' has had currency at particular historical junctures (Holmes, 2001), a significant body of work has more directly challenged film studies' mantra about the impossibility of television stardom.

Primarily this work has considered the historical forms of early television stardom in the USA, such as Susan Murray's (2005) work on early US television and broadcast stardom, Diane Negra's study of Hedy Lamarr (Negra, 2002), Lola Bratten's examination of Dinah Shore (Bratten, 2002), Christine Becker's investigation of the interplay between film and television fame (Becker, 2009), and Denise Mann's analysis of the recycling of Hollywood stars on 1950s television (Mann, 1991). Whilst Murray convincingly argues that 'television used its stars to define itself' during the 1950s, Mary Desjardins has examined the circulation of film star images by television during the same period. She argues that performers such as Gloria Swanson developed a televisual image that drew on their cinematic star image, but was distinctly informed by television's production and reception contexts (Desjardins, 2009). Like the work of Negra, Mann and Bratten therefore, the study by Desjardins is illustrative of the way in which such work has tended to focus on the way in which television circulates film stars' images. More directly, Deborah Jermyn's analysis of *Sex & The City*'s (HBO, 1998–2004) Sarah Jessica Parker has argued that with the growth of American quality television it now 'seems indisputable that this status [of stardom's presence absence] has been conferred by television' (Jermyn, 2006: 81).

Nevertheless, despite the useful interventions that each of these authors have made in terms of understanding and establishing a distinctly televisual regime of stardom, I do not wish to treat the performers under discussion across this book as 'TV stars' for a number of reasons. Primarily, this is because the term 'star' is too loaded – and well theorised in film studies – to be helpful in this context. For example, Murray's otherwise excellent history of early US television does not interrogate the use of the term 'star' in relation to television – preferring simply to adopt it as the most prevalent term used to describe prominent performers on television in the popular press of the time. Whilst Murray makes it clear that, what she terms, 'TV stars' were pivotal in the formation of the televisual, understood as an aesthetic as well as a set of production and reception practices, the performers she discusses come primarily from light entertainment and variety and do not conform to the regime of stardom as discussed in film studies. Moreover, although she suggests that the multiple roles a television star had to maintain 'required the star to simultaneously remain extraordinary whilst asserting his or her ordinariness' (Murray, 2005: 132), this argument is made without reference to Ellis's extraordinary/ordinary paradox of stardom. Indeed, her discussion of Arthur Godfry's fall from grace, brought about by revealing a disjuncture between the likeable on-screen persona and a hard-nosed off-screen self, underscores the way in which television's personality system tends to emphasise the continuity of performers' on- and off-screen image. As she suggests, this was connected to 'broadcasting's economic goals and its presumed aesthetics', which:

> encouraged intimacy in television performance style along with an enhanced conflation of a star's 'real life' with that of his or her character's textual history and personality in order to promote viewer identification with both a program's star and products.
>
> (Ibid.: 129)

As I shall discuss across this book, the lack of such a distinction is no barrier to considering television personalities' on-screen personas as worthy of attention nor any less constructed; indeed, arguably it is more appropriate to think of television personalities as 'extraordinarily ordinary'. Whilst an invaluable study of broadcasting history and fame, clearly the use of the term 'star' in Murray's work is not conceptually theorised here.

In contrast to Murray's use of the term 'star', Jermyn more purposefully sets out to establish that television can confer 'stardom proper', in producing forms of fame that correspond to cinema's regime of the paradoxical film star image: extraordinary/ordinary. Jermyn's analysis perhaps most pertinently challenges Butler's, Langer's and Ellis's arguments regarding the television actor, whereby, as Jermyn goes on to argue, we can understand recent 'quality' American television drama as having potentially extended the paradoxical ordinary/extraordinary terms of stardom to television. Insofar as this is accurate, Jermyn is correct to argue that these performers might be perceived as formulating a category of television stardom. Whether this is as new as Jermyn suggests is something of a moot point as far as my argument here is concerned, but it is worth noting that the work of US scholars listed above, as well as Alexander Doty's study of Lucille Ball (Doty, 1990), have pointed to a similar form of televisual stardom apparent in the movement of performers between film and television screens during the 1940s and 1950s. However, in thinking about this category of television star, I do not think that it is insignificant that Sarah Jessica Parker's, Hedy Lamarr's, Gloria Swanson's and Lucille Ball's careers started in film, and then moved back and forth between film and television. Indeed, whilst it might no longer be necessary for a career to start on film in order for stardom to be achieved or conferred on a performer, the examples of George Clooney, Jennifer Aniston and Gillian Anderson that Jermyn lists do suggest that the (successful) film appearance does remain pivotal to 'stardom proper'.

However, what remains apparent from this analysis is that the term 'television star' has remained problematic and its use has tended to start from the presupposition that television's regime of stardom should conform to that of film. This is not to say we should now simply discard the term 'television star' and adopt the moniker 'television personality'. Indeed to propose one catch-all term for television fame would be erroneous: television produces actors, presenters, contestants, celebrities, stars and personalities. Without creating a rigid typology we need to separate forms of fame, televisual or otherwise, circulated and produced by television. The term 'television personality', as I am using it across this book, is therefore restricted in three important senses: relative fame; work, which I will discuss across the book as 'skill', 'knowledge' or 'expertise', and 'labour'; and, finally, performance mode.

First, in relation to the distinctions that frame studies of stardom in film and television, the category of the television personality is necessarily limited to those performers whose image enters into subsidiary circulation, such as appearances in magazines, newspapers, adverts and books (for example, 'how to' merchandising surrounding a vocational skill, such as gardening, DIY or cookery; or autobiographies and biographies; or more rarely, exploits into fiction). Of course, such subsidiary circulation should also include television appearances, such as David Attenborough's guesting as a celebrity on *Friday Night with Jonathan Ross* (BBC, 2001–2010), or in turn when Ross himself appears as a celebrity panellist on *The Apprentice: You're Fired* (BBC, 2006–ongoing). Moreover, increasingly this intertextual circulation of the television personality persona includes its multiplatform dissemination across digital media formats such as Internet television, Twitter, Facebook and other social media sites; which, in turn, offer spaces for the construction of various forms of 'DIY celebrity' discussed in Chapter 7 (Turner, 2004). In turn, such publicity, promotion and coverage should clearly feed back into their on-screen appearances. In this sense, the television personality can be defined as those who develop a 'televisual image', which distinguishes them from the mere 'presenter', akin to the 'star image' of film theory that Richard Dyer proposes separates stars from actors (Dyer, 2001).

Second, as Christine Geraghty has noted, a television personality's fame remains distinct from that of the 'celebrity', which 'indicates someone whose fame rests overwhelmingly on what happens outside the sphere of their work and who is famous for having a lifestyle'. Whilst reality TV contestants might be readily subsumed within this category, Geraghty goes on to suggest that television personalities belong to a category of 'professionals', 'whose fame rests on their work in such a way that there is very little sense of a private life and the emphasis is on the seamlessness of the public persona' (Geraghty, 2000: 187). This notion of work is an important category for my delineation of television personalities from other forms of fame – televisual and otherwise. By invoking an understanding of work in the form of different kinds of skill across the book – discussed as *televisual skill*, *vocational skill* and *vernacular skill* – I want to suggest that far from the simple presentation of an authentic, ordinary self, the construction of a television personality's fame involves both labour and achievement, often taking the form of promotion, publicity and performance. I will return to this question of achievement in Chapter 5. But for now it is worth noting how this category of skill again delimits the category of the television personality from both television actor and television celebrity.

This point about performance leads me to the final distinction I want to make in terms of the use of the term 'television personality': that is, between the television celebrity, actor or star, and the television personality. Understanding the presentation of the authentic, ordinary self as a performance, worked at over time, intertwines with Geraghty's assessment of the professional's fame and persona being characterised by the seamlessness of their public persona. The television personality as a category, therefore, consists of those performers who play themselves, making little distinction between on-screen and private persona: Jamie Oliver as 'Jamie Oliver', etc. In this sense, the category of the television personality is essentially comprised of presenters of various non-fiction genres and formats: the chat show host, the game show or talent show host/judge, the magazine show presenter, the factual programme presenter (history, natural history, science, etc.), light entertainment performers and lifestyle programming presenters (cookery, motoring, gardening, DIY, etc.). The most problematic categories here are those of the newscaster or journalist, and the comedian – both of whose position on television and within television studies has already been the subject of much sustained study and debate.[2] I return to the category of comedy throughout this book but the newsreader or journalist remains largely absent for reasons of space and personal interest. However, it is possible to understand both newsreader and television journalist as practising a vocational skill: journalism.

At the time of writing, the category of the television personality is exemplified by personalities such as Jonathan Ross and Oprah Winfrey, Anne Robinson, Simon Cowell, Richard Madeley and Judy Finnegan, Simon Schama, David Attenborough, Robert Winston, Ant and Dec, Bruce Forsyth, Nigella Lawson, Jeremy Clarkson, Alan Titchmarsh, Jeremy Paxman and Graham Norton. Whilst many of these examples remain nationally specific, television personalities' fame has always extended beyond national borders. Indeed, as we shall see in later chapters, working within non fiction genres increasingly leads to such personalities seeing their televisual image circulated internationally as part of the exchange in television formats globally (for example, the decision to keep Anne Robinson in the US version of *The Weakest Link*, but replace her in international versions in Holland, Australia and elsewhere). In summary, therefore, the term 'television personality' will be used throughout this book to refer to *presenters* of television programming, whose *fame* has developed a high degree of intertextuality and longevity that is strongly connected to their *work* in, and on, television.

However, these distinctions between television personalities and other forms of television celebrity do not remain rigid and fixable. Rather, as Karen Lury has observed:

> [the] personality and the actor are ... entangled, and individuals may oscillate from one position to another. The actor may perform as a celebrity when they guest on a game show, whereas the celebrity may act in a dramatic fiction. On top of this ... the personality is always in some sense 'acting'.
>
> (Lury, 1995: 117)

I will return to this issue of acting in Chapter 5, as for now I want to concentrate on the particular kinds of performers subsumed within the term 'television personality' as defined here.

It seems an obvious point, but nevertheless worth making, that not all presenters are the same and their presence on television is often predicated on the different talents they hold. The category of the 'television personality'

Figure 1.1   The lack of vocabulary in relation to studies of the television personality means we currently subsume performers as diverse as Graham Norton ... (screen capture from *The Graham Norton Show* [So Television, 2007–ongoing]).

therefore contains a vast array of performers, which we need to account for and delineate further, if we wish to think about the meaning, pleasure and function of a particular television personality's image. There seems little point in comparing the performance of David Attenborough as natural historian with the deployment of Graham Norton's camp naughtiness as a chat show host (Figures 1.1 and 1.2); or in turn, comparing the verbal dexterity of David Letterman and his ringmaster-like hosting of *Late Night with ...* against the performances of Delia Smith's or Jamie Oliver's cookery expositions. Clearly, therefore, we must pay attention to questions of genre in undertaking such analyses, but also how the schedule differentiates kinds of television personalities and modes of performances. I want to therefore suggest that we can usefully distinguish between what I have termed the *televisually* skilled performer and the *vocationally* skilled performer (Bennett, 2008). Although this distinction should be understood as neither absolute nor a catch-all typology, it does help us understand distinctions between the kinds of performers subsumed within the wider category of the television personality.

Increasingly, in an era of DIY celebrity, these two categories of performer are appended by the notion of *vernacular* skill that is examined in Chapter 7. I use the term 'vernacular skill', drawing on Jean Burgess's work on vernacular creativity, to refer to the common, ordinary and everyday practices of cultural production that exist 'outside the cultural value systems of either high culture (art) or commercial creative practice (television, say)' (Burgess, 2006a). These vernacular skills go towards the construction of ordinary

Figure 1.2 ... with David Attenborough, as if there were no discernible difference in the way television's register of fame operates in relation to each (screen capture from *The Life of Mammals* [BBC, 2002–2003]).

people as celebrities who, whilst not necessarily or always television personalities themselves, such as Jade Goody, impact on the meaning and structures of the television personality system. In contrast, televisual skill refers to the performance mode of presentation – all television personalities must therefore have this skill to some extent in order to be successful and popular – whilst vocational skill refers to an expertise, knowledge or skill that is held by the television personality as a professional within a particular field; for instance, cookery, gardening/DIY, zoology or history. Whilst a personality may possess all three forms of skill – such as Kevin Rose, discussed in Chapter 7 – these final two categories of performer are distinguished by the televisually skilled performers' *lack* of any skill, external to that of television presenting, that *informs* their performance. The content of the show is largely irrelevant to their 'real' life or any 'skills' they may hold therein. For example, *Blind Date* (LWT/ITV, 1985–2003) was not reliant on Cilla Black's (well-known) ability as a professional singer, but is instead hinged on her ability to 'present'.[3] Similarly, Oprah Winfrey's success as a chat show host is divorced from her appearances as an actress. Whilst such an external vocational skill may have contributed or informed their celebrity status, it is not crucial to their continued presence on television or successful career as a television personality. What is important is how such a skill, singing or acting or comedy, is deployed as a form of televisual skill that enables them to hold the viewer's attention, marshalling

Table 1.1 Televisually skilled versus vocationally skilled performers

Televisually skilled	Vocationally skilled
• Cilla Black, Ant and Dec, Graham Norton, Arthur Godfry, Ryan Seacrest (light entertainment) • Anne Robinson, Pat Sajak, Eddie McGuire, Noel Edmonds (game shows) • David Letterman, Jonathan Ross, Michael Parkinson (chat shows) • Oprah Winfrey, Trisha Goddard (talk shows) • Sylvia Peters, Mary Malcolm, Noelle Middleton (announcing)	• Delia Smith, Jamie Oliver, Julia Childs, Martha Stewart (cookery) • Alan Titchmarsh, Don Burke, Tye Pennington, (gardening and DIY) • Trinny and Susannah, Gok Wan, Carson Kressley (fashion) • Simon Schama, David Starkey (history) • Steve Irwin, David Attenborough (natural history) • Richard Dimbleby, Jeremy Paxman, Walter Cronkite (journalism) • Milton Berle, Benny Hill, David Mitchell and Robert Webb (comedy)

forms of direct and indirect address, orchestrate other performers on set, host the procession of guests a programme might utilise and scale their performance to the intimacy of the domestic television viewing experience. This category is most easily understood in relation to the careers of performers who have 'fronted', presented or hosted a number of different programmes during their career. Predominantly, therefore, such televisually skilled presenters work within the broad genre of light entertainment and variety. By contrast, the vocationally skilled performer is largely, but not exclusively, tied to the presentation of lifestyle or documentary programming. So we can see presenters such as Julia Childs, Alan Titchmarsh and David Attenborough as vocationally skilled performers whose authenticity of character is tied inextricably to the *credibility* of their professed skill. Table 1.1 may therefore usefully demonstrate this division of television personality and its broad relationship to genre.

As I have suggested, the demarcation between performers, like the distinction between actor and personality, is not fixed: both Cilla (singing) and Graham Norton (comedy)[4] have been vocational performers at different points in their career, whilst Alan Titchmarsh has fronted natural history programming and the BBC's annual coverage of the Proms away from his vocationally based gardening programmes such as *How to Be a Gardener* (BBC, 2002–2003). Most recently this has extended to his presentation of the chat show *The Alan Titchmarsh Show* (Spun Gold TV for ITV1, 2007–ongoing) as well as a slot DJ-ing on BBC Radio 2.[5]

There are therefore two trends to note in the way this loose distinction works: first, that there is increasingly an emphasis on televisual skill, and second that this emphasis can lead to a detachment between a personality's original vocational skill, which predicated their appearance on television, and their televisual fame. For example, Graham Norton's early appearances on television were closely linked to his vocational skill as a *professional* comedian incorporating many of his stand-up routine's elements, such as the use of phone calls to classified ads found in gay magazines. Whilst he continues to host a similar programme on the BBC, his main appearances have increasingly taken place in primetime light entertainment programming, such as *How Do You Solve a Problem Like Maria?* (BBC, 2006) or *Any Dream Will Do* (BBC, 2007), and his professional appearances as a stand-up comedian have almost entirely ceased. This is not to say that Norton is no longer funny (although it is increasingly debatable), but that this has been folded into his televisual skill – a similar trajectory might be followed by *Late Night with ...* host Jimmy Fallon, or a reverse path trod by Alan Titchmarsh if he ceases to make gardening programming altogether. Comedy, as I indicated earlier, is clearly one of the most difficult categories to accommodate within this distinction and this is largely because of the diverse array of performers we might assemble under the heading 'comedy' or 'comedian'. This might include the sitcom star, the sketch comedy artist and the chat show host, with performers moving across this continuum. Nevertheless, as I shall discuss further in Chapter 2, it is possible to understand comedy as both a vocational and televisual skill. For example, the sketch artist's fame resides largely in their vocational performances of comedy routines that have a long heritage in vaudeville and music hall but, as I discuss in Chapters 2 and 3, such performers must master televisual skill in order to become a television personality; in turn, the role of comedy to the chat show host may have been crucial to the personality's initial appearances on television and infuses his/her performance, but it predominantly becomes deployed as a form of televisual skill.

To return to the first of the two trends I noted, Titchmarsh's oscillation between vocationally and televisually skilled performer is emblematic of an increasing emphasis on televisual skill, so that vocationally skilled personalities are no longer simply divulging their specialised knowledge, but many are now capable of managing a performance similar to the televisually skilled performer. This is most notable in lifestyle programming's increased reliance on the ability of one of its vocational performers to present the programme, rather than have a presenter who is solely televisually skilled acting as an intermediary between expert and ordinary contestant/viewer. Whilst David Bell and Joanne Hollows are correct to surmise that the adoption of a conversational mode of address by UK lifestyle presenters – which plays on 'chattiness and matiness' delivered in a variety of regional accents and the use of slang – serves to 'de-emphasize authority' (Bell and Hollows, 2005: 15), it is also important to understand that such a shift also *emphasises* televisual skill. For example, on British television Carole Smillie's position as the televisually skilled host of *Changing Rooms* (BBC, 1997–2004), was increasingly supplemented and eventually replaced by the performances of

Laurence Llewellyn-Bowen, who originally joined the series as a vocational expert in design. Thus, whereas the many early-to-mid-1990s makeover programmes, discussed by Rachel Moseley in her foundational study of lifestyle programming, were generally presented by a televisually skilled performer, such as with *Changing Rooms* or *Style Challenge* (BBC, 1996–2000), by the turn of the millennium programmes such as *Ground Force* (BBC, 1998–2004) and *What Not to Wear* (BBC, 2002–2008) were carried on the performances of vocationally skilled performers alone (Moseley, 2000). Jacob Smith's (2009) analysis of the 'titans' of 1950s US educational television, particularly Dr Frank C. Baxter, suggests that this emphasis on televisual skill – often over and above professional expertise or knowledge – has a much longer history, which I pick up in Part I's historical excavation of early forms of British television fame.

In a similar vein, one can think of the trend of the 'ordinary' person on television, most obviously the reality show contestant, developing (or exhibiting) the televisual skill necessary to become a television personality. However, whilst many former *Big Brother* contestants may go on to a briefly successful celebrity career, fewer make the transition to work as a television personality because of the skills and personas required. For example, Craig Phillips, the winner of the UK's first *Big Brother* series, moved from 'ordinary person' to a vocationally skilled performer as a DIY expert on various makeover programmes but has lacked the necessary televisual skill to become a television personality. Similarly, Jade Goody, despite remaining in the media spotlight for an unprecedented length of time for a former reality TV contestant (something which she to some extent undoubtedly *achieved*), was not a television personality. Her celebrity might best be understood as specifically configured by television so that, as Su Holmes has argued, the furore around the *Celebrity Big Brother* race row partly emerged as a reaction to 'the fact that the race row had apparently exposed an undesirable *disjuncture* between' on- and off-screen persona (Bennett and Holmes, 2010: 71). However, to my mind it is not helpful to describe her as a 'television personality': her television programmes, such as *Just Jade* (Granada for LivingTV, 2006) and *Jade's PA* (Ruggie Media for LivingTV), dealt in observational docu-tainment formats, rather than the presentational performance modes that characterise the television personality; in turn, cultural intermediaries – rather than a skilled performance per se – were the central driver in maintaining her celebrity status. This is not to suggest a complete lack of skill or labour – as I suggest below the presentation of the self in front of cameras and other media technologies is an increasingly shared vernacular skill – but that it is more helpful to understand Goody as part of the wider celebrity economy of the television personality system than as a television personality herself.

In this section, I have been keen to emphasise that the television personality is best understood as a particular kind of television performer whose fame is specifically configured by their work in television. However, this attempt to judge such personalities 'by television standards', does not mean a return to medium theory. One of the welcome results of celebrity studies move from the specific to the general has been the conception 'of celebrity as less a trait of a particular person than a discursive *mode of representation*' (Turner *et al.*, quoted in Bennett and Holmes, 2010: 68). As Graeme Turner's analysis of celebrity has argued, the growth of modern celebrity has taken place within the broader contexts of globalisation, particularly the international circulation of television formats, and convergence (Turner, 2004). These conditions play into any analysis of contemporary celebrity, including one addressed solely at television; indeed the question of media convergence and fame is dealt with explicitly in Chapter 7. Moreover, as Jason Jacobs (2000) and others have persuasively shown (Boddy, 2004; Spigel, 1992), television is after all a hybrid medium, and this shapes its formation of celebrity too. Jacobs' excellent history of early British television drama production demonstrates how three key discourses were constructed around television during the pre-war period in Britain, whereby live immediacy was coupled with discourses of intimacy and hybridity (Jacobs, 2000: 28). These discourses formed a complex understanding of television so that the simultaneity of transmission and reception were understood to create a relationship of authenticity, reinforced by the privileging of the close-up and direct address as devices of intimacy. These tactics were complemented by television's value being placed on its relay ability: to act as a hybrid of other media forms, such as opera, newspapers and national events, by allowing the viewer live access to them through television's window-on-the-world. The formation of television's personality system during this period was therefore equally shaped by this hybridity and its entwinement with the other key discourses of immediacy and intimacy. For early television fame, this often meant performers moved between platforms: from radio to television, or from the stages of music hall and vaudeville to television, as well as from television to film and vice versa. As I shall go on to discuss in Chapter 2, this was far from a secure or easy relationship for both performers and institutions.

Whilst these back and forth relationships have persisted to the current day – particularly between radio and television – television's hybridity has been extended further by its convergence with digital media. John Caldwell's work is suggestive here of how digital convergence renews this hybridity: television is a 'hybrid … media art form … regularly seen – even in the digital age – as a combinatory medium; a venue in which historically discrete art forms are aggregated into and presented as part of a complete whole' (Caldwell, 2004: 55–56). Such a conception moves beyond an understanding of television as a mere relayer of other art or media forms and constitutes it as an amalgam of these: a convergence with other media technologies. Thus besides looking at the historical connections between television, film, radio and music hall, I shall consider 'multiplatform fame' in relation to Internet television and social media platforms, such as Twitter, in Chapter 7. Such an analysis draws our attention to the way authenticity and intimacy structure our access and understanding of mobile and digital forms of television, as well as returning us to the question of what the extension of fame to an increasingly diverse and 'ordinary' array of celebrities means in relation to the debates about the democratic or adverse nature of contemporary celebrity. In turn, paying close attention to the discourses that I map out below allows us to move beyond these debates and consider the ideological, economic and cultural meaning of such fame more specifically. Primarily, however, what I hope to have set out in this section is the way in which television personality fame can be understood as *achieved* as well as distinct from other forms of celebrity produced and circulated by television. These other forms of celebrity are no less part of television's personality system and, whilst my focus across the book will be on 'television personalities', we can only understand the specificities of their fame by paying attention to this broader context.

Ordinariness, authenticity, intimacy and work: Taking the television personality seriously

Throughout this book I shall be discussing television personalities in relation to key discourses of ordinariness, authenticity, intimacy and work. In the remainder of this chapter I set out some of the key theoretical understandings that underpin their use throughout the book. These are expanded on, nuanced and at times challenged across the following chapters, but the discussion below provides a map for the exposition of how television personalities function in relation to ideology, performance, ontology, aesthetics, economics and cultural values.

Ordinariness

Raymond Williams famously declared that 'culture was ordinary', and yet this is a term that often has negative connotations. In his *Keywords*, Williams's etymological excavation of the term 'ordinary' shows how its original application to describe 'persons able to act "in their own right" … was extended, not at first in any contradictory way, to something done by custom'. This extension eventually led to a largely class-based understanding of the term, which connected ordinariness with a lack of education and social inferiority. Williams quotes Daniel Defoe's eighteenth century use of the term to describe the vulgar language and expressions he encountered 'such as … even the worst and ordinariest people in the Street would not use' (quoted in Williams, 1983: 225). Equally however, the term 'ordinary' – and in particular as applied to people – can express an opposite attitude. To position people as ordinary therefore is also to describe them as 'sensible', 'regular' and 'decent', 'as distinct from the views of some sect or of intellectuals' (ibid.: 226). In turn, understandings of ordinary people have depicted them as part of the 'masses' – a term with equally ambivalent meanings. Thus on the one hand, as David Morley has suggested, this tends to envisage the mass 'as Others – the poor, the mob, the crowd, the uneducated – all those who constitute the antithesis of the educated middle-class white adult male, who (naturally) encapsulates the tradition of enlightenment reason' (Morley, 2005: 208). On the other, Williams's entry on mass points to the way 'English radicals' have used the term 'the people and its variations – common people, working people, ordinary people – as their primary positive terms' so that as much as connoting a low, ignorant and unstable mob, the masses can stand as a 'description of the same people but now seen as a positive or potentially positive source' (Williams, 1983: 194–195). As we shall see, in the British context, television personalities' claims to ordinariness are particularly associated with notions of working-class-ness – with equally ambivalent meanings apparent in the way it is connected to notions of common knowledge, the masses or the popular.

The use of the term 'ordinary' in relation to television and the television personality, and its attendant implications, is further complicated by the medium's status as one of, if not *the*, mass media of the twentieth century. In negative understandings of the term 'mass', such as the Frankfurt School's description of the culture industries, the mass media are understood as manipulative, purveyors of propaganda, alienation, 'dumbing-down', disempowerment and inauthentic cultural forms – including personalities, who are distinguished only by pseudo-individuality. Moreover, for those who perceive the democratisation of celebrity negatively, television is at the forefront of fame's extension to ordinary, seemingly undeserving, people. In this view ordinary people are manufactured for celebrity as a form of commercial property that exploits both the celebrity themselves, as well as consumers. Yet, as Morley points out, 'against all this negativity, there is ... a more positive view ... seeing popular culture as having an important democratic dimension, in its drive (even if in commercialised forms) towards extension and inclusiveness' (Morley, 2005). As Su Holmes has suggested, reality TV celebrity often functions as evidence of this democratising ethos drawing on Jon Dovey's claim that the form acts as a 'challenge to "established paternalisms" in its bid to boldly release "everyday voices into the public sphere"' (quoted in Holmes, 2004a: 112). Whilst reality TV may have accentuated the place of ordinary people on television, beyond the stark debates about the value of contemporary celebrity, television has long dealt in the currency of ordinary people: from audiences on programming as diverse as light entertainment to political debate through to vox pop pieces in news reporting or documentaries. However, although this leads Frances Bonner to conclude that television's 'conception of the [ordinary] often draws on the definition of "ordinary" as a shared culture' (Bonner, 2003: 30), equally the term has been used as a negative evaluation of television's regime of fame in comparison to cinema. Television, and television personalities in particular, therefore arguably function at the contested boundaries of these meanings of the ordinary.

The contestation of the meaning of ordinary in relation to television's production of celebrity is particularly apparent in the way the extraordinary/ordinary dialectic established by film studies for understanding film stardom has been extended to create a hierarchical dichotomy between film and television fame: extraordinary/ordinary. It is instructive here to dwell briefly on how this understanding of ordinariness has informed our understanding of the television personality, and why its negative connotations are resisted by scholars such as Jermyn who have argued for a category of television stardom. Her work, like Andy Medhurst's on Gilbert Harding before it, demonstrates that the television personality is capable of achieving the kind of intertextual coverage assumed to be the preserve of stars. Medhurst argues that Harding's appearances as a straight talking and often rude panellist on *What's My Line?* (BBC, 1950–1967) in the 1950s had made him Britain's 'first unequivocal media personality'. As with Jermyn's analysis of the intertextual coverage of Sarah Jessica Parker, Medhurst finds that the extent and kind of media coverage that accompanied and built Harding's fame must therefore fit Ellis's 'basic definition of a star as a "performer in a particular medium whose figure enters into subsidiary forms of circulation and then feeds back into future performances"' (Medhurst, 1991: 72). In Jermyn's analysis she suggest that this intertextual coverage of SJP marks a clear distinction between on-/off-screen self, creating a star image in line with cinema's ordinary/extraordinary paradox. In turn, she goes on to challenge the devaluation of television's fame as merely ordinary by suggesting 'some of the differences that were once held to exist between TV "personalities" and cinematic stars have been eroded' (Jermyn, 2006: 82). In contrast, Medhurst finds that '... something pulls me back from calling [Harding] a star'. That 'something' turns out to be precisely the present absence of the cinema Ellis enunciates as central in defining a star's extraordinariness: as Medhurst goes on to articulate, 'film stars have an aura of mystery, of other-worldliness, of sexual desirability, that is enhanced by the size of the screen and the darkness of the cinema' (Medhurst, 1991: 72–73).

In celebrity culture the television personality system's ordinariness is therefore devalued twofold: because it is part of the everyday, lacking cinema's ordinary/extraordinary paradox but also because it has been at the forefront of the extension of fame to ordinary people. Yet what Langer describes as television's 'will to ordinariness' is precisely the site of the personality system's economic, textual, cultural and ideological value. Again, I want to resist the binary of suggesting that the ordinariness of television's celebrity is a democratisation of fame, nor merely the demotic circulation of diversity for its own sake or in the interests of media conglomerates (Turner, 2004). My use of the term 'ordinary' throughout the book suggest that the devaluing of television's ordinary, everyday fame has happened at the expense of understanding the way ordinariness, as Holmes and Couldry have argued, 'clearly functions as an ideological category' (Holmes, 2006b; Couldry, 2002: 102). In this context, and following Richard Hoggart's work, the ordinary becomes a category worthy of attention firstly for revealing the way in which film stardom's paradox has been enlisted to restrict scholarly analysis to a category 'so narrow that only the exceptional in society were worthy of study' (Hoggart, paraphrased in Gregg, 2007: 95). One response, as with Jermyn's work, would be to attempt to elevate television fame to the same plane as cinema's extraordinary stardom. However, Hoggart's work suggested that the ordinary is a category worthy of attention for the way it was intimately connected to working-class lives, helping draw 'a barrier between "them" and "us" in everyday dealings is a way of making a subordinate position acceptable' (quoted in ibid.). As such, in line with Williams's and Morley's analysis of the relationship between the masses and ordinary above, the category has often been enlisted as part of a Marxist critique by academics that demonstrates the potential positive power of the masses to deflate, rebel, reject and overturn authority. Such a view of the ordinary might easily be aligned with the celebrity as democracy perspective for the power it confers to the diverse masses.

However Melissa Gregg's work cautions against the continuance of such an easy relationship. She demonstrates how cultural studies' adoption of the ordinary has been confounded in Australia by the way former prime minister John Howard co-opted the meaning of the term as part of a conservative ideology that enabled him to govern in the name of ordinariness in opposition to 'the so-called intellectual "elite" ... special interest groups [such as Indigenous Australians] ... "politically correct" [society] ... [or] Muslims ... who refuse to "integrate" into "ordinary Australia"' (Gregg, 2007: 101). For Gregg therefore, the ordinary is a complex category whereby:

> Reclaiming the conceptual rigour of the term therefore involves a 'shared rejection of fixed, static and foundational presuppositions' of ordinariness, to allow for 'an awareness of the complex mediated nature of "ordinary life" situated in class, gender, ethnic and sexual differences'.
>
> (Gregg, quoting Sandywell, 2007: 99)

Television's personality system similarly enlists the ordinary in myriad ways that the predominant understandings of the term in this context (as an elision of on-/off-screen self and a purveyor of 'ordinary' celebrity) fail to account for. As we shall see in the discussion of national identity and multiplatform fame in Chapters 6 and 7, understandings of ordinariness as a valued form of 'sensible' or 'common' knowledge play an important role in the construction and performance of vocational and vernacular skill that underpins how television personalities function in relation to cultural and ideological values.

Moreover, the analysis of a range of television personalities' claims to ordinariness suggests the concept is not static. As with Holmes's study of 1950s television fame, my examination of the 'invention of the television personality' in Part I disrupts the taken-for-granted-ness of ordinariness as a hallmark of this fame by examining a moment when 'the apparatus itself is not yet entirely "ordinary"' (Holmes, 2006b: 285). Such an examination demonstrates how ordinariness functions as an ideological marker of class and gender, which worked to reconcile television fame with the institutional and economic parameters of public service broadcasting. Ordinariness is therefore a discursive category constructed across television personalities' intertextual image. In turn, therefore, these complex ideological and cultural functions of television personalities' ordinariness nevertheless remained tethered to the way personalities form part of television's everyday-ness, affecting intimate connections with audiences by appearing 'just-as-they-are'.

Authenticity

> Authenticity: as being authoritative or duly authorised; as being in accordance with fact, as being true in substance; as being what it professes in origin or authorship, as being genuine; as being real, actual.
>
> (*Oxford English Dictionary*, online)

The use of the term 'authenticity' in celebrity studies, as established by Dyer's work, has suggested that we are encouraged to locate the 'real', 'true', 'private' stars away from their public persona. As Su Holmes has explicated, Dyer's analysis of the role of authenticity in the construction of stardom articulated the 'notion of individualism upon which capitalist society depends' whereby 'the perpetual attempt to lay claim to the "real self", was organized around a desire to suggest a "separable, coherent quality, located "inside" consciousness and variously termed "the self", "the soul", "the subject"' (quoted in Holmes, 2005a: 27). To a large degree, as Holmes acknowledges, Dyer's notion of authenticity draws both on the ordinary/extraordinary paradox of stardom, which suggests the separation of on- and off-screen self, as well as on modern understandings of the authentic self. As Charles Guignon has explained, this posits 'a split between *the real me* – the true inner self – and the *persona* (from Greek for mask) that one puts on for the external world' (Guignon, 2004: 35). Most importantly Guignon's work, reviewing a range of philosophical writing from Lionel Trilling and Stanley Cavell through to popular sources such as the discourses purveyed by Oprah Winfrey and Dr Phil McGraw, suggests how authenticity has been positively *valued* across postmodern, modern, Romantic and pre-modern societies. As Trilling suggests, the authentic self is seen as 'something that is worth accessing and raising to expression' (quoted in Guignon, 2004: 12). Thus whilst Guignon's work demonstrates the mutability of the concept of authenticity – including the way in which postmodernism has challenged the notion of a stable, centred, 'core' identity – he suggests that notions of remaining true to oneself and understanding the authentic self as a source of strength and value have remained; even if that meant to '*be* that lack of self with playfulness and ironic amusement' (ibid.: 119).

Challenges to the notion of authenticity in relationship to celebrity studies have tended to come from two main arguments: postmodernism's understanding of the self as de-centred; and the extension of fame to ordinary people, whose celebrity is apparently based on the revelation of the authentic self from the outset of their fame. Holmes's work deals effectively with a number of the problematics that both critiques apply to the perceived centrality of authenticity in the meaning of celebrity. In relation to the extension of celebrity to ordinary people, as Sean Redmond has noted, the dominant rhetorical device of 'being ordinary, authentic or "real" ... has increasingly found its logical point of reference in the onscreen and online antics of extraordinary and ordinary people supposedly *just* being themselves' (Redmond, 2006: 28). In contrast to the condition of film stardom that Dyer sets out therefore, in such a situation there is apparently little need for a search for the 'real' or authentic self as fame has already been predicated on its exposure. Nevertheless, Holmes's analysis of *heat* magazine suggests how authenticity remains a predominant concern in celebrity culture, albeit one that is carefully negotiated to acknowledge both the manufactured, pervasive and ordinary nature of modern fame. Thus she suggests that *heat*'s coverage of all celebrities, including those ordinary or manufactured by reality TV, demonstrates the continued search for an authentic, inner self but no longer with the belief that it 'is indeed truly special or extraordinary' (Holmes, 2005a: 36).

Indeed, the extension of celebrity to ordinary people speaks to the second challenge to notions of authenticity posited by postmodernism which, like the decontextualisation of fame engendered by ordinary celebrity, emphasises an anti-essentialist view of the world and a lack of guarantees over any pre-determination (Grossberg, 1987). In postmodern thought, the self is understood to be something always 'in play' – a process of 'becoming' as Stuart Hall has argued in relation to diasporic identities in the late modern condition (Hall, 1993). This notion of the self as changeable has perhaps been most influentially theorised by Anthony Giddens's work. Focusing on what he terms 'late modernity', but has clear overtones of postmodernity's conditions of instability and flux, Giddens argues that in this period 'self-identity becomes a reflexively organised endeavour. The reflexive project of the self, which consists in the sustaining of coherent, yet continuously revised, biographical narratives, takes place in the context of multiple choice'. Of particular importance to Giddens is the notion of lifestyle, which 'implies choice within a plurality of possible options, and is "adopted" rather than "handed down"' (Giddens, 1991: 81). For Giddens, as with Ouellette and Hay's analysis of reality TV discussed further below, in modernity the self is constantly asked to 'reskill' as part of lifestyle projects that are mediated by experts – whose knowledge and skills affect a connection with the authentic self as ordinary, by professing to be self-made experts via the application of common knowledge. The self, particularly of ordinary people, is therefore one that is constantly asked to transform. However, this is a process managed and presided over by experts, discussed here as vocationally skilled performers, who offer solutions to the problem of the self. In such debates authenticity, like in Guignon's work, is based on remaining 'true to oneself' but through a process of self-actualisation (Giddens, 1991) that involves growing through lifestyle projects as discussed in Chapter 6.

Whilst such notions of authenticity function helpfully to explain the role of vocational performers, their emphasis on the mutability of the self also suggests how we can understand authenticity as a performance. Erving Goffman's work has suggested how the self is constantly performed even in face-to-face encounters (Goffman, 1969). Yet as Holmes has suggested, his approach 'offers a rather abstract and dehistoricized account of social interaction and performance' in which mediation plays no part (Holmes, 2008a: 17). Drawing on Abercrombie and Longhurst, she goes on to analyse the role the mediated self plays in the relationship between viewer and performer in *Big Brother*, suggesting that mediation itself can be 'positioned as a source of privileged "truth" and revelation, or as a conduit which facilitates a transparent and immediate connection between audience and screen' depending on the context (ibid: 18). Holmes's work is useful in that it demonstrates the way authenticity can be performed, and acknowledged as such – even in the realms of the ordinary (person).

Yet, for television personalities, the performance of authenticity must be understood as a professional problem and, as I show across the book, this is constructed both discursively and via signs of performance that it is possible to analyse, both in terms of their economic and ideological function as well as their *achievement*. Thus I draw on film studies' paradigms, such as Andrew Klevan's (2005) and Richard Dyer's (2000, 2001) work on performance, to demonstrate how authenticity – or the appearance of it – is also a palpable mode of performance and achievement. As Dyer has argued, authenticity as a mode of performance is 'established or constructed in media texts by the use of markers that indicate lack of control, lack of premeditation and privacy' (Dyer, 2000: 137). Most importantly, what such analysis reveals is that to describe a *performance* of authenticity need not be seen as a contradiction in terms. As British television critic Mark Lawson has suggested, understanding the television personality as a performance does not amount to 'insincerity ... [as] certain elements of [their] nature' are exaggerated 'while others [are] play[ed]down'.[6] In particular, if we adopt a postmodern approach to the self, Lawson's comment that personalities may 'play up' certain aspects of their persona fits with more pervasive discourses of the self as something that is constantly worked at and refashioned. This notion of the display of authenticity and the self being both a form of performance and work turns me to my final two concepts relevant to the television personality: intimacy and work.

Intimacy

> 'Pleased to meet you'... Say five million viewers.
>
> (*TV Mirror* headline, August 27, 1953: 4)

Intimacy is a key discourse of not only television celebrity but also, as Chris Rojek's work demonstrates, of modern fame more widely. Rojek suggests how, prior to the mass media, a form of 'pre-figurative' celebrity was circulated through state-sponsored sources, such as proclamations and decrees, which 'did not carry the illusion of intimacy … [that makes] the veridical self a site of perpetual public excavation' in contemporary celebrity (Rojek, 2001: 19). The connection between intimacy and the revelation of the 'veridical self' that Rojek makes evidences the inextricable link between discourses of intimacy and authenticity. As Sean Redmond has argued, the prevalence of the 'celebrity confessional' is demonstrative of the importance placed on celebrity's affecting an intimate connection with fans that assures the validity of the authentic self (Redmond, 2006: 32).

Television, however, has been understood to accentuate these qualities. As suggested by Jacobs' work on early British television, the techniques and technologies of television have been key in underscoring intimacy (Jacobs, 2000). On the one hand, the technological base of television's 'simultaneity of transmission and reception' together with the use of direct address served to create a relationship of intimacy and authenticity between performer and audience. On the other, the predominant technique of direct address also served as a device of intimacy. Thus in an article that appeared in *TV Mirror* under the quote that opens this section, Elizabeth Gray – a regular performer on British panel shows during the 1950s – suggests that whilst 'stage and film stars had their fans throughout the years', the impact of television 'beats them both' by bringing a performer 'into millions of homes at once'.

Television's emphasis on intimacy is therefore connected to its domestic viewing situation and the way in which it delivers its performers into the milieu of everyday life via the regularity and repetition of the schedule. This goes towards what Marshall (1997) has described as television's familiarisation function, which as Susan Murray has suggested, helps facilitate the economic goals of broadcasting. Thus from its very outset television performance has 'overtly courted the conflation of on-stage/off-stage by a breaking of the boundaries of theatrical realism', via the use of direct address, in order to create an intimacy 'between performer and audience' (Murray, 2005: 72). In turn, this functioned to 'naturalise the performers in the domestic setting so as to make them appear less aberrant in the context of the everyday', so as to engage audiences in a continuing story and 'draws positive attention to the sponsor's product' (ibid.: 130–131). Whilst television's regime of fame may therefore be understood to be part of what Rojek suggests is a wider turn to intimacy in modern celebrity, it is also clear that it functions quite distinctly from other forms of fame that preceded it, such as theatre or cinema (Rojek, 2001). As Holmes argues, the extraordinary/ordinary paradox of cinema stardom worked as 'an economic strategy intended to encourage repeat trips to the cinema. But the regular flow of television culture demands a different economy of viewing' (Bennett and Holmes, 2010: 69). Intimacy is therefore inextricably linked to the domestic context of reception that cultivates an informality between celebrity and viewer, who is no longer 'humble before the image'. Television's liveness – both real and simulated – in turn, tends to emphasise this intimacy by connecting the regular appearances of television personalities into the viewers' home with the discourses of authenticity discussed above, which emphasise the continuity of on- and off-screen persona.

Discussing the importance of liveness in television, Philip Auslander has suggested that in establishing televisual form in relation to drama, 'although the question of authentic television form remained unresolved, early writers on television generally agreed that TV's essential properties as a medium were *immediacy* and *intimacy*' (Auslander, 1999: 17). Drawing on Lynn Spigel's work on the way early television drama sought to simulate the experience of being at the theatre, Auslander goes on to argue that the televisual has come 'to *replace* live performance', so that television has become the dominant ideological reference of liveness. As I suggest in Part I, beyond the genre of drama liveness played a key role in the emergence of both televisual fame and televisual skill. Liveness is therefore integral to the creation of intimacy and, in turn, the display of an authentic self: it offers both the promise of access to the unmediated self 'when things go wrong', and paradoxically may also affirm their televisual skill in performance. Although concerned primarily with a particular mode of female performance, Bonner helpfully suggests how the 'elevation of the qualities of liveness effectively sanctions, if not requires, a roughness around the edges' that goes towards affecting an intimate connection, yet simultaneously 'most hosts of live programmes vaunt their ability to transcend glitches of various kinds' (Bonner, 2003: 70).

However, our understanding of intimacy in relation to the television personality must not remain static. If Richard Schickel is correct to argue that each 'new development in communications has increased our illusion of intimacy with the celebrated' (Schickel, 1985: 49), whereby television has reduced the barriers between the other-worldly and the audience as well as their own private personas, then it is also true that many forms of digital media work to continue this trend. Thus whilst Su Holmes's analysis of *heat* and reality TV contestants discussed above attests to the way in which authenticity continues to function as a key site of understanding fame, despite its extension to an increasingly diverse and ordinary celebrity sphere through reality TV, the creation and maintenance of celebrity via social media technologies and platforms such as Twitter and blogs continues to emphasise the intimate connection between audience and a celebrity's 'authentic' persona. Such technologies place a greater cachet on interactivity than liveness but, as I shall come to in Chapter 7, the construction of DIY and digital fame continues to draw on the discourses, performance tropes and values of television's intimate, authentic personality system. At the same time, whilst such technologies promise DIY fame to all, mastering them is undoubtedly a form of vernacular skill that few achieve in establishing and sustaining a celebrity image.

Work: Skill, labour, knowledge and expertise

Ideals of work and talent have been understood as crucial to the construction of celebrity. As Dyer argues, the success myth:

> tries to orchestrate several contradictions: ordinariness is the hallmark of the star; the system rewards talent or 'specialness'; that luck, 'breaks', which may happen to anyone typify the career of the star; and that hard work and professionalism are necessary for stardom.
>
> (Dyer, 2001: 42)

Most importantly, the myth also 'suggests that success is worth having – in the form of conspicuous consumption' but also, as Barry King points out, through providing stars with social mobility (King, quoted in ibid.). As Su Holmes argues, the success myth has effectively 'narrativised' the ordinary/extraordinary paradox of cinematic stardom (Holmes, 2005b). In contrast the narrative of predominant forms of television celebrity, most particularly that from reality TV, tends to elide questions of hard work or talent: instead, fame is merely attributed to them via the work of cultural intermediaries, such as publicists, managers and PR gurus (Biressi and Nunn, 2004; see Turner et al., 2000 on the role of cultural intermediaries). Beyond reality TV the intertextual emphasis on authenticity and ordinariness discussed above, which positions television personalities as 'just-as-they-are', equally serves to erase any notion of talent, skilled performance or hard work that goes towards the construction of their on-screen persona. Whilst the success myth's emphasis on the on-/off-screen personas of film stars allowed for a discourse on screen acting to develop, which valued acting as an achievement (deCordova, 1990), this has simultaneously worked towards establishing the hierarchical dichotomy with television fame and performance. Again, we are returned to the question of 'what do television personalities do' if they merely play themselves?

The consequence of this dichotomy has been the failure to develop an acknowledgement of, and vocabulary for, the concept of performance in relation to television presentation. Whilst the turn to American quality drama by not only television scholars but film counterparts increasingly comes to recognise the distinction between on-/off-screen self in television, and thus deem television performance as a site worthy of study, the notion that presenting involves a performance that might sustain critical attention and reward has not been equally explored. Yet as the BBC's Head of Light Entertainment Ronald Waldman recognised in 1954, presenting or introducing is 'a highly skilled professional job'.[7] Thus in proposing the various categories of televisual, vocational and vernacular skill that I have set out above, I want to go further than simply reveal that the television personality's persona is a constructed performance. We can understand it both in terms of achievement – with the resultant pleasure it provides – as well as a form of labour and expertise – with the consequent reward and exploitation that attends it. These forms of skill are therefore pivotal to the commodity *and* aesthetic function of the television personality. Indeed, televisual skill is crucial to the longevity of television fame: whilst television may produce a plethora of celebrity and confer 'ephemeral' fame, it is those who master the techniques necessary to create an intimate, spontaneous, immediate performance style that may be understood as 'television personalities'.

Susan Murray's and Karen Lury's work provide useful correctives in this regard. Murray examines historical discourses of television performance that aligned the success of early performers with the 'ability to represent what the industry believed were [television's] primary aesthetic properties – immediacy, intimacy and spontaneity' (Murray, 2005: xv). Discussing performance as a 'marriage of spectacle and intimacy', Murray's work demonstrates how performers faced the problem of developing 'televisual skill' in seeking to move from vaudeville, music hall and radio to television and I discuss this further in Part I. More conceptually, Lury pays close attention to the construction of various performers' televisual image as an interplay between performance technique and production technology. These two elements are crucial in understanding televisual skill, whereby the former are 'aligned to [the performer's] given physiology [technique], as opposed to technology … [which comprises] the process of filming and recording' (Lury, 1995: 118). As I suggest in Part II, by analysing these signs of performance we can understand how 'sustaining a performance – over three hours, a run in the theatre, over weeks of filming – starts to look like a professional problem' (Thompson, 1985: 68). However, televisual skill is but one form of the labour and expertise that we need to recognise and pay greater attention to if we are to fully understand the television personality system.

Where studies of labour and work in television have occurred they have tended to focus on reality TV and the place of ordinary people. For example, Mark Andrejevic (2002) and Nick Couldry (2004) draw on Foucauldian conceptions of power to suggest that the aesthetics of surveillance in both reality TV and digital media place the revelation of the authentic self at the heart of a 'value-generating labour' exchange that underpins corporate marketing strategies in an age of convergence television (Andrejevic, 2002: 266). In this view, the work of the ordinary person attempting to gain celebrity is understood as a form of labour that is bootstrapped into media conglomerates' commercial strategies, with the fleeting and ephemeral fame of the 'celebs' an unequal and exploited reward in terms of the media industries' profit participants and the structures of capital. Such a perspective provides an important reminder of the political economy of celebrity. But it is also one in which value judgements remain latent. Alison Hearn's work is useful here, recognising on the one hand that 'the constitution of the self is now an outer-directed process, which involves our *skill* at self-production', but on the other that such work 'does not produce commodities per se … [instead] furthering the corporation's colonization of the "real" ... and the real subsumption of social existence by capital' (Hearn, 2006: 631, emphasis added). And yet, whilst the commercialisation of the real, and by proxy the 'authentic' self, might be something accentuated by reality TV, these economic relations of labour and capital are those that have structured stardom (proper) from its very inception as a twentieth-century commodity form.

Whilst this emphasis on the commodity form of celebrity is certainly a useful way of understanding the labour performed in reality TV, it again draws our attention away from the 'television personality'. In particular, in understanding the celebrity and function of the ordinary person in such programming, we must also acknowledge that the presenters of such programming play an equally important role in negotiating the meaning of television celebrity. For example, if John Hartley (2004a) is correct to argue that *Big Brother* contestants must come out into the real world to discover what they 'mean', then the show's host (for example, Davina McCall in the United Kingdom) plays a vital role in negotiating this meaning. Whilst not directly concerned with celebrity, Laurie Ouellette and James Hay's recent study of reality TV provides fertile ground for considering the work that is performed in different forms of the genre by not only contestants, but also presenters (Ouellette and Hay, 2008). Their study demonstrates how television functions as a cultural technology that governmentalises participants' behaviour in order to encourage self-regulation and allow for a Foucaldian form of 'governing at a distance'. Basing their analysis on the reinvention of government during the 1990s as a neo-liberal enterprise, Ouellette and Hay suggest reality TV is a 'civic laboratory' for experimenting with 'the best way to govern liberal capitalist democracies'. It does so by promoting 'privatization, personal responsibility and consumer choice ... [in order to] shows [sic] us how to conduct and "empower" ourselves as enterprising citizens' (ibid.: 1). They position the main participants in reality TV as governed by 'the development of expertise', whereby presenters and professionals represent the power 'to authorize and administer it' so as to shape and guide 'human beings toward "better" strategies of self-regulation that was [sic] not tied to state power' (ibid.: 13).

Predominantly focused on lifestyle television, their argument implicitly recognises the vocational skill of presenters as 'experts' in their chosen profession, whilst simultaneously positioning 'ordinary people' as what Paul du Gay calls 'entrepreneurs of the self' (quoted in ibid: 103). Drawing on du Gay and McRobbie they suggest this entrepreneurial self is a response to the devaluation of organised labour and the loss of job security in the flexible economy of neo-liberal government, which replaces the public sector with an emphasis on 'competition, "the seeking of self-advancement in work, and, in commercialized leisure spheres, self-improvement techniques" ... [in order to promote] self-fashioning as a requirement of work' (McRobbie, quoted in ibid: 103–104).

Their study has two implications for my argument here. First, as they suggest, the emphasis placed on expertise positions the vocationally skilled television personality, such as Alan Sugar, Donald Trump, Gok Wan or Alan Titchmarsh, as '"self-made" authorities trading in applied forms of business, lifestyle, and therapeutic knowledge' (ibid.: 3). Such an approach chimes with the way ordinariness functions as a form of common knowledge for many television personalities, working to reduce the distance between expert and viewer. Yet, as Ouellette and Hay's analysis suggests, their role is crucial in fashioning the entrepreneurial selves sought by neo-liberal government and as such, are worthy of more sustained attention than has so far been given in studies of both celebrity and television. In particular, as I go on to argue in Chapter 6, the very ordinariness of the television personality is central to the way expertise – as a form of vocational knowledge or skill – is administered as part of these lifestyle projects of the self.

Second, as Su Holmes and I have argued elsewhere, reality TV appears to embrace the concept of the 'entrepreneur' of the self, and a culture which demands strategic self-fashioning and remaking – a subject who can adapt and respond to change at will – while at the same time it invests in more conservative discourses on an essential, 'inner' core (Bennett and Holmes, 2010). As work by Sternberg suggests, this discourse of entrepreneurialism intersects with one of self-presentation, whereby 'workers and managers raise their value through calculated self-presentation, using techniques originally meant for the making of celebrities' (Sternberg, 2006: 418). Similarly, Ouellette and Hay argue that 'today's Reality TV focuses on instilling self-management techniques in individuals' (Ouellette and Hay, 2008: 65) that turns 'the self into a commodity or managerial "resource" for securing "payoffs" such as satisfaction and success' (ibid.: 80). Such work builds on Goffman's influential analysis of the presentation of the self in everyday life, which suggests that we are always in some sense performing. However, in combination with the existence of books such as *The Reality TV Handbook* that promise an 'insiders' guide' to self-presentation for contestants, including 'how to perform emotion on cue', it is apparent that a skilled (or at least knowing) performance in front of cameras is increasingly ordinary.[8] At the same time, the acknowledgement of performance in such transformational forms of reality TV invests the notion of authenticity with a sense of postmodern play with the 'self', to suggest that it is constantly worked at, refashioned and adapted. Of particular import to Ouellette and Hay's discussion of the way such programming emphasises 'self-help and do-it-yourself entrepreneuralism' in the citizen-consumers it seeks to cultivate is the way in which these lessons extend beyond the confines of the broadcast programme text to the web. Thus television's convergence with the web promises ordinary people the tools of self-empowerment and entrepreneurialism that, as they suggest, connects television with ideals of democracy through participation. In an argument that is critical of the approach taken by Henry Jenkins (2006a) and John Hartley (2004b) regarding the democratic potential of interactive media, Ouellette and Hay argue that forms of DIY television and digital media promise freedom and participation not as a democratic endeavour, but rather as 'an objective of a governmental rationality that values self-enterprise, self-reliance and lessons to be learned in privatized experiments and games of self-constitutions and group government' (Ouellette and Hay, 2008: 224). In Chapter 7 I suggest how this can help us understand the nature of labour and skill that go into television and digital media's promise of DIY celebrity. As with my concern across this book, such an approach moves us beyond the immediate binaries of whether the extension of celebrity to ordinary people is good/bad for democracy and society and helps us understand the ideological and cultural function of television fame.

Part I

'TV must train its own stars'

The invention of the television personality

Writing in a November 1953 issue of *TV Mirror*, Jack Payne exhorted television to train its own stars. His call provides a useful starting point for considering to what extent television has developed its own specific regime of fame. As set out in the previous chapter, for some, television has never achieved this goal, being merely a relayer of celebrities from other spheres or of authentic, ordinary personalities. Yet, as part of a series of articles appearing in *TV Mirror* in 1953, Payne suggested how a concern to not only develop televisually specific forms of fame, but also move beyond simply relaying existing forms of celebrity and talent, was evident from the advent of television as a mass medium. Payne, the former director of dance music at the BBC, set out how the need for television to train its own stars was a concern for the institutions of television, music hall and the performers themselves. He argued:

> ...we must protect our interests if the BBC is not ... to take all the best talent. If this continued it would destroy the whole financial structure of the profession [of music hall and variety] ... Instead of taking artists *only* from variety bills and then televising them in opposition to the theatres, the BBC could start to train its own team of budding variety stars.[1]

Moreover, Payne went on to suggest that performers themselves needed to be wary of this new medium and the fame and rewards it promised because – due to its emphasis on liveness, intimacy and mass reception – *'just one bad appearance on TV can kill'* (ibid., emphasis author's own). Payne's call therefore points to the way in which the institutions of television not only required 'star names' to attract audiences, which in turn threatened to cannibalise the music hall, but also that such performers needed to adapt to the technical and aesthetic possibilities of television. That is, to develop *televisual skill* in order to be successful.

The chapters in Part I aim to set out some of the ways early television fame was understood by performers, institutions and the popular press in the United Kingdom. In so doing, I am concerned to engage with the question that the work by Su Holmes on 1950s British televisual fame poses, namely: 'Where do ... later conceptual claims of television fame locate their historical roots?' (Holmes, 2007a: 428). As discussed in Chapter 1, since Andy Medhurst's (1991) account of Gilbert Harding's fame in the 1950s, Harding has been understood as the test-case for the definitions and limits of televisual stardom. This has foregrounded notions of authenticity and ordinariness, understood in relation to the elision of on- and off-screen self, which has been central to differentiating television fame from the cinema (Ellis, 1992). Yet, not only were the meanings of authenticity and ordinariness worked out across a number of different sites, these were far from the only registers within which televisual fame was constructed. I am therefore concerned to demonstrate three key developments: first, the way in which performance – including of the ordinary and authentic self – was recognised as a form of televisual skill that went towards distinguishing television's own regime of fame as distinct from radio, film and the music hall; second, how a discourse of glamour emerged in relation to early female television personalities; and, finally, the way in which the institutional parameters of the BBC's public service obligations shaped the meaning and structure of televisual fame during the early 1950s in the United Kingdom.

The appeal to the popular of television personalities and the role of glamour in early television fame has arguably been overlooked or dismissed because they are seemingly incompatible with the discourses of not only ordinariness, intimacy and authenticity that have described television fame, but also the BBC's public service remit, which Jerome Bourdon has suggested had to carefully negotiate the popular (Bourdon, 2004). Bourdon's analysis ranges across a number of sites – from game shows, to seriality and Americanisation – but suggests that 'stars' constituted one of the central problematics for public service broadcasting's accommodation of the popular. Bourdon focuses on the early 1960s and the tension between the popularity of newsreaders and the public service obligations of early European broadcasters to argue that public television only 'reluctantly gave a place to its hosts, but never fully accepted them or rewarded them in proportion to their appeal' (ibid.: 289). However, a study across the three sites of interest noted above suggests the negotiation between public service and the popular was already more complex than this during the 1950s. Far from being 'considered as some sort of necessary evil' or as 'persons "without quality" [who] did not have a place in a television culture that emphasized culture and education' (ibid.), key personalities were cultivated, recognised, rewarded and, with the emergence of ITV in 1955, fought over by the BBC and its commercial rival. Nevertheless, Bourdon's notion of public service broadcasters *negotiating* the popular remains useful for understanding early television fame in the United Kingdom and the way it was shaped by institutional parameters. Thus whilst Espen Ytreberg is right to argue that public service broadcasters communicated 'public legitimacy ... through persons of authority' whereby broadcasting can be understood as concerned with 'converting institutional legitimacy into conventions of self-presentation, focused particularly around functions like hosting and anchoring', personalities were often a site of struggle and negotiation (Ytreberg, 2002: 759). The chapters in this section are therefore concerned with the way in which a register of television's own regime of fame was worked out during the post-war period in the United Kingdom, focusing predominantly on the period 1953–1956 and making references to developments in pre-war broadcasting that fed into these structures of television fame.

As with any historical and archival work, it is worth making a note about method and time frame here. Although the standard rationale of the availability of the archive, and archivists' time, pertain to the limitations of this study, the choice of this period relates to three key factors. First, I would suggest that this period is particularly illuminating because it marked television's transition to a mass medium, including the Queen's coronation in 1953, the coming of Independent Television in 1955 and the development of a regular mass viewership. For example, during this period broadcast hours rose from approximately 35 hours per week to 50 with the arrival of ITV (Thumin, 2004: 23–24). The *Daily Mail Television Handbook* of 1951 reported that there were around 1 million sets in circulation in 1951, but by the end of 1956 (one year on from the launch of Britain's second television station) there were an estimated 4 million 'television homes' with a cumulative viewing population of around 12 million (Heap, 1951: 9). Second, 1953 saw the launch of the first independent television listings and gossip magazine, *TV Mirror*, which commenced in August 1953. This magazine represents one of the earliest archival sources which, unlike the popular and broadsheet press that archivists have relied upon in constructing understandings of early television culture, was wholly dedicated to covering television. Moreover, it was largely dedicated to coverage of television's personalities, featuring gossip, rumour, bios, interviews and details of forthcoming vehicles and programming for television's emergent forms of fame. To this end, *TV Mirror* represents an important archival source for understanding television culture that stands outside the BBC sources one might otherwise rely upon: the BBC Written Archives and the BBC's *Radio Times*, although these and newspaper archival sources are also drawn upon in what follows. Finally, I have extended the period to cover to the end of 1956 so as to make some kind of assessment of the impact of Independent Television on the United Kingdom's emergent regimes of television fame. This reveals the way in which competition led to the poaching and development of new personalities by ITV, prefiguring practices that have continued to affect the political economy of television fame discussed in Part II of this book. Such an approach to the archive addresses two of Helen Wheatley's key criticisms regarding historical work in television (Wheatley, 2007): the canonisation of particular programme texts, often removed from their viewing context, and the (over)-privileging of institutional histories. It does so by engaging in the ephemera surrounding television, newspapers, listing magazines, etc., rather than canonised texts, and by supplementing and testing the institutional histories supplied by the BBC's Written Archives Centre (WAC) with these other sources.

Andy Medhurst's analysis of Gilbert Harding as 'the first paradigmatic television personality', similarly relies on such a framework to set out the way ordinariness and authenticity functioned in relation to televisual fame's elision of on-/off-screen private/public persona (Medhurst, 1991). However, in looking across the construction of televisual fame during a period in which the meaning of the medium itself was being worked out, rather than focusing on the persona of one television personality in particular, it is apparent that Medhurst's work – corroborating as it does Ellis's and Langer's star/personality dichotomy discussed in Chapter 1 – fails to account for the range of sites, genres and discourses over which television fame was constructed. My intention here is not to refute the arguments that have distinguished television personalities from stars. Rather, I aim to demonstrate not only how television fame is more complicated than simply positioning Harding as an archetypal figure from which all other television personalities followed, but also how this entailed more than simply playing oneself. Instead, it involved the negotiation of institutional parameters, the development of televisual skill and the emergence of a diverse array of discourses that celebrated televisual fame as different from the ordinary world of the viewer.

Susan Murray's account of US television stardom begins to offer such a picture of televisual fame. Her study draws out the way in which television was never simply understood as the purveyor of ordinary and authentic personas, but rather worked to develop its own regime of stardom that married spectacle and intimacy, authenticity and commercialism in television performance. In particular, Murray demonstrates how the emphasis on the authenticity of persona was as much an economic function of television – used to help sell the sponsor's product by promoting 'viewer identification with both a program's star and products' (Murray, 2005: 129) – as it was an aesthetic or performance property of the medium. Moreover, in examining the relationship between television and vaudeville, Murray elucidates how the discourses of intimacy Medhurst indelibly links to Harding's perceived ordinary and authentic persona were more complicatedly married with a discourse of spectacle in early television programming and celebrity form. Murray's analysis suggests that performance tropes that included expressive gestures, spontaneity, slick vaudeville routines and quick tongues were not only imported from vaudeville, but also worked over in the television medium to provide a form of spectacle that highlighted what the industry saw as television's key attributes: visual immediacy, liveness and intimacy. For Murray, therefore, the development of US television stardom was negotiated over three stages: first, the recasting of many of radio's advertising and programming practices for television; second, the television industry's poaching of ex-vaudevillians from stage, film and radio for creating presold stars; and finally, the rise of the telefilm, and the creation of the domestic sitcom and its stars in the mid-1950s.

In the United Kingdom a similar trajectory might be mapped, whereby, as histories such as those by Andrew Crisell and Asa Briggs have attested, early television borrowed heavily from radio practices (Crisell, 2002; Briggs, 1995). This included, as Stuart Hood has observed, the transposition of a 'television talks' department whose longevity epitomised both 'how difficult the BBC found it to come to terms with the fundamental difference between radio and television ... and how little the top echelons of the television service understood the new medium' (Hood, 1983: 40). As Richard Dyer's foundational study of light entertainment has suggested (Dyer, 1973), during this phase early television poached the talents from radio and music hall, particularly in comedy and light entertainment – where performers such as Terry Thomas and Arthur Askey made the transition from radio to television, whilst others, such as Benny Hill, Tommy Cooper and Eric Morecambe, successfully pack aged the music hall mode of performance for television (see Medhurst, 2007 for further examples of this trend). As in the US system, this phase was followed by the rise of the domestic sitcom star in the mid-to-late 1950s. As Peter Goddard's excellent analysis of *Hancock's Half Hour* (BBC, 1956–1960) demonstrates, 'a number of formal, stylistic and technical breakthroughs helped to develop situation comedy as a televisual form' during this period (Goddard, 1991: 75). Until this point, as Goddard notes, 'most television Light Entertainment consisted of nothing more adventurous than the presentation of variety and musical comedy artists before cameras' (ibid.:76).

However, if we broaden our examination both beyond the archetypal figure of Gilbert Harding and the realms of comedy, it is apparent that the meaning of televisual fame was worked through across a number of genres, institutional parameters and discourses. In particular, it is important to recall that not all of television's personalities were poached from film, theatre, radio or music hall: some, such as announcers, were distinctly televisual. The chapters in this section aim to offer a broader understanding of the way in which early television fame was constructed and informs contemporary conceptual understandings. In Chapter 2 I examine the way in which television began to develop its own regime of fame attached to the notion of televisual skill, which enabled the transition from a reliance on the star performers from music hall and radio to the emergence of the television personality. This chapter traces the ways in which televisual skill was recognised and valued by both the popular press and the institutions of television at the time. In Chapter 3 I focus on the BBC's 'in-vision' announcement team, particularly its roster of female personalities during the early to mid-1950s, to further explore this notion of 'televisually skilled' performers – appearing neither because of, nor validated by, the holding of some vocational skill external to that of television, such as cooking, the comedy tropes of vaudeville or music hall, or, as Jake Smith has argued, education (Smith, 2009). Such an analysis suggests how, contrary to understandings of television personalities as simply ordinary and authentic, a register of glamour intertwined with notions of authenticity, ordinariness and intimacy in the construction of these performers' fame. Across these two chapters I examine the way in which the BBC's monopoly informed the construction of the early television personality system, so that the meaning of popular television fame, televisual skill and glamour were negotiated within the parameters of the Corporation's public service ethos.

Chapter 2

An 'irreconcilable opposition'

Music hall, radio and the emergence of televisual skill

We do not pretend that Television Light Entertainment is a complete art-form in itself .... On the other hand, too close an adherence to the forms of Sound Radio, the theatre, or the cinema will prevent the growth of T.V. as such and although most of the authoritative and experienced comedians in this country have had considerable experience of Sound Radio, we should be careful to avoid using the methods of Sound Radio when employing them. Similarly a purely 'theatre' comedian is no use to us, unless we use a 'theatre' technique, e.g. *'Music Hall'*.

(Memo from Ronald Waldman, BBC Head of
Television Light Entertainment, 1951)[1]

In this chapter I detail how pervasive discourses sought to understand what was specific about forms of television performance in contrast to radio and music hall. Whilst many of the performers who briefly appeared on television during this period were posited as famous, long-lasting celebrity was often tied to mastering the televisual skill required to ensure regular appearances. As the quote from Waldman suggests, this period was clearly one in which the form of television and light entertainment was being worked out, including the role and nature of television performance – and the production techniques used to broadcast them. Eventually, as television developed into a more confident medium, critics saw music hall and radio performance modes as irreconcilable with the demands of television.[2] The first section of this chapter concerns the emergence of a discourse of televisual skill that is linked to the genre of light entertainment and, in turn, the establishment of particular performers as *television* personalities – famous for, and attuned to, the specificities of the new medium. In the second section, paying particular attention to Benny Hill, I suggest how the persona of performers which developed through intertextual circulation had to be commensurate, or reconciled, with the BBC's public service ethos. Whilst I suggest that this led to an emphasis on the ordinariness and authenticity of a personality's persona, this did not rule out a stress and value placed on the popular. In the second section of the chapter I therefore deal more explicitly with the way competition, in the form of ITV's arrival, led to a battle over key television personalities that demonstrated the importance of televisual skill and the role of the BBC in shaping television fame.

Susan Murray's study of early US television fame suggests that, what she terms its 'vaudeo stars', 'came about logically because of the industry's desire to differentiate itself aesthetically from other mediums [particularly radio], while still balancing the financial interest and needs of the networks' (Murray, 2005: 2). However, the stars of US television remained relatively obscure for British viewers during the early 1950s; viewers, who, as Su Holmes has demonstrated, were more likely to be exposed to American cinema stars' appearance 'as they really are, and in close-up' on programming such as *Film Fanfare* (ABC TV, 1956–1957) and *Picture Parade* (BBC, 1956–1962) (Holmes, 2001). Thus, an interview with BBC producer Richard Afton in *TV Mirror* suggested that whilst Milton Berle, Jackie Gleason and Arthur Godfry might be 'all star names in New York TV', they were relatively unheard of in the United Kingdom; indeed, for Afton at least, the popularity of Godfry was baffling given 'most of the time he just sits at a table and talks'.[3] Of course, part of this relative obscurity was due to the limited recording, and consequent trade, of television programmes on both sides of the Atlantic during the early years of television. However, the development of the United Kingdom's own register of television personalities owed as much to national specificities of performance mode, genre and the intertextual circulation of celebrities by national press. A key staging ground for the development of the United Kingdom's television personality system therefore was the relationship between the British traditions of music hall and the development of 'light entertainment' programming. As Eric Maschwitz, who took over from Ronald Waldman as Head of Light Entertainment at the BBC in 1958, noted in surveying the growth of the genre by 1960, light entertainment is a term 'strange to American ears', consisting 'mainly of comedy shows, musical shows and Quiz or Panel games … I remember telling American friends two years ago that I had become Head of Light Entertainment … and their answering: "What's the rest of it then – Heavy Entertainment?"'.[4]

As a programme category 'light entertainment', as Frances Bonner has summarised, primarily relates to a British tradition with 'ties to popular theatrical forms like variety, music hall and vaudeville, even if mediated through radio' that encompasses a wide array of shows but places variety shows 'at its core' (Bonner, 2003: 17). These ties to music hall, variety and vaudeville meant that early television performers were often poached from London's, and to a lesser extent, the region's music halls.[5] As Medhurst argues, music hall was therefore 'the motherlode of English popular comedy' (Medhurst, 2007: 63). For the performers on the music hall circuit, the new medium of television represented both competitor and show case, involving considerable risk as well as potential reward. Television held the appeal for new and established acts to move from the local stage of the music hall to the national, at least in terms of the imaginary.

This might be understood in relation to Nick Couldry's (2002) arguments about the process of media ritualisation and the separation of those in the 'media sphere' from us, as somehow more important and exciting than us, 'ordinary' people. Arguably the newness of the medium of television and the fame that one broadcast could generate, compared to performances in front of vastly smaller music hall crowds,[6] led to the over-extension of the term 'television personality' or 'star' during this early period whereby nearly every performer was labelled as such by the popular press. Thus long before current debates about the worth of reality TV celebrity, *TV Mirror* complained in 1953 that 'the trouble with some radio and TV "discoveries" is that they are not discoveries at all. One appearance is followed by oblivion'.[7] Nevertheless the appeal to be part of this new form of celebrity for many was clear. As an 'Old Stager', writing into the letters pages of *TV Mirror*, lamented the following year:

> Music-hall bills reflect the times. They used to describe So-and-so's "stupendous act". Then the description changed to something like "Your favourite of Radio fame". Now it seems that nearly every bill contains at least one artist who is a "Star on TV". A manager friend of mine tells me that a good "viewer appreciation" figure is a passport to bookings and success. So far from killing the music-hall, TV is making it. Laddie, if only I were a few years younger![8]

Programmes such as *Music Hall* (1952–1954), *Variety Parade*, *The Good Old Days* (BBC, 1953–1983) and later *Sunday Night at the London Palladium* (ATV, 1955–1969) on ITV relayed live shows from theatres across the country or re-staged them with a live studio audience and were seen as 'a shop window for the variety stage of the country'[9] (see Figures 2.1 and 2.2). However, as Dagmar Kift's history of music hall suggests, television ultimately landed the 'death blow to the halls during the 1950s' (Kift, 1996: 27), with not only the theatres themselves closing but such programming either disappearing from the schedules or moving away from the live outside broadcast format that initially characterised *Music Hall*. This 'death blow' to music hall, conversely, also saw the establishment of televisual performance modes, as a roster of televisually skilled personalities developed during the early to late 1950s who became famous *for* their television performances. Figures such as Benny Hill, Bruce Forsyth and Bob Monkhouse all emerged during this period and, in the case of Forsyth, have continued to figure prominently in the UK television schedules up to the present day.

However, this transition from music hall to televisual fame and performance modes also involved considerable *risk*. David Lusted has recognised that

Figures 2.1 and 2.2 Programmes such as *Sunday Night at the London Palladium* (ATV,
1955–1969) relayed live shows from theatres across the country
or re-staged them with a live studio audience.

'much of the pleasure of television's light entertainment forms comes not
only from recognising the skills of personalities (from physical dexterity to the
verbal constructions) but also the *risks* at stake'. Primarily this risk pertains to
the potential 'failure to maintain … an individual performance', which threat-
ens to undermine the 'faith in success and talent underpinning showbiz itself'

(Lusted, 2000: 253). As the quote from Jack Payne at the head of Part I suggests, early television performers were acutely aware of this risk and the threat it posed to their careers both on- and off-screen. For example, Tommy Cooper recognised that television was great for him because 'my act is entirely visual' but worried about the staleness that might arise because of the everyday-ness of television, which made appearances regularly available to a much wider audience than music hall and made an artist '*too* well known'[10]. Similarly, music hall star Florence Desmond felt the risk of television was to 'kill the novelty value' without commensurate economic reward:

> The artist is paid so little in relation to time spent at rehearsals etc, that his or her salary is barely more than that paid to an office boy. Thus in one performance – for extremely little money and almost solely for the sake of publicity – she is giving away to a wide audience valuable material, while simultaneously killing novelty value.[11]

Benny Hill further outlined the challenges and risks to performance and livelihood television posed for established acts, suggesting that 'for those who already have a "name", [television] demands careful preparation if years of hard work on the halls are not to be ruined in five minutes on the TV screen'. This ruin was understood to have dire economic implications, with Hill suggesting that if 'you are not a howling success' on television public talk and the popular press may immediately suggest '"He's going off. I think he's had his run" … causing the music-halls thinking twice before signing you up'.[12] The economic importance of the music hall circuit for many artists meant that they could not afford the risk of television performances: a 1954 interview with Jon Pertwee to promote a live appearance in *Music Hall* later that year revealed that whilst the BBC had sought a series with Pertwee, he could not afford to leave his music hall tour arrangements to do so.[13]

Exact figures for industry-wide norms of salaries and performance fees for appearing on television and music hall are difficult to ascertain. A 1953 article in *TV Mirror* reported on how the viewers' licence fee was spent suggested, in a far cry from the outrage that accompanied the release of BBC television personality salaries discussed in Chapter 4, that 'a good fee for a single appearance, with rehearsal, of a well-known variety star would be about £100, though in exceptional circumstances it might rise as high as £500'.[14] However, certainly during the early 1950s, television remained a site of potential additional revenue and exposure, rather than a replacement for work on the music hall circuit. As an internal memo from Ronald Waldman in 1955 makes clear, it was only 'possible for a very few artists (the Lyon Family, Wilfred Pickles) to earn their major income from the BBC combined Sound and Television contracts' alone.[15] As Desmond alludes to, such performance fees were to cover rehearsals and often meant a performer's schedule was incompatible with a music hall tour, where according to *The Times* it was still possible for average performers to earn £30–£40 a week playing in regional music halls and seaside venues in 1956–1957.[16] The relative decline in pay for such performances is undoubtedly linked to the increased competition for talent that the advent of ITV brought, which certainly contributed to the end of the music hall as a direct economic competitor to television. Nevertheless, as I shall come to below, the relationship between television and music hall pay was never so straightforward, particularly with the advent of ITV in 1955 and the role of Lew Grade and Val Parnell in the battle over light entertainment between the new upstart and the BBC.

If music hall performers were faced with an economic dilemma in considering television performances, radio stars had the difficulty of moving from what Andrew Crisell has described as a 'blind medium' to a visual one (Crisell, 1994: 3). As Bransby Williams, a former music hall star, surmised in a series of articles written in 1954 for *TV Mirror* on the correlations between music hall, radio and television performance: 'Broadcasting sounds easy – because they can READ their scripts .... How many fail when they are SEEN. The television artist must learn all the time-repose, diction, easy delivery, and facial expression.'[17]

Indeed, the challenge of moving from music hall and radio to television led to some performers, such as popular Lancastrian comedian Al Read, steadfastly refusing to appear on television. In particular, criticism was levelled at those performers who relied simply on 'patter'[18] that was thought to 'somehow entirely evaporate on television ... [and] gain nothing when translated to the home screen'.[19] By 1958, the show business correspondent for *The Times* declared that television 'had brought to a head the irreconcilable opposition between music hall technique and broadcasting technique', arguing that television required comics, deprived of the physical connection of the audience in the music hall, to find new ways of creating proximity and intimacy with the television viewer. Moreover, television's weekly schedule required the stretching and narrativising of a comic persona that 'few comedians have the necessary equipment for', going on to cite both Tony Hancock and Benny Hill as leading proponents of the new televisual style.[20] In this sense, we can understand comedy as a vocational skill practised by artists in their vocation as music hall or radio performers. As Ronald Waldman noted in lamenting recent failings in the performances of Wilfred Pickles and Vic Oliver, 'To see Bob Hope doing this job was a lesson entirely disconnected with his ability as a comedian'.[21] The televisual skill to present this comic knowledge or vocational expertise, therefore, had to be learnt and formed a key discourse in production and popular press in understanding the new medium of television and the forms of performance and fame it produced.

Waldman, as Emma Sandon has noted, is a key figure in the development of early television entertainment in the United Kingdom, pushing the BBC's light entertainment producers to improve the televisual presentation of programmes (Sandon, 2009). Thus in a memo to all light entertainment producers written in 1954, Waldman emphasises the importance of televisual skill in presentation. Recognising, as per Lury's (1995) analysis of television performance, that part 'of this presentation is technical – good camera-work, lighting etc', Waldman went on to argue that:

> another form of presentation is that which is provided by a compere or an 'introducer' of some sort. Obviously, this is a highly skilled professional job .... Points have to be made, tempo has to be established or varied, vital information has to be given, 'flow' has to be maintained – all these functions have to be performed by the presenter. Skill and efficiency in this direction, when allied to a pleasing personality, can work wonders for a show.[22]

Waldman explicitly lays out the elements and importance of the presenter's performance to the programme's 'flow'. Later that year, Waldman had become so confident in the development of the televisuality of light entertainment that, when 'asked if light entertainment would be better if professional producers from the world of show business were involved, responds [sic] with an outburst against this "malicious lie"', which failed to acknowledge television variety performance and programming was a form distinct from music hall.[23]

As with Murray's analysis of early US television fame, the development of televisual skill and performance modes can be understood as a marriage of spectacle and intimacy. As I discuss in the next chapter, whilst the form of spectacle associated with light entertainment conformed to the performance tropes described by Murray, it also extended to discourses and the display of glamour in relation to female announcers. However, primarily this spectacle related to emphasising the qualities of visual immediacy, liveness and intimacy of television in a way that drew on, but distinguished itself from, music hall. Richard Dyer's study of light entertainment suggested that it was in the movement away from the audience in the transition from music hall to television, and the simultaneous fact that 'television is small' in comparison to both music hall and film, which called for 'new ideas of what constitutes spectacle' (Dyer, 1973: 13). Murray's study details the problematic helpfully, arguing it led to an emphasis on a 'presentational mode of address', as opposed to exaggerated performance, and a careful negotiation of the place of the studio audience, who had the potential to both *represent* and *supersede* the home audience. (I shall return to these aesthetics of performance in Chapter 5.) Similar points have been made in a UK context by studies such as Andrew Crisell's (1994: 165–168) and rather than repeat the ground that Murray treads in her study here, transposing the various performance tropes to UK television, I want instead to focus on just one such element that negotiated the need for both intimacy and new forms of spectacle: direct address.

Direct address has long been understood as cultivating an intimacy between performer and viewer in television. However, it was also linked with forms of

spectacle in order to set television apart from radio and music hall. At the time
Dyer was writing on light entertainment in 1973, he suggested that direct
address – whilst rarely *not* used – was rarely used in a way to address the
'home-orientated situation' in such a way as to be a 'distinctive use of television'. That is, he suggested 'few performers address the camera in the actual
performance of their act: they either address no-one or else the unseen studio
audience'. He goes on to argue that the failure to do so is intimately linked
to such performers' roots in music hall and variety, suggesting such a lack is
'not surprising, since so very few entertainers are products of television itself'
(Dyer, 1973: 18). As Dyer implicitly suggests, direct address is a key marker
of the televisual – something that early performers were acutely aware of in its
exploitation for both spectacle and intimacy.

   Here, spectacle is no longer the reproduction or adaptation of music hall
performance modes for television, but instead is closer to Gunning's assessment of spectacle as a moment whereby narrative is suspended or secondary so
as to become a 'frame upon which to string a demonstration of the magical
possibilities of cinema' (Gunning, 1986: 65). For the emerging televisual
comic and light entertainment performer, this involved the use of the conven-
tion of breaking the fourth wall to surprise the viewer, rather than as a mere
'aside'. In an interview with *Radio Times*, Arthur Askey emphasised the importance of direct visual address to the camera in both creating intimacy and distinguishing television performance from the music hall and radio broadcasting,
arguing that in creating a distinct televisual performance 'comics should use
the camera more and talk directly to it'. On the one hand, Askey stresses the
potential for creating an intimate connection with the viewers that direct
address offers by noting how, when a performance goes wrong, he will always
reach out to the audience at home by stating: 'everyone is a little gem – it will
go better next time'. However, he also recognises the more performative
potentialities of direct address, by going on to describe its different uses: 'Even
if I am supposed to be in the middle of the Sahara I like to shove my face right
up into the camera and make some crack'.[24] As James Naremore has argued in
relation to 'certain types of vaudeville-inspired comedy', performers may 'use
direct address to disrupt illusion' (Naremore, 1988: 36). In early television this
could be used to emphasise the visual immediacy of television and create a
form of spectacle. A letter from a reader of *TV Mirror* is illustrative here:

> We were all watching Arthur English on 'music hall'. The picture went a
> little dim. I went forward on my knees, face practically touching the
> screen, and he roared out: 'What cher looking at, Big Head?' I rocked
> back on my heels, there was a startled silence, then my family burst out
> with a roar of laughter. I was too astonished at first to join in.[25]

Such uses of direct address are suggestive of both the marriage of spectacle
and intimacy that Murray finds characteristic of early television performance,

but also the experimentation and development of televisual style and perform
ance modes.

However, as Crisell has argued, the 'very term "spectacular" reveals their
[sic] predominantly theatrical concerns' of variety forms of light entertainment, making some elements of such performance 'too vast, too detailed, for
the small screen' (Crisell, 2002: 102). It was those acts, therefore, that were
able to marshal the intimacy and immediacy of address that made the transition to television personality. Goddard and Crisell have demonstrated the
importance of *Hancock's Half Hour* in creating a 'more progressive, more
telegenic' (ibid.) style that allowed for the development of 'sitcom naturalism'
via a focus on 'greater "reality"' that stressed the importance of detail. In
particular, this included the use of the close-up to emphasise facial comedy
and 'create an intimate comic style ideal for television, in which many of the
funniest moments came from reactions or facial expressions rather than from
dialogue' (Goddard, 1991: 80–81). Nevertheless, the continuation and
popularity of variety forms of light entertainment television suggests that
televisual modes of performance within this genre were able to be developed;
I shall return to this in Chapter 4. Whilst the above discussion of light entertainment performance modes does suggest the way spectacle could be married with intimacy in the development of a discourse about televisual skill, it
was also the importance of the discursive construction of television personalities' fame as ordinary and authentic that helped locate the televisuality of such
performers within the institutional parameters of the period.

'The comedian you made a *TV star*': Authenticity, ordinariness and competition

As Janet Thumin's study of 1950s' television culture suggests, competition
between the newly emerged ITV and BBC 'extended beyond the evaluation
of programming and quantification of audience to the struggle to recruit,
train and keep personnel – particularly skilled technicians and writers, actors
and presenters' (Thumin, 2004: 16). In this struggle, as Jonathan Bignell has
argued, 'light entertainment was a key battleground on which both the perceived dominance of ITV over BBC and the concerns about Americanization
were played out' (Bignell, 2005b: 62; see also Crisell, 2002). Bignell illuminates the key role Lew Grade played in this battle; he has been described as
'Britain's nearest equivalent to a Hollywood showbiz mogul' and was particularly powerful in the field of light entertainment due to his control of the
Palladium theatre in London, which provided the acts and contacts for the
successful *Sunday Night at the London Palladium* (Potter, quoted in Bignell,
2005b: 61). Grade's ownership of the theatre and connection to variety manager Val Parnell was arguably central to ITV eventually usurping the BBC in
the field of light entertainment and in establishing television personalities
such as Bruce Forsyth, who hosted the programme for over twenty episodes

between 1959 and 1964. More widely than the one programme and theatre, however, Grade and Parnell gave ITV considerable 'pulling power' for personalities. As a BBC memo from Ronald Waldman to Kenneth Adams (Controller of Programmes–Television) set out, 'in order to earn a living they must all work with the Managements of Theatres'.[26] Lew Grade's and Val Parnell's agencies, described as 'the largest ... in the country' and 'able to make life extremely uncomfortable for any Variety artists who are outside their sphere of influence', respectively, were of particular significance in delimiting the BBC's access to variety and light entertainment artists (ibid.).

Key to the battle over light entertainment therefore, were television personalities. For example, in 1956 Ronald Waldman wrote an anxious memo to the Controller of Programmes–Television, over an audience research bulletin that showed 'two of three viewers declared the ITA was "better than the BBC" in the matter of Variety', suggesting that this loss of initiative was down to either a lack of variety in the schedule or to the 'stars' the ITA had assembled. In late 1958 this issue remained problematic with Kenneth Adams arguing in a memo to Eric Maschwitz that a slump in viewing figures for BBC light entertainment was caused by a lack of television personalities:

> The size of audience for the Saturday Light Entertainment shows at present makes melancholy reading ... who wants to watch music hall without a single well known name on BBC .... We must try and get some *personalities* back *before* the autumn. The Saturday night habit of watching BBC has gone.[27]

However, two years later in January of 1960, Maschwitz was boasting of 'the BBC not only holding its own but ... winning back the audience', in spite of the fact that commercial rivals – particularly through the figures of Grade and Parnell – could offer 'many inducements apart from that of appearing on their programmes'. Central to this success, Maschwitz argued, was the retention 'under exclusive contract for TV of an ever-growing family of top television performers'.[28]

Benny Hill was a central figure in this battle over light entertainment between the BBC and ITV. Although Hill never appeared on a programme like *Sunday Night* ... itself, he was increasingly unavailable to the BBC during the late 1950s as he either appeared directly for its television competitor or in Lew Grade's and Val Parnell's theatres. Thus by the time Hill signed permanently to ITV in 1969, *The Benny Hill Show* (originally BBC, 1953–1963; ITV, 1964–1989) had last appeared on the BBC in 1963 having been made sporadically for the Corporation up to that point. In the remainder of this chapter I focus predominantly on Benny Hill to suggest how such performance modes discussed above functioned in the creation of televisual fame, intersecting with discourses of authenticity and ordinariness that were negotiated within the public service and the emergent competitive television landscape during this period. Hill was arguably a key transitional figure in the development of not only television's own regime of fame, but also of televisual skill and of some of the ways in which the BBC negotiated the demands of the popular. As I shall go on to show, the arrival of ITV did not simply result in 'crass Americanisation' or 'commercialisation' whereby, as Bourdon has argued, 'the market replaces supply and entertainment replaces integrity' (Bourdon, 2004). Rather such a discussion is suggestive of how a form of fame developed that was understood as specifically televisual and which emphasised a number of facets – such as ordinariness, authenticity, mass appeal – that have been taken for granted in later conceptual understandings of television personalities as inferior and incommensurate with cinematic stardom, but are in fact better understood as the result of complicated institutional, economic, aesthetic and historical configurations.

The politically incorrect and sexist comedy (not to mention the relative lack of laughs – at least for me), associated with Benny Hill has meant that he has largely been neglected by the academy. Medhurst finds him too risible – deadpanning Hill's omission from his study as causing 'a little less grief' than the omission of others – whilst other studies of early television comedy have tended to focus on the sitcom (Krutnik and Neale, 1990; Goddard, 1991) or the personas of performers like Tommy Cooper and Diana Dors (Lusted, 1998). It is not my intention to 'recuperate' Hill here, or even provide a complete analysis of his persona – one that changed considerably from his first appearances on television through to his most popular incarnation as a naughty old man chasing semi-clothed young women across identikit sketches.[29] Rather I aim to show how Hill, along with Gilbert Harding and others discussed below, was constructed as one of the first 'television personalities' on British television – a figure whom Milton Birle described as the standard by which to measure his own success and popularity during the 1950s (Slide, 1996: 102). Indeed Hill was the first solo recipient of the *Daily Mail* 'television personality of the year' award in 1954–1955; the award having previously been shared by Gilbert Harding and Richard Dimbleby. Hill's early career on television emphasised the links and continuities with the music hall tradition, but also the way in which television developed its own regime of performance tropes and fame during this period. Leon Hunt notes how Hill's 'rise to power is often paralleled with that of television' quoting *Observer* critic and former BBC producer Ken Carter's 1967 article, which described him as 'really the first star comedian to be made entirely by television' (Hunt, 1998: 46).[30] Hill, therefore, was arguably the earliest British comic to successfully make the transition from music hall to television, first appearing in 1953 and becoming one of the few British television personalities to gain fame internationally, particularly in the USA, across a long career that lasted until 1989.[31]

Up until this period comedy was, by and large, a vocational skill taken from the performer's external activities to television – whether radio, music hall, vaudeville or a combination – that was both separate to, as well as no guarantee of, televisual skill. As *TV Mirror* proclaimed in a March 1954 issue, this transition positioned Benny Hill as 'The Comedian You Made a *TV Star*'.[32] Hill's career began in music hall and radio, but soon moved to television where he acted as a compere for Ken Carter's – who would remain his producer throughout Hill's time at the BBC – *Nuffield Centre Shows* in 1953. Described by Carter as having 'that certain something which makes the good compere',[33] Hill was immediately championed by *TV Mirror* as 'the Bright New Hope of Lime Grove'.[34] As Dyer's analysis of direct address in relation to the televisual suggests, the compere, host, linkman or announcer is the performer most likely to have had their career 'predominantly [built] in professional broadcasting' and thus best able to 'exploit' televisual forms that link performer and viewer effectively (Dyer, 1973: 18). Across his early career, Hill was positioned as having quickly mastered the televisual – understood in terms of spectacle and intimacy. *TV Mirror* described his performances as 'in the grand tradition of the music-hall, with burlesque as its trump card'.[35] Hill's act at this stage contained an element of the risqué, sexist comedy that we associate with our popular imagination through his later, and long-running, series with ITV (Thames, 1969–1989). However, such elements were more toned down – though certainly present (see Figure 2.3) – and negotiated as much by Hill's own cherubic appearance as the BBC's widely perceived middle-class taste codes. Thus *TV Mirror* went on to declare Hill had learnt the 'secret of being a television comedian', stressing the intimate connection made with audiences via his televisual skill. This meant 'being a family comedian, which means that your humour can, without offence, be heard in the home ... [and second] you are a television comedian – visual, playing to the camera and therefore to the viewers'.[36]

By the late 1950s the success of Hill's performance style had led to ITV creating a series of 'spectaculars' to promote his televisual image, with *TV Times* announcing Hill's return to television to 'star in a spectacular show screening on ITV on Sunday night', after an eighteen-month hiatus on the music hall circuits in late 1956.[37] Similarly, discussing the development of television light entertainment from music hall, *The Times* argued that performers had to create intimacy – which 'survives only if it is present on both sides of the footlights' – but that such forms of entertainment 'cannot afford to be less than dazzling'. In such a context, the reviewer 'welcomes ... Mr Benny Hill's periodic returns to sink his teeth into the rich crop of unsatirized material; or the way in which the Goons apply logical shock tactics to topics long immune from straightforward attack' to create a successful performance of 'intimate revue'.[38] Hill's performance mode, therefore, can be understood as a successful mix of the spectacular with the intimate, the presentational with the vaudeville.

As I have suggested in Chapter 1, the intimacy of television personalities' performance mode is inextricably linked to notions of authenticity and ordinariness. This discourse of authenticity was understood in relation to both

Figure 2.3 Benny Hill's televisual image was understood 'in the grand tradition of the music-hall, with burlesque as its trump card', but successfully mixed these with presentational and intimate modes of early television (publicity still from *The Television Annual 1956*).

the cultivation of a performance mode – where it intertwined with an ideal of sincerity – and the intertextual circulation of the personality. Thus, returning to Bransby Williams's article on television performance, he argued that 'the camera was the all-seeing eye ... [which] can detect sincerity and insincerity'.[39] Similarly, Askey posited that 'broadcasting ... tests your sincerity to the utmost. It is like a doctor's stethoscope'.[40] Such an approach to performance resonates with Auslander's critique of the way performers have understood the presentation of the 'actorly self as "honest" or "self-revelatory", "truthful"... which is produced by the performance it supposedly grounds', which I shall return to in Chapters 3 and 4 (Auslander, 1997: 29–30).[41] Authenticity was therefore understood as a performance mode that had to be mastered in the confluence of technique and technology.

In terms of technology the fact that, as Goddard's work demonstrates, television comics became more adept at using the close-up during this period is important in this context. As Su Holmes's work on the use of the close-up in television for the presentation of film stars has argued, the emphasis on this technical possibility in television suggested that whilst it may have been associated with filmic moments that promise '"access" to the star's private self … this is what *television* was seeking to present … defined in opposition to the constraints and "mediation" of the stars' film performance of "big screen roles"' (Holmes, 2001: 168). Whilst Holmes is discussing the appearance of the film star here, the possibilities of such unmediated access to the performer's 'private', authentic self chime with the way intertextual coverage of stars and television personalities seeks to offer such intimate connections with celebrities. Moreover, as Holmes's later discussion of the troubling use of close-ups in *Face to Face* to 'unmask' the real personas of Tony Hancock and Gilbert Harding suggests, television's aesthetic regime of the close-up suggested a desire to rip away the public image and peer beneath the public 'mask' of not only film stars and other celebrities, but television personalities too. As Holmes goes on to suggest, both the intertextual coverage and technical attributes of television tend to stress a 'collapse [in] the distance between the "real" and the role' (Holmes, 2007a). Thus personalities often complained of being greeted as friends or as if known by audience members. As Wilfred Pickles argued, the 'announcers and various personalities' on television 'have become friends who regularly visit' viewers – 'they are not merely pictures on a small screen, but living people in the room'. Similarly Hill complained of being constantly 'conscious of a row of faces looking at me …. It gets a bit embarrassing after a while'.[42] As *TV Mirror* summarised, 'ask any TV star and they'll tell you that there's never been anything like television for making friends'.[43] These technical modes of television production (the close-up), combined with the techniques of performance (the marriage of spectacle and intimacy, the use of direct address), mixed with the intertextual coverage of early performers that stressed their 'just-as-they-are-ness' and authenticity around a discourse of ordinariness.

As I have suggested in Chapter 1, this notion of ordinariness is intimately connected to ideals of working-class-ness in the United Kingdom. Thus in a reflection on his rise to fame penned for Kenneth Bailey's *The Television Annual* 1956 Hill recalls: 'It's not so long ago, really, since I was sharing lodging with honest workmen like those chaps on that building. The salt of the earth! I recall this without any sense of big-headedness, but just as fact' (quoted in Bailey, 1957: 19).

Other articles and interviews with Hill equally stress the ordinariness of his persona. For example, Anthony Slide's interview with Hill describes him as 'an extraordinarily down-to-earth person', stressing his humble roots and a narrative of success commensurate with star mythology, which saw him sleeping rough in London before finding his lucky break as an understudy in an East London theatre when the lead failed to appear on the play's final night (Slide, 1996: 100–106). This suggestion of being 'down-to-earth' is indicative of how such understandings of ordinariness are inextricably tied to both class (as I shall discuss in Chapter 6), ideals of authenticity and the continuousness of the television personality's on-/off-screen self. Thus the 'open

Figure 2.4 Those television personalities, such as Eamonn Andrews, who were positioned as 'the face' of the BBC, were positioned in terms of authenticity and ordinariness that stressed hard work and a persona that remains unchanged by fame (*Radio Times*, December 31, 1954).

letter to Benny Hill' by *TV Mirror* discussed above, concludes by praising Hill for being 'a hard worker' and 'hope that you survive – as yourself. We can ask for nothing more'.[44] The fame of other high profile BBC television person-alities was treated in similar terms. An article in the *Radio Times*, detailing how Eamonn Andrews, the host of *What's My Line* and regular face of the BBC (Figure 2.4), followed the traditional star mythology narrative in setting out the lucky break that saw him 'spotted as the "central figure in a 'double or nothing' quiz"', describes Andrews as unchanged by his fame. Thus, despite the fact 'these activities have introduced Eamonn to internationally famous stars', the reporter finds that '… They have not changed him a bit. He is still the friendly, sincere "broth of a boy" I first met five years ago'.[45]

Such an understanding chimes with Su Holmes's argument that much of the pleasure audiences derive from celebrities and their intertextual coverage is 'that the "exposure" of the "ordinary" self appears to pivot on the delight in "penetrating" the usual celebrity façade, and thus closing the potential gap between "them" and "us"' (Holmes, 2005a: 31). In particular, those who 'appear to be fundamentally *unchanged* by wealth and fame' tend to receive approving treatment from press coverage (ibid.). Such treatment was evident in the descriptions of personalities such as Hill in the 1950s, who is described as possessing a 'modesty that impresses you right away'.[46] In turn, drawing on Dyer, we can understand how such approval is granted because it bears 'witness to the continuousness of [the self]' whereby the 'ideology of the self' is reinforced via a stressing of 'sincerity and authenticity [as] two qualities which have historically been "greatly prized" in a star' (Holmes, 2005b: 16). Notions of sincerity, authenticity and ordinariness were therefore pre-eminent in discourses about both television fame and performance.

To some extent, such discourses helped negotiate the relationship between the public service obligations of the BBC and the popularity of performers like Hill. The stress on the authenticity of the personality's persona emphasised a range of different values that were commensurate with public service broadcasting: hard working, remaining unchanged by fame, down-to-earth, authentic and ordinary. As Charles Guignon has suggested of Stanley Cavell's work, authenticity is 'clearly central to [Cavell's notion of] "moral perfectionism", an approach to moral thought that is, he says, "directed less to restraining the bad than to realising the good"' (Cavell quoted in Guignon, 2004: vii). As Guignon goes on to argue, notions of authenticity that attach it to moral behaviour suggest that authenticity 'calls for owning oneself as well as self-loss and releasement – looking beyond personal needs to give yourself over to something greater … often around different … conceptions of togetherness'. Such a view of authenticity might be easily aligned with conceptions of public service broadcasting as concerned with moral and educational 'uplift' as embodied by Lord Reith's tripartite of 'inform, educate, entertain' and edict to 'make the nation as one man' (quoted in Keane, 1998: 168). In this context it is worth recalling the way in which Dyer's work on the way forms of light entertainment that evidence a connection with the music hall do so to stress a form of togetherness that evokes a notion of a common good (Dyer, 1973, 1981). As Ytreberg's analysis of 'ideal types in public service television' suggests, charismatic personalities produce 'feelings of intimacy and rapport … a sense that the viewer unites with the personality-host onscreen' (Ytreberg, 2002: 765).

However, whilst Ytreberg argues that a consequence of charismatic personas is to suppress some institutional capacity (ibid.), Hill's ability to amass a large, popular audience was seen as crucial by the BBC in its competition with ITV. Although Hill was largely ignored by external publicity up until his 'Television personality of the year' award in 1954–1955, he then became the first television personality to appear on the front page of the notoriously conservative *Radio Times* in February 1955 (Figure 2.5). Hill was by no means the first personality from television to grace the magazine's front cover, notably Richard Dimbleby, Gilbert Harding, Eamonn Andrews and Wilfred Pickles had all preceded him. However, Hill was the first of these to be celebrated for his television work alone – the others having all previously appeared to promote or celebrate a radio performance. Coverage in the magazine focused on his humble beginnings and notions of service, from a job as a milkman to a career in the army, through to the hard work he had put in to *achieve* his fame.[47] Internally the popularity of his image with the public was increasingly recognised by the BBC, as Ronald Waldman argued in an October 1955 letter to Hill's agent, Richard Stone, that offered Hill a new series with the Corporation: '... many millions of viewers whose support and "applause" were so vital to Benny in his exciting rise to stardom are obviously beginning to feel that they have a "right" to demand him on their home screens again!'[48]

By mid-1956, Hill had been placed on a '"highly" paid list' at the Corporation that provided for a 'top limit offer' of £500/programme.[49] However, the arrival of ITV during this period quickly led to inflation of performer pay as the BBC sought to secure its top talent. As Shirley-Long, editor of *TV Mirror*, noted shortly prior to the arrival of ITV '... you can hear a new, unattractive word being whispered in BBC conference rooms these days. The word is – Exclusivity ...'.[50] The continued importance of the music hall, and ITV's connections to it through Grade and Parnell, however, meant that Hill was reluctant to sign exclusively for the BBC – and despite a letter from Waldman to Stone that noted how the schedules had come to 'rely [sic] on *The Benny Hill Show*',[51] the Corporation could only secure a four show run for the start of 1958, at the cost of £693/programme, in return for limited exclusivity during the three months of filming and broadcast of the programme.[52]

The success of this show led to a further letter – this time from Acting Head of Light Entertainment, Tom Sloane – which implored for more appearances from Hill and urged Stone not to let 'a sordid little thing like money come between us because we may even offer more!'.[53] By late 1959 and early 1960, the importance of Hill to the BBC led to the Corporation pursuing one of the first 'golden handcuff' deals for a television personality, which sought to tie Hill exclusively to the BBC for a twelve-month period at a sum of approximately £15,000 – described by Tom Sloane as 'far higher than any fee we have ever paid previously to any British Artist'.[54] This developed into a series of protracted negotiations over what Hill was to deliver as part of his obligations for 'A shows' and 'B Shows', including an attempt by Hill to establish himself as the BBC's 'consultant on Light Entertainment'.[55]

Figure 2.5 Benny Hill's status as the *Daily Mail* 'Television personality of the year' in 1954–1955 confirmed his popularity and led to a protracted battle for his services between the BBC, ITV and the music halls (*Radio Times*, February 4, 1955).

However, wariness concerning both the cost of Hill's contract – particularly given he was in the process of completing a series of ITV 'spectaculars' – and the potential for Hill 'exaggerating [sic] his own importance in departmental set-up', led to a failure to conclude negotiations.

Conclusion

The battle over Hill both calls into question the notion that the BBC was irrevocably the place of staid, middle-class entertainment that was unable, or only reluctantly able, to accommodate the popular. Whilst this view might have been apparent in the higher echelons in the BBC, with Cecil Madden

(Controller of Television Programmes at the BBC) dismissing music hall as 'indigenous and nobody's idea', this view was certainly not shared pervasively in the BBC.[56] As a *Times* article in 1958 proclaimed, programmes like '*Whacko*, *The Benny Hill Show* and the cup final' could be enjoyed by 'the most cultured people … as anyone else', banishing what BBC Director of Broadcasting Gerald Beadle described as 'one of the most pernicious modern heresies' regarding the incompatibility of public service broadcasting and popular programming.[57] Beadle went on to argue that 'anyone who is frightened of the word "popular", who feels there is something derogatory about it, has no place in television' (ibid.). The prominence given to Hill by the BBC, in both its internal and external communications, as with Holmes's work on the presentation of the BBC's 1950s cinema programmes *Film Fanfare* and *Picture Parade*, challenges the 'long held view that "ITV forged a friendly style of presentation which the BBC had always found elusive"' (Stokes quoted in Holmes, 2007b: 67).

Moreover, the place of Hill within debates about the development of televisual skill suggests how the importance of television personalities was recognised from the outset by television's institutions; not as 'persons "without quality"' or personas merely trading on one aspect of their personality, but as skilled performers who had to turn their vocational comic skills learnt on the boards of music hall and studios of radio into a form of televisual entertainment. Their value was evident in the production discourses that surrounded light entertainment and contract negotiations such as Hill's, which contradict Bourdon's claim that 'the value of hosts would be fully recognized only in the years of deregulation, after "star wars" between channels had pushed the salaries of television figureheads high' (Bourdon, 2004: 289). Such a history suggests that television did develop its own specific regimes of fame from the outset and that, whilst our later conceptual theorisations of it may be right to emphasise notions of authenticity, ordinariness and intimacy, their configuration is worthy of much greater and sustained attention in order to understand the various forms of fame television produces and the way specific institutional and national parameters inflect its formation. Overall, what is apparent is that television's own specific forms of fame and performance mode were recognised as professional problems. That a discourse of televisual skill emerged in relation to the genre of light entertainment is perhaps unsurprising in some respects, given the emphasis on performance in such programming. However, discourses around the presentation and performance of the ordinary, authentic self also emerged more problematically in relation to other programming that had strong ideological implications for our understanding of television fame. These are issues that I turn to in the following chapter.

Chapter 3

'Too much glamour?'

Glamour, gender and 'in-vision' announcers

The Battle still rages over announcers. First they were to be faded gradually from the screen, with off-screen voice only in the middle of the evenings. Their role was generally to open and close proceedings. But now, I notice the announcers do appear – that is, the girls – they are being 'presented' in a big way. We see them with backgrounds of drapes and curtains and flowers, and with side-face camera angles. Well, I am all for a bit of presentation and dressing up. But in the BBC there are as usual Two Views. I can reveal that on the evening when flowers were first used to surround the night's announcer a Certain Top Executive telephoned TV presentation studio and said 'who's dead?'.

(Shirley-Long, 1955: 7)[1]

In-vision announcers were introduced on the BBC with the arrival of television before World War II, lasting until the late 1950s when they were phased out by simple voice-over continuity announcers. Making appearances usually no longer than a few minutes between programmes or at the start and end of an evening's viewing – and then only to inform viewers about programming – the fleeting appearances of in-vision announcers would seem an unlikely site for exploring television fame; let alone an argument that such fame has been constructed as glamorous. The ephemeral nature of their performance has left few traces of their appearances in the archive – or at least little footage that is tagged and collated separately from programming. Yet, apart from the fact that their appearance was a major site of pleasure for audiences, and concern for industry, a focus on in-vision announcers is revealing for understandings of television fame for a number of reasons. First, the BBC's decision to have announcers appear *in*-vision speaks of a key distinction between television and radio, and television and film: on the one hand, their in-vision appearance emphasised television's visuality in contrast to radio – as early television critic Kenneth Bailey asserted, 'nobody will ever be able to deny that they [the first female announcers] gave television a *distinctly visual* flying start' (Bailey, 1950: 7; emphasis added). On the other hand, their performance style emphasised an intimate connection with the audience, largely through the use of direct address. This use of direct address continues my interest from the previous chapter in the development of a discourse of televisual skill, which emerged here in relation to a more presentational mode of address that stressed the ordinariness and authenticity of persona in different ways. However, a focus away from the well-explored genres of light entertainment, comedy and drama in television history illuminates and broadens not only our historical understanding of television performance and fame, but also the ideological and cultural meanings of television fame.

The primary concern of this chapter, therefore, is to examine the way in which a discourse of glamour emerged and examine its relationship to our understandings of televisual fame and the institutional parameters of public service broadcasting. In particular, I demonstrate the way in which glamour was accommodated within these confines as a process of reconciling issues of femininity, class and technical and televisual performance with the BBC's institutional culture. As the opening quote from *TV Mirror* editor Shirley Long suggests, for female personalities this involved the negotiation of their very *visuality* and gender. Such a negotiation reveals historically obscured discourses of glamour, which speak to the hierarchical organisation and valuation of celebrity, not only between film and television but along gender divisions as well. As I shall go on to argue, the construction of female television personalities during the 1950s as glamorous demonstrates that our understandings of television celebrity, as characterised by authenticity, intimacy and ordinariness, mask the complexities of televisual fame. This is not to suggest that we should understand television fame to be as glamorous or akin to the extraordinary lifestyles of film stardom. Rather, attention to the way discourses of glamour were negotiated in the 1950s suggests they were not incommensurate with notions of ordinariness and authenticity, revealing recurrent themes to do with class and gender that have characterised television fame. As Long's article attests, this was a contested space that deserves greater attention in television historiography.

In *Stars* Richard Dyer sets out how certain discourses of 'conspicuous consumption' that surround female stars, particularly those in relation to clothing that 'would make any form of industry impossible', can promote 'the notion of woman as spectacle' (Dyer, 2001: 38).[2] Dyer's point about female clothing and the positioning of female stars as a form of visual spectacle comes in a section that establishes 'stars as stars', who have become 'idols of consumptions' which, in combination with the emphasis on success inherent in the star system, goes towards the construction of the film star's paradoxically extraordinary/ordinary image. Whilst Dyer does not set up this paradox explicitly himself, the discussion of lifestyle and the emphasis he places on analysing female clothing as indexical of conspicuous consumption lead him to the question of 'ordinariness – are stars "different?"'. Dyer's answer to this question is crucial to positioning the extraordinary/ordinary paradox of film stardom, whereby dress has been positioned as emblematic of the 'extravagant lifestyle' of stars that goes towards understandings of them as 'people who live more expensively than the rest of us, but are not essentially transformed by this'. In turn this has allowed us to study them for the way they 'isolate certain human qualities' and 'represent what are taken to be people typical of this society' (ibid.: 43), with fashion having undoubtedly become one of the key areas of scholarship (see Moseley, 2002, 2005; Berry, 2000). In turn, such a discourse has been taken as incompatible with television's production of personalities whom, unlike stars, are understood as part of the ordinary, everyday world – received in the domestic, familiar and familial confines of the home. As Denise Mann and Diane Negra have argued, television could be understood to destabilise images of Hollywood stardom, particularly so-called '"auratic stars" ... whose image of glamorous distance from spectators worked well in the context of cinematic stardom but appeared strikingly out of place in the domestic context of television' (Mann quoted in Negra, 2002: 109). Thus, whilst film studies has developed a tradition of understanding the relationship between fashion, stardom, identity and film, there is much less of a concern in television studies with such issues: because personalities, and their appearance, are seen as part of the everyday, existing within the mundane nature of television's flow.

As Su Holmes has recently suggested, where there has been interest in the relationship between television and glamour it has tended to focus on female performers associated with film. She cites the example of scholarship on Diana Dors in a UK context, with studies such as Pam Cook's placing her amongst a 'host of exotic, glamorous blonde starlets', such as Sabrina, Belinda Lee, Shirley Eaton and Sandra Dorne, 'who "offered similar exhibitions of excessive sexuality" modelled on the likes of Marilyn Monroe, Jayne Mansfield and Lana Turner' (Cook, quoted in Holmes, 2010). But as Lusted's description of Dors as a 'film star of the sub-species "sex-symbol"' suggests, her positioning as the most studied British face amongst this contingent reflects a hierarchy that has ensured 'film history has been more visible than that of its television counterpart' (quoted in ibid.). In the USA a range of recent scholarship has begun to examine the way in which particular female television personas inflected emerging American ideals and identities during the 1950s (Desjardins, 2002; Negra, 2002). Such studies have tended to focus on the repackaging of the glamour associated with former Hollywood stars for the television screen. Indeed, even where the focus is away from connotations of glamour, the focus has tended to be on former film stars (Doty, 1990; Bratten, 2002). It is worth noting, as essays in Bruce Babington's *British Stars and Stardom* suggest, that a different, and less glamorous, form of stardom was associated with British cinema during this period (Babington, 2001) – as Marcia Landy's essay on Gracie Fields suggests there, British female film stars were more likely to be 'extraordinarily ordinary' than 'inaccessible goddesses' (Landy, 2001: 56). Such notions of extraordinary ordinariness chime well with the forms of glamour circulated by television fame during this period, evidencing the way in which television did produce its own forms of glamour, away from the recycling and repackaging of film stars.

As I have suggested in Chapter 1, the hybridity that has been understood to shape the formation of television is also central to its construction of fame. Thus, during the 1950s, television's hybrid form resulted in the predominant discourses of ordinariness, intimacy and authenticity mixing and interweaving with understandings of its personalities as glamorous. This produces television's own form of glamour; for which we can usefully draw on Beverley Skeggs's notion of 'respectable glamour' to understand (Skeggs, 1997). Rather than the unattainable and extraordinary image of the film star's lifestyle, television's discourse of glamour allows its personalities to function as figures of identification and 'reachable' ideals of wealth, extravagance and glamour. Moreover, Skeggs's study of the formation of class in relation to gender demonstrates how respectability, as an almost ubiquitous signifier of class, has been an overwhelming concern of those who do not have it; namely the working-classes (ibid.: 1). In this sense, sexuality becomes an inherently difficult concept to resolve with the display of respectable attributes by the working-class. However, Skeggs argues that a certain form of glamour is capable of 'holding together sexuality and respectability ... [that] is difficult to achieve ... unless "protected" and defended by other marks of middle class respectability (such as education or wealth)' (ibid.: 110). Such a discourse is evident in the construction of the BBC's female in-vision announcer team during the 1950s – and in the short period of television transmission before World War II as well. However, popular discourses of glamour, as well as the appearance of female personalities themselves, had to be negotiated by the institutional parameters of the BBC and later ITV. This had important implications for the representation of femininity, class and how we understand the value of both televisual skill and fame.

This chapter is divided into three sections: in the first, I briefly discuss the emphasis placed on both glamour, in the selection of announcers, and televisual skill in the development of their role. There I argue that these two registers were crucial in developing their intertextual fame. In the second section I go on to examine the intersection of these discourses with those of public service, detailing how production practices and an emphasis on authenticity, respectable glamour and 'extraordinary ordinariness' helped to negotiate their televisual fame in terms of the BBC's accommodation of the popular. As I set out in this second section, class was an inseparable part of this negotiation. In the final section I pick up on the way glamour became, and has remained, an increasingly problematic category for female television fame. Overall, whilst there has been an eventual disavowal of glamorous femininity, a discourse of glamour nevertheless emerged as compatible with television fame during this early period that can helpfully inform our contemporary understanding of television personalities' fame.

'Learning the unheard of art of talking and smiling straight into the goggle eye of a television camera lens'[3]: Presenting the glamorous television personality

The BBC appointed three permanent announcers before the war – Jasmine Bligh, Elizabeth Cowell and Leslie Mitchell – and although Bligh briefly returned to viewers' screens in 1946, making the first post-war broadcast to welcome audiences back to television, all were eventually replaced by a permanent roster of Sylvia Peters, Mary Malcolm and McDonald Hobley. These three were joined by guest and temporary announcers, such as Nöelle Middleton, Bronwen Pugh and Peter Haigh – although it was only Middleton who had an extended period as an announcer. My focus is predominantly on the female announcers – Peters, Malcolm and Middleton – who were the most regular faces in viewers' homes during the period of this study (1953–1956). As Figures 3.1 and 3.3 suggest, female announcers conformed to a particular (middle-class, white) notion of female beauty. As I shall go on to discuss below, these women came from more elevated social strata – with their upper-middle-class taste codes and backgrounds proving pivotal in the negotiation of glamour.

From the initial search for what the *Daily Mail* called an 'It' girl in the BBC's first recruitment of announcers before World War II, it was clear that, both popularly and institutionally, female announcers were to be understood in terms of both glamour *and* televisual skill. Kenneth Bailey's 1950 account of the arrival of television, *Here's Television*, corroborates such an understanding of the role of glamour. Bailey details how Gerald Cock, the first director of television at the BBC, '… believed in glamour, but knew that television comes intimately into the home, and that warmth of personality, without either affectation or artificiality, would be required of its announcers' (Bailey, 1950: 6–7). Thus Earnest Thomas, the BBC's first press officer for television, described the pre-war announcers as having undergone careful 'grooming', to become 'the first two girls in the world [specifically trained] … for television announcing'. Thomas goes on to highlight the visual appeal of these announcers: 'Jasmine Bligh (blonde) and Elizabeth Cowell (brunette) were learning, with Leslie Mitchell, as male colleague, the unheard of art' of television presenting.[4] If the throw-away line to Bligh and Cowell's male colleague and the detailing of their hair colour is suggestive, it is Thomas's description of Cecil Madden, BBC Programme Organiser, as 'blessed as no other man' to have these 'girls' that is more revealing of the institutional discourses of glamour that were attached to women in early television. Indeed, it was almost institutional policy that announcers be beautiful: a 1935 policy edict declared that whilst the frequency of announcers' appearance was to be experimented with, 'attractive announcers are obviously of first-class importance'.[5] This approach to announcers carried through to the selection of Sylvia Peters, Mary Malcolm and Nöelle Middleton after the war – the last of whom Cecil McGivern, Controller, Television Programmes, personally recommended for an announcing role, describing her as 'attractive charming,

Figure 3.1 BBC television production policy stipulated 'attractive announcers [were] obviously of first-class importance'. The selection of Mary Malcolm and Sylvia Peters (see Figure 3.3) conformed to a particular notion of female beauty (Anon. [1954] *TV Mirror*, January 30, 2(5): 1).

capable'.[6] The appointment of beautiful women to the announcing roster continued until the role was phased out during the mid-to-late 1950s, but perhaps reached its height with the appointment of Bronwen Pugh; already a successful model when selected in 1956, she went on to become what *The Independent* described as 'the Kate Moss of her day', having been notoriously caught up in the sexual intrigue around the Profumo affair in the early 1960s.[7]

Of course not all the announcers were female, and the appointment of Leslie Mitchell before the war and McDonald Hobley when broadcasting recommenced in 1946, also played a crucial part in the development of televisual skill outside of the genres of comedy and light entertainment. Indeed, whilst their looks might not have been as strongly emphasised as their female counterparts in production notes, male announcers *were* admired by viewers for their handsome good looks. As *TV Times* noted in covering his switch from the BBC to ITV in early 1956, Hobley is 'lean, good-looking and is never lost for words, or "stumped" by a situation'.[8] As Figure 3.2 suggests, like the female announcers, their male counterparts had clear sex appeal to the audience. Thus whilst they may not have been as strongly imbricated in the discourses of glamour themselves, their visual and performance style were nonetheless important in the negotiation of the popular with the BBC's public service remits. As I have suggested in the previous chapter, direct address was a key site for developing televisual modes of performance. Whilst comics and vaudevillians might have had some experience of the technique from their music hall appearances, the majority of announcers had no such experience. Thus, whilst Mitchell had some limited experience (though not training) as an actor before joining the BBC's radio service in 1932, Bligh and Cowell were selected by McGivern himself on the basis of audition, having been amongst over 700 applicants for the role (Bailey, 1950: 7). Although Sylvia Peters had some training and experience in theatre, female announcers were generally selected on the basis of their visual appeal – for example, in 1951 BBC producer Richard Afton sent Nöelle Middleton's 'particulars' to Presentation Editor Clive Rawes for consideration, which included her address, age, one line on her experience as an announcer at Radio Eireann, and details of her bust, waist and hip measurements along with photographs of Middleton. Similarly, Bronwen Pugh came from a modelling background with no theatre, radio or television experience – having been appointed after writing to the Presentation Editor at the BBC 'on impulse'.[9] However, the emphasis on visual appearance tied in closely with discourses about production technique, performance mode and the presentation of the authentic, ordinary self. As the quote from Earnest Thomas at the head of this section suggests, announcers' use of direct address spoke to the very concern of developing television's own performance techniques: learning an *unheard of* art.

On the one hand it would seem obvious to simply suggest that announcers, given they were neither playing any fictional role nor performing in a variety programme, were very much presented 'just-as-they-are'. On the other hand, the importance placed on announcers' direct address is unsurprising given, as Andrew Tolson has argued, it 'acts as the central point for a whole institutional system' (Tolson, 1996: 62). Whilst their appearances were only fleeting, announcers were stitched in to the way we associate television with the rhymes and rhythms of the everyday more than any other performer: they opened and closed the evening's viewing – welcoming viewers to television and bidding them goodnight at the close of programming; presented information between programmes at regular intervals; and provided a reassuring face when transmission or other technical difficulties interrupted programming.[10] Announcers were arguably understood as the very personification of the BBC (Ytreberg, 2002). However, as Philip Purser noted in writing occasional announcer Peter Haigh's obituary in *The Guardian*, this style was often in contradiction to the tendency to characterise early BBC television performance and personalities as 'stuffy':

Figure 3.2 Similarly to female announcers, their male counterparts had clear sex appeal to the audience (Alison Pressley [1999] *The Best of Times* London: Michael O'Mara Books, 106).

It is fashionable today to assume that its dinner-jacketed announcers and 'comperes' then were all stuffy Oxbridge snobs. On the contrary, several of them imparted a distinct whiff of the second-hand car forecourt or the cashiered officer-class.[11]

Whilst none of the announcers discussed below could be understood as carrying such a 'whiff', their performance style did go towards cultivating a friendly and familiar style that others have argued the BBC found elusive (Stokes, 1999). Letters from readers to *TV Mirror* suggested such a view was present at the time, with announcers positioned as creating an intimate connection with the audience. Thus one reader described how 'one tends to look on announcers as friends. They give the impression of speaking to each of us personally', whilst another suggested the announcers performance – from Mary Malcolm's 'little wicked look through her dignity' to Peters' 'charming chuckling eyes' and Hobley's 'wonderful nearness, poise and neatness' – all combined 'to form that wonderful intimacy of television as against radio'. As the reader concluded, the announcers 'have informality and formality mixed to a fine art – please keep these proportions'.[12] Similarly, an article on Leslie Mitchell as 'the man for great occasions', described his fame as 'gained ... as a Master of Ceremonies ... his easy confident manner, unfailing charm and genuine friendliness have kept him a firm favourite in the public's eye'.[13] In an article on 'what it's like being a TV announcer', Sylvia Peters reflected on the way announcers are trained to create intimacy with the audience via direct address. Stating that she is often asked 'what it feels like to address a huge television audience, perhaps running into millions', she goes on to suggest that:

> This may sound odd, but I really don't know. Like other announcers I never think of it. When announcers are trained they are told to visualise a group of two, maybe three, people sitting round a set and when I say 'Good night' I like to think of the elderly gentleman who once wrote to me that we waited up every night to be able to reply 'Good-night' to me.[14]

Thus whilst Ytreberg's study of ideal public service types challenges 'notions of public service history as a "slide" from the excesses of paternalism to the excesses of charisma', he is only able to recognise alternative, avant-gardist or charismatic personas as existing outside of mainstream or highbrow programming (Ytreberg, 2002: 760). A study of the BBC announcers suggests popular and charismatic personalities, who were able to exploit the intimate performance modes of the new medium, were also evident in the spaces that anchored the schedule.

The importance of the in-vision announcers' televisual skill is underscored by a number of internal BBC memos and policy files. For example, the BBC's general television policy file for 1934–1939 laid out some of the key parameters for announcers' performance from the outset of the television service. A statement on announcements in 1935 therefore read:

> More initiative must be left to the announcers than in sound broadcasting. Normally announcements cannot be read but must be memorized. Judging by pic. technique, few things are more irritating to an audience than read announcements, speeches or talks. It is essential, therefore, that announcers should have a good memory and develop a pleasant personality and informal manner for actual Television appearance.[15]

As Philip Auslander has demonstrated, surveying 1950s' discourse on television performance, although 'the question of authentic TV form remained unresolved, early writers on television generally agreed that television's essential properties as a medium are *immediacy* and *intimacy*' (Auslander, 1999: 15). Appraisals of the achievement of this performance style during the period, however, were not always positive. For example, Ronald Waldman asked for announcers to avoid the phrase 'parlour games' in announcements for programmes such as *What's My Line?* and *Down You Go* (BBC, 1951–1956) and eschew the term light entertainment entirely, which gave 'an impression, for me at any rate, of a local vicarage concert!'[16] Similarly, Janet Thumin quotes producer Doreen Stephens in 1958 as objecting to Sylvia Peter's becoming the predominant face of afternoon television announcements on the basis that 'her milk and water voice and face' are uninspiring, leading Stephens to 'prefer no announcement' at all than Peters (Thumin, 2004: 87–88). I shall return to the phasing out of announcers and its implications for female celebrity during this period in my conclusion.

For now, it is worth noting that during the early to mid-1950s announcers were generally understood as important performers in developing both the institutional image of the BBC as well as modes of televisual skill. Indeed, such was the recognition of the televisual skill of the announcers that in 1957, when the Queen finally conceded to pressure to deliver the Christmas broadcast on television, Sylvia Peters was asked to make a special film 'demonstrating the five best ways to make a speech on TV'.[17] Discourses of the work and labour involved in the duties of the announcers are prevalent in their institutional and intertextual coverage, with audiences often wanting to know what the duties and hours their role entailed. In response to a recurring series of letters on this topic in *TV Mirror*, the editor penned a short editorial that highlighted the long hours and hard work announcers put in:

> Sounds like a cushy job doesn't it? But here are the facts. The announcers have sixteen full days a month in the studio (some of them from 9:30am until close of transmission at 11pm). On the other days they have recording duties for BBC newsreels etc ... BBC public relations ... appearances at functions and at demonstrations organised by the radio trade. Many hours of duty are worked by the announcers when they are not visible on the TV Screen.[18]

A series of articles later that year from Peters, Malcolm and Rawes in the magazine along with coverage in the *Radio Times* similarly emphasised the amount of work and preparation that went into announcing. As Rawes suggested, such hard work went towards ensuring announcers '*know* [sic] *the facts*', so as to ensure their performance was commensurate with prevailing discourses of immediacy and liveness that characterised understandings of early television: 'hesitancy [was] an irritant to viewers'.[19]

Arguably this televisual skill contributed to viewers wanting to see more of the announcers, as one reader noted in a letter to *TV Mirror* that praised a rare performance by McDonald Hobley away from announcing duties, '[B]oth my husband and myself agree that McDonald Hobley is wasted just as a TV announcer'. Such intertextual coverage spoke of the announcer's rising fame, as one reader posited in relation to the possibility of losing in-vision announcements: 'Have the announcers become so popular, by their individual charm, that the TV controllers are fearful of losing them to some other form of entertainment?'[20] Indeed, such was the popularity of the announcers that Hobley was given the *Daily Mail* personality of the year award in 1953–1954 and was eventually poached by ITV to become the new face of the channel. Others, however, were less sure given the role announcers played in cultivating an institutional image, complaining that Hobley's appearances as announcer and in light entertainment were 'sadly incompatible', with the latter causing viewers to take him 'less seriously … in his official capacity as an announcer …. After all he speaks with the authoritative voice of the corporation'.[21]

Nevertheless, by the mid-1950s it was clear that the announcers had developed a level of intertextual circulation and interest that positioned them as television personalities. Central to this was an interest in their appearance. A letter from one reader to *TV Mirror* that called for more appearances from Sylvia Peters is indicative of this interest. Complaining that Peters's role as announcer provided 'little opportunity for displaying her charm, grace and beauty' compared with other personalities, the reader suggests that despite this limited exposure she looks 'so lovely just announcing' that she must be 'termed a natural beauty'.[22] However, as the previous quote suggests, the increasing intertextual circulation of their image was one that had to be controlled and negotiated by the BBC, as I shall turn to now.

'Under-dressed?': Negotiating femininity, fame and public service broadcasting

> I wonder if I am alone in thinking [announcers] are over-dressed. Or, in the case of our women announcers – under-dressed? I loathe these low necks, showing about half a yard of material and a great display of weird and wonderful necklaces.[23]

Whatever the focus on presentational modes of performance, it was clearly the announcers' appearance – most particularly the female announcers' dresses – that was of central concern to both the BBC and audience. Evidencing the central problematic glamour caused for the BBC, Kenneth Bailey noted in 1950 that from the outset 'there was a lot of injudicious publicity about the glamorous wardrobes being collected' for Bligh and Cowell (Bailey, 1950: 8). Read in conjunction with the discourses that surrounded the appointment of female announcers detailed in the previous section, these opening quotes suggest the BBC felt that such performers had to be attractive and glamorous, but recognised that such an emphasis might disrupt the 'public service' ethos of the Corporation, or indeed be incongruent with its promotion of (upper) middle-class taste codes. Issues of class, in conjunction with the authenticity and ordinariness of announcers' on-/off-screen persona, were therefore pivotal in negotiating the meaning and limits of glamour in television fame. As Skeggs's study of 'respectable glamour' suggests, markers such as education or wealth are necessary for the display of femininity as glamorous in a way that can hold together sexuality and respectability (Skeggs, 1997: 110). Early television critic Kenneth Bailey's account of Gerald Cock's, the first director of television at the BBC, selection of Jasmine Bligh and Elizabeth Cowell as the BBC's first pre-war female announcers indicates this choice was motivated by such factors: 'both young women were well-born adornments of what used to be called "London Society"', going on to suggest 'Cock would probably have said that for *savoir faire*, dignity of bearing and charm you could not beat the socialite strata of hard Mayfair training' (Bailey, 1950: 7). Post-war announcers were equally 'groomed' from higher social echelons, with Mary Malcolm having an off-screen identity as Lady Bartlett (discussed further below), whilst Bronwen Pugh was the daughter of a judge and eventually became Viscountess Astor when she married Viscount Astor in 1960.

More than just the intimacy and familiarity between audience, institution and personality that such announcements – with the direct address of their delivery and framing in television's mid-close-up – have been understood to create, the interest in announcers' glamorous appearance reveals a much overlooked popular understanding of television as providing visual spectacle. Other historical excavations of television's archive, such as Susan Murray's, have similarly suggested that notions of spectacle were not incompatible with television performance style or fame. However, Murray's insightful study of spectacle is limited to the manner in which (the predominantly comedy) stars of the time emphasised the physicality of their routines in relation to the visual immediacy, liveness and intimacy of television. As I have suggested in the previous chapter, much of this understanding of spectacle could be transposed to an account of early British light entertainment television personalities. However, a study of the BBC's female announcers reveals that we should understand that the spectacle Murray suggests intimacy is married with as being inclusive of glamour.

To be sure, this is no argument that television promoted a form of scopophilia that positioned woman as object-spectacle. The psychoanalytic theories of Laura Mulvey's work (1989) have long been discredited and I do not want to rehearse the debates on this matter here. Rather I would suggest it is more helpful to draw on two key arguments about female performers that are pertinent here: first, Denise Mann's study of the recycling of Hollywood film stars in early US television variety programmes, which demonstrated the way direct address could be seen to subvert 'Hollywood's representations of the woman as erotic spectacle of the male gaze' by imbuing her with agency

(Mann, 1991: 351). My discussion of performance above is suggestive of such agency; however, as I shall go on to demonstrate, this was not without limits that suggest glamorous femininity was nevertheless problematic for broadcasters. Second, Jackie Stacey's work on the identificatory positions offered to female audiences by the glamorous and spectacular appearances of stars, which can usefully be applied to the female announcers (Stacey, 1994). As Peters detailed, her 'fan letters run to hundreds each week', but these are often from women interested in her outfits, going on to describe the many requests she received from audience members for a fur coat she once wore at an outside broadcast – although tellingly, in terms of the construction of announcers as extraordinarily ordinary, this particular garment turned out not to belong to the BBC wardrobe but was in fact her own (a point I shall return to shortly).[24] Indeed, one of the ways that the BBC sought to reconcile the announcers' glamorous appearance with the institutional culture of middle-class paternalism and citizenship was to detail how the married Sylvia Peters and Mary Malcolm 'receive more fan mail from women than men'.[25] The interest in the look and style of these announcers as figures of identification and pleasure for female viewers is evident in readers' letters to *TV Mirror*. As one reader complained in relation to an article that had previously appeared on Sylvia Peters's new dress, 'I do wish we could have a few full-length shots of the TV announcers. I read in last week's TV *Mirror* about Sylvia Peters' evening dresses. But what do we see of them? The shoulders!'.[26]

Announcers took the obligation to look glamorous to be a serious aspect of their duties. As Sylvia Peters argued, attending 'dress shows regularly may hardly seem part of the job, but it certainly is because the BBC, who buy our dresses, naturally insist on a certain amount of variety combined with simplicity'.[27] Similarly, the article on Peters's 'new TV dresses' evidences the way glamour must be negotiated within the confines of production practices. The article describes the dresses chosen by 'lovely Sylvia Peters' as 'based on three prime considerations: first, the television cameras (they have a stringent set of rules all of their own); second, the kind of person she is – feminine slender, with a fresh-dark beauty; and third, the current fashion'.[28] Indeed, Rawes himself understood the importance of such costuming for the female announcers, going so far as to prioritise it over their male counterparts. Thus in a letter to the BBC Make-up and Wardrobe Manager regarding the appointment of Nöelle Middleton, Rawes suggests that 'as we hope to see her fairly frequently on the screen in 1954' it 'would be sensible to buy her a new afternoon dress and, if possible, two new evening dresses'. However, noting that there was only £10 budget left for guest announcers' wardrobe, Rawes decides it prudent to 'spend up to £50 of [Mac Hobley's] allowance on Noelle', as they had 'so far only spent six guineas' on him.[29] Indeed, one of the primary reasons for continuing to find work for Middleton appeared to be that she was 'exceedingly good to look at'.[30]

I am not, however, suggesting that glamour was *the* dominant discourse in early television fame – but it was certainly negotiated by television producers

Figure 3.3 Intertextual coverage of the BBC's female announcers, such as Sylvia Peters, represented them in terms of a 'respectable glamour' (Anon. [1954] *TV Mirror*, February 26, 2(8): 1).

and audiences, with the BBC's public service remit, understood in terms of Reithian values of educate, inform, entertain in order to uplift moral and taste codes to middle-class standards, playing a large part in the construction and limitation of glamour. For the BBC, the negotiation of public service and glamour became a clear production problem. Such a negotiation is evidenced by a 1953 *Radio Times* interview with Clive Rawes on the features of the new Lime Grove studio as part of both the establishment of a new Presentation Department and the BBC's move from Alexandra Palace. Describing the studio as 'quite small', Rawes went on to add the caveat '... but just big enough to allow the cameras to track back for shots of Sylvia Peters and Mary Malcolm in full-length'.[31] Rawes's statement can be read as an admission that costuming, understood in terms of the glamorous full-length evening gowns that announcers wore, was a major attraction to the audience of these short continuity announcements. As I have suggested, this is underscored by intertextual coverage of Peters and Malcolm in newspapers and gossip and listings magazines; *TV Mirror* included front covers depicting them in formal evening wear with plunging neck lines and features on feminine star style (Figures 3.1 and 3.3).

Returning to the quote from Clive Rawes, he goes on to suggest that despite the popular interest in the announcers' clothes, such long shots 'won't happen often ... Sylvia and Mary have a first duty – to announce. I do not intend to turn them into television clothes pegs'.[32] A similar theme to that of Rawes is picked up by Nöelle Middleton in an early 1954 interview with *TV Mirror*, suggesting that:

> [dress] has to be considered in relation to the type of programme we have to announce. In the main a not too elaborate evening gown is suitable most evenings .... But there are rather solemn occasions where an off-the-shoulder creation and jewellery might not be in keeping ... .[33]

Middleton's answer displays an investment in middle-class taste codes congruent with a respectable glamour that chimes with understandings of the BBC's paternalist culture at the time. Yet, as she goes on to reveal, audiences' interest in the glamour of television threatened to disrupt the attentive citizenry the BBC sought to address and cultivate. Middleton explains the paradox:

> I am often asked by women viewers why we are so rarely shown on the screen full-length, so that our dresses can be seen in full. The main reason for this is the very nature of the announcer's job. She is there to link the programmes together as smoothly and as simply as possible. I'm afraid she is not there to display herself or the dress! Moreover, the BBC found out that when an announcer *is* shown full-length, the viewers' eyes are so occupied taking her in that what she says may not be properly heard.[34]

Viewers apparently disagreed: the announcer *was* there to display herself and after Middleton first featured on television and the front cover of *TV Mirror*, the magazine reported receiving 432 letters from men asking her for a date. Moreover, a postcard competition for readers run by *TV Mirror* in 1954 to 'make your own choice of television beauty', named both Malcolm and Peters in the winning three names.[35] Thus, by the time Nöelle Middleton had become a regular (although not permanent) announcer in early 1954, the problem of viewers' interest in the look of in-vision announcers had become a clear production guideline in line with Rawes's reservations about showing the women in long-shot to reveal their full-length gowns. Middleton again explains:

> In fact, when we do get the luxury of a 'long shot', the Presentation Department quite deliberately gives us a 'throw-away line' at the beginning of the announcement. This is a few seconds of padding, put in before the essential part of the statement. If viewers don't hear it properly, it doesn't matter, and by the time it is over, they are ready to attend to the announcement.[36]

Indeed, reservations about the announcers' dress were evident from the very outset of television broadcasting, with a 1936 BBC memo on television policy noting that there would be occasions 'where the appearance of our announcer would be inappropriate', citing the example of the 'ludicrous' juxtaposition that might be created between the announcer in 'normal clothes' and the Archbishop of Canterbury 'in his robes'.[37]

The above discussion demonstrates the problematic position of the feminine as glamorous and its negotiation within production parameters. Indeed, beyond the immediate concerns of demonstrating the importance placed on performance discussed in the previous section, arguably the emphasis on the work required of announcers aimed to dispel any notion that they lived an extraordinary or more glamorous lifestyle than the audience. Production practices, therefore, were not the only site at which glamour was both promoted and controlled – with the intertextual circulation of female announcers' image another key site of negotiation. It is worth noting here that announcers' contracts required them not to speak in public or give publicity without the written consent of the Corporation.[38] As a result it might be implied that there was an attempt to ensure their intertextual persona was congruent with the middle-class taste codes of the BBC, so as to reconcile promotion of their glamorous femininity with the ordinary and everyday of television. Such control is evident in Su Holmes's discussion of the way in which the Corporation attempted to limit the 'semiotic base' of the actors who appeared in *The Grove Family* in line with moral discourses of family life (Holmes, 2007a). Thus, one finds a counter discourse to glamour emphasising the 'extraordinary ordinariness' and continuity of on-/off-screen persona in the intertextual coverage of female presenters. For example, many articles also stressed their identities as wives and mothers, such as the *Radio Times Annual's* yearly publication of personality portraits of key personnel, which described Malcolm and Peters in terms of their marital status, simple home life and children. In a self-penned article by Malcolm on the 'problems involved in being a household face', she describes how she has given up attempting to keep her identity as Lady Bartlett and Mary Malcolm separate as too many people recognise her in very ordinary situations, such as on the London Underground – 'I have to get around too'.[39] Dismissing any viewers' fantasies that her life is full of meeting famous people and 'a giddy round of dress shows, film premiers and dinner-in-the right-places-with-the-best-people', she asserts her life is 'just as humdrum as' everyone else.

Nevertheless, in a UK context, allusions to a slightly more glamorous lifestyle persisted in a way that was commensurate with upper-middle-class taste codes and the display of a respectable glamour that appeared reachable to viewers and readers of television gossip magazines. For example, an article on Malcolm moving house from the 'Sussex countryside', to a 'tall, narrow, very attractive house on London's Campden Hill', emphasises its ordinariness in terms of size and location but also that its 'tiny garden' has 'a fountain, *no less*'

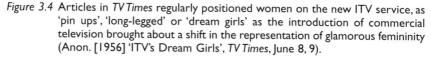

Figure 3.4 Articles in *TV Times* regularly positioned women on the new ITV service, as 'pin ups', 'long-legged' or 'dream girls' as the introduction of commercial television brought about a shift in the representation of glamorous femininity (Anon. [1956] 'ITV's Dream Girls', *TV Times*, June 8, 9).

(emphasis added).[40] Similarly, Peters's revelation that the fur coat viewers enquired about was her own has connotations of an extraordinary ordinariness. The promotion of announcers as 'ordinary people' therefore differed slightly from our conceptual understandings of television fame – allowing for a recognition of upper-middle-class connotations so as to not only reconcile feminine glamour with respectability but also, I would argue, the BBC's culture of the time that aimed at civic and class improvement.

'They're ITV's dream girls': Gender, hierarchical fame and ordinariness

Whilst such a negotiation of feminine glamour and respectability might have been largely successful in producing a distinctly televisual form of fame that was commensurate with the BBC's accommodation of the popular, the place of

Figure 3.5 The role of 'announcers' was replaced with the rather un-public-service title of 'air hostesses' on ITV (Anon. [1955] 'Air Hostesses', *TV Times*, September 30, 9).

glamour on television has not remained so easily reconciled. Indeed, the promotion of announcers as glamorous was but one site of a range of discourses that positioned female personalities in these terms. For example, *TV Mirror* ran a 'Girl of the week' feature for most of 1953 that promoted a range of 'beauties', from Eve Boswell to Petula Clark and Bronwen Pugh. For much of its publication run the magazine featured a 'Star choice' fashion feature that allowed famous personalities – including men – to comment on female fashion. Away from the BBC, articles in *TV Times* regularly positioned women on the new commercial service as 'pin ups', 'long-legged' or 'dream girls', whilst *TV Mirror* noted that the introduction of advertising on ITV had brought 'more and more pretty girls into our homes and they are proving good sales women'.[41] Indeed when ITV launched, they replaced 'announcers' with the rather un-public-service title of 'air hostesses' – who despite never appearing in-vision were nevertheless promoted in terms of glamour (see Figures 3.4 and 3.5). As one critic reflected on the absence of these 'beauties': 'More's the pity'.[42]

It would be wrong, however, to suggest that it was simply the commercialism of ITV that promoted more problematic notions of feminine glamour. The decision by ITV not to use in-vision announcers eventually led to a change in practice at the BBC. In an editorial noting that announcers were soon to disappear from viewers' screens, Long notes that they will 'continue to open and close the night's entertainment, give us the weather and a sweet good night', but appear less frequently between programmes because 'TV programme timing is being speeded up and tightened'. This move was evidently a reaction to ITV's decision that 'announcers should be heard but not seen', as such appearances slowed 'continuity of programmes and by-and-large seeing the faces does not add enough to make it worthwhile'.[43] However, the BBC's move away from in-vision announcers was more gradual, with the decisions underpinning the transition revealing the way a discourse of glamour that constructed the female announcer's celebrity persona was also a gendered and hierarchical one. Thus, despite the visual appeal of female announcers, it was they who were initially removed from in-vision announcing, with those 'at Lime Grove [feeling] that a man's voice is preferable'.

As Janet Thumin details, this decision had a gendered agenda whereby even female producers and Rawes himself had come to accept the 'proposition that female announcers were, somehow, second best' by 1958. Thus Thumin quotes Doreen Stephens as not only reminding Rawes of his reassurance at the programme board that 'the less acceptable announcers, particularly women, would not now be appearing after 7.00pm in the evening', but also chastising him for implying that women's afternoon programmes would now be 'subjected to undiluted introduction by Sylvia Peters' (Thumin, 2004: 87). Whilst the female presenters were clearly valued throughout the early 1950s – as Sylvia Peters and Mary Malcolm argued, during this period 'the only thing they would not let us [women] do was read the news' (quoted in ibid.: 172) – the position of famous female personalities became increasingly problematic. Thumin argues, 'as the television institution developed through the fifties so, too, did its internal hierarchies and, despite the consensual emphasis on the importance of the family and of woman's place at its centre, women and the feminine were increasingly marginalized' (ibid.: 87). Indeed, whilst Long might have noted that there was 'nothing more pleasant than a beautiful woman's face on the screen', the decision that their appearance 'merely slows up the momentum of the evening's programmes' also implicitly recognised that these spots therefore only served to promote the glamorous celebrity persona of the announcers. As Holmes's analysis of the 'television celebrity' Sabrina's glamorous sexuality suggests, such a promotion of the female celebrity persona – particularly if notions of skill or work were evacuated – were incommensurate with not only the BBC's public service culture, but that of television more generally. As Holmes argues, Sabrina became 'famous within a social and media economy which values women for their physical appearance, only to find herself derided for successfully fulfilling this role' (Holmes, 2010).

Her study suggests that Sabrina's fall from grace was not just indicative of earlier discourses that questioned the value of celebrity 'without the requisite degree of work', but also how female celebrity is 'circumscribed by wider hierarchies of gendered power' (ibid.).

Rachel Moseley (2008), in one of the few pieces to address post-war femininity and television in the United Kingdom, suggests how the problematic of glamorous femininity on television had wider ideological bearings in the way it was negotiated by the BBC. Discussing how Marguerite Patten's cookery programming addressed working women during this period, she demonstrates how Patten's intertextual persona attempted to resolve 'the apparently impossible – or at least remarkable, in BBC production – figure of the working woman who also ran a home' with official institutional discourse and culture (Moseley, 2008: 23). Positioning television as a 'technology of gender', Moseley describes Patten's interest in enabling working women to make the gendered division of domestic labour 'more manageable' as 'proto-feminist', whereby Patten 'as one of the first public women of British television' embodied modern woman as a 'figure of negotiation ... unequivocally one of anxiety and disruption, which television discourse attempted repeatedly to contain' (ibid.: 25–26). In particular, Moseley notes an 'anxiety registered over the appropriateness of Patten's appearance', with a clear dispute between presenter and producer evident over the wearing of nail varnish and impractical aprons, which suggested 'certain modes of glamorous modern femininity [were] understood as problematic in conjunction with domestic femininities and food' (ibid.: 26).

The position of female television personalities in the 1950s suggests that whilst a certain amount of glamour might be accommodated, it needed to be reconciled with either upper-middle-class taste codes, such as markers of wealth and education, or an intertextual persona that could be understood in relation to more traditional notions of domestic femininity. This is particularly true of performers operating in light entertainment formats, where women – such as Sabrina – were often reduced to 'stooging' for comics. Disconnected from discourses of work, skill or the 'respectable glamour' that I have discussed in this chapter, their celebrity persona was never as highly valued as their male counterparts. For example, in a 1955 article on what I have termed 'televisually skilled' performers, *TV Mirror* lists those as not presenting any vocational skill, such as Catherine Boyle, Isobel Barnett, Gilbert Harding (all panellists on *What's My Line* at the time), as 'in fact amateurs. They cannot act, sing, dance or play instruments'. Whilst recognising that '[t]hey have looks, charm and personality in their various styles', the article returned to the question of 'what do they do?' As a result, it suggested that those in Lime Grove did not know what to do with these television personalities 'when people demand that these favourites be given series to themselves'. It is significant, therefore, that whilst Harding was given a number of vehicles that saw him 'front' a series – such as *Gilbert Harding Finds Out* – Barnett largely disappeared from viewers' screens whilst Boyle was reduced to stooging for Benny Hill and being the glamorous assistant on *It's a Knock Out*. The problematic of negotiating glamorous femininity, and its role in constructing famous television personalities, with the institutional cultures of early television therefore speaks to the long-standing equation of femininity with both spectacle and 'distraction' – and there has been a continuing concern throughout television history about women reading the news precisely because their appearance might 'distract' viewers from the 'gravitas' of a television news report (Holland, 1987).

This chapter has demonstrated that such long-standing issues relate to the way in which female television personalities' fame emerged in the context of the BBC's institutional parameters and the intertextual construction of television fame during the 1950s. Far from televisual fame merely emphasising some particular aspect of an individual personality's persona, or authenticity and ordinariness being the only registers in which such fame was understood, such a history suggests television was capable of producing, and promoting, glamorous personalities. Rather than authenticity and ordinariness being understood as central to the way in which television personalities' personas must elide any distinction between on-/off-screen self in order to appear familiar, authentic and in keeping with the intimate, domestic modes of television, the suppression of such discourses of glamour and forms of television fame is better understood as the result of specific institutional, economic, aesthetic and ideological conjunctures. Indeed, the discourses of ordinariness and authenticity that we take for granted as central to television fame were in fact crucial in negotiating this glamour. Such an unearthing of the historical archive provides us with an enriched understanding of the contemporary mediascape, going towards unpicking the reasons television fame has been discursively constituted in the terms we may now too readily take for granted.

Moreover, the sheer scale of interest and commensurate valuation of television personalities during this early period evidenced across both chapters in this section indicates that television was, and is indeed, capable of producing its own form of fame. Far from a mere relayer or recycler of other forms of celebrity, close attention to the discourses of television fame during this period suggests there was a concern with the specificities of not only television fame, but the televisual skill that went towards the construction of a successful persona and performances. Overall what the chapters in this section demonstrate is that the taken-for-granted discourses attached to television fame, which have largely functioned to devalue it, were in fact complex cultural discourses that went towards constructing the economic, ideological and aesthetic meanings of television fame. In turn, paying greater attention to them demonstrates the way in which television personality fame was understood as *achieved*, and in turn, valued by both audience and institution alike. As Ronald Waldman argued:

Is it not true that Gilbert Harding, Barbary Kelly, Patricia Curtis, Eamonn Andrews, Catherine Boyle, Helen Cherry and their companions are today almost better known (and more loved or reviled) than many a 'movie star'? *What's My Line?*, *Down You Go*, *Guess My Story* and the others are successful with viewers because they deal in 'personalities' – the life blood of good television.[44]

This 'life blood' is picked up in the next section's discussion of the political economy of television fame and the question of achievement and pleasure in televisual performance.

Part II

'Oooh, I'm an entertainer … it's what I do'

Political economy, performance and pleasure

In the Christmas special finale of the BBC-HBO co-production *Extras* (2005–2007), Ricky Gervais's character Andy Millman has a moment of self-realisation about the value of his 'celebrity' status. Having apparently 'made it' as a 'TV star', Millman is now out of work after quitting his successful, but catch-phrase driven, *When the Whistle Blows* sitcom.[1] Despite complaining that this has made him famous with the 'wrong audience' by 'shouting a catch phrase to a bunch of morons', Millman finds himself desperate for the fame and attention that this success has granted him and has subsequently agreed to appear in *Celebrity Big Brother*. Stuck in a D-List celebrity hell, Millman has a (long overdue) epiphany. Sitting on the couch and surrounded by his fellow 'celebs' he launches into a scathing monologue on the ills of modern fame. Delivered predominantly in television's familiar mid-close-up to the house 'CCTV' cameras, Millman directly addresses the watching home audience: both 'us' – the viewers of *Extras* – and those in the narrative world of the programme, represented here by Millman's best friend Maggie. Declaring that the 'Victorian freak show never went away' he suggests it is now simply called '*Big Brother* or *X Factor*'[2] where 'we wheel out the bewildered to be sniggered at by multimillionaires', before going on to insist that the producers, audience and he himself should all be ashamed of their part in this culture. Millman's vitriol becomes primarily aimed at himself, because 'I'm the worst of all … one of those people that goes "Oooh, I'm an entertainer, it's in my blood". Yeah it's in my blood cause a real job's too hard …. So I go "it's what I do"'.

Via his use of direct address, Gervais's performance as Millman draws our attention to the way 'ordinary' people, such as *Big Brother* contestants, have become more adept at managing a performance under the aesthetics of surveillance that characterises reality TV.[3] In so doing, the performative nature of authenticity in television fame, which has also been greatly prized in reality TV, is exposed (Hill, 2002). Thus through gesture Millman makes us aware of the range of cameras filming the sequence (Figure II.1), but then focuses his performance on one which, via its acute angle, emphasises reality TV's 'fly

Figure II.1 Through gesture Millman makes us aware of the range of cameras filming the sequence ... (screen capture from *Extras* [BBC-HBO, 2005–2007]).

Figure II.2 ... but then focuses his performance on one which, via its acute angle, emphasises reality TV's 'fly on the wall' aesthetic as he builds towards his crescendo (screen capture from *Extras* [BBC-HBO, 2005–2007]).

on the wall' aesthetic as he builds towards his crescendo (Figure II.2). This takes the form of Millman answering a stupid question Maggie had asked earlier in the episode about being a flying fish or a penguin. Choosing the latter to quite surprising comic and emotional effect, Millman is able to reveal his true, authentic, self and finally find validation in the 'right' audience:

Maggie. However this 'authentic' self is immediately perceived by a fellow housemate as an 'amazing' performance, which can be rewarded in the form of commoditisation. Thus she seizes on Millman's announcement that he is leaving the *Big Brother* house to try and come with him, 'just give me 5 minutes, there's paparazzi out there, I'll put on a bikini'.

Millman's diatribe, its narcissistic self-loathing and setting in the *Big Brother* house, draws our attention to one of the central ways in which television fame, particularly its conveyer belt production of reality TV 'stars', produces celebrity and its resultant value: that is, television fame is premised on people appearing 'just-as-they-are', without any extraordinary talent, and/or the revelation and commoditisation of the authentic self: 'it's what I do'. Whilst obviously played for comic effect in *Extras*, this 'playing oneself' is precisely what has been criticised in describing the hallmarks of television's register of fame, setting it apart from, and inferior to, cinema. Yet the appearance of film stars alongside a plethora of British television personalities who are all 'playing themselves' draws our attention to how all celebrity appearances are a performance; and, in turn, the impossibility of television personalities' on-screen personas being an authentic image of such personalities 'just-as-they-are'.

In turn, the relationship between the Millman character and Gervais persona is raised. Lisa Kelly (2010) and Brett Mills (2005) have both pointed to the way in which comedians' celebrity personas operate with a continuity of image so as to elide any distance between 'self' and on-screen performance. In a *Flow* column on *The Office*, a follow-up comment posits Millman as an extension of the Brent persona Gervais established there, suggesting that *Extras* similarly places a priority on friendship over fleeting fame in determining the meaning of 'success'.[4] Whilst this appears to be confirmed by the ending of the series – which sees Gervais's character refuse the devalued currency gained as a celebrity reality TV contestant and instead drive off into the sunset with his best friend Maggie – such a comment is also suggestive of the continuousness of persona associated with television fame's elision of on-/off- screen self. Indeed, Gervais has described *Extras* as his 'study of fame years',[5] admitting the diatribe on celebrity discussed here did not involve 'a huge veil of character .... That was me'.[6] To a large extent, the series works on the premise that it is poking fun at the excesses and self-aggrandisement of stardom's 'extraordinariness'. However, it does so at the same time as conferring this success on Gervais. Thus as the curtain closes on *Extras*, Millman sets out in search of a place where 'no one knows me', to which Maggie sarcastically offers the possibility of 'Hollywood?'. Of course, this is where Gervais himself has headed in search of the legitimisation, and financial reward, of Hollywood stardom. This suggests that, like the devalued audience Millman finds his fame amongst via the success of a derivative television sitcom, 'stardom proper' for Gervais remains a quality to be conferred by cinema.

Whilst *Extras* itself falls outside the non-fiction genres within which I have suggested television personalities deal – and I am not suggesting Gervais falls within this category, he is perhaps best understood as a television 'star' as discussed in Chapter 1 – I find it suggestive to start here because the programme draws our attention to the intertwinement of political economy, performance and evaluative judgements in understanding the television personality system. For the television industry, as Ronald Waldman's quote at the end of the last chapter suggested, television personalities have always been recognised as the 'life blood' of good television. Yet the economic value, the skill and pleasures of performance of television personalities has largely been ignored or dismissed. These failures are partly due to the registers of authenticity, ordinariness and 'just-as-they-are-ness' that characterise the television personality system, which do not lend themselves easily to critical scrutiny. Indeed, so absent has a discussion of the achievement and pleasures of performance been in relation to the television personality system that I find it necessary to start with a fictional narrative in order to suggest that television's markers of authenticity are capable of sustaining close critical scrutiny. *Extras* returns us, more alive to the possibilities of performance and its attendant economic value, to the question I opened this book with: if television personalities merely play themselves, then 'what do they do?'. As I suggested there, 'being oneself' on television has hardly been applauded or recognised as a skill.

And yet, as Gervais's performance of a contestant in *Big Brother* suggests, being authentic is not only a skilled performance but is also a prime commodity within which television's economy of fame deals. In the United Kingdom the scale of this investment in on screen talent is sizeable: the report by Oliver & Ohlbaum Associates for the BBC Trust's investigation into presenter pay discussed in Chapter 4, which was instigated following the scandal that emerged in 2006 about the cost of television personalities' contracts to the BBC, estimated that of the £580 million spent annually on initial appearance and contribution fees in radio and television in the United Kingdom, £388 million of this was on television talent. This was in addition to a further £170 million paid annually for residual and royalty payments. As the report summarised, talent fees 'can be less than 10 per cent of programme budgets in TV genres such as sport (excluding sports rights fees), children's and documentaries, to 15 per cent in news programming, to 20 per cent or more in TV drama, comedy and panel shows' (Oliver & Ohlbaum Associates, 2008: 60–61). The association of narrative-based television forms such as drama and comedy with high profile 'star' salaries may be widely acknowledged – the US$1 million per episode the cast of *Friends* were reported to be earning by the series' final season is but one recent high profile example. However, it is perhaps more surprising to find 'panel shows' and non-narrative forms of comedy as amongst the most expensive in terms of on-screen talent costs.

Indeed, as I shall go on to discuss in Chapter 4, the furore over the amount the BBC paid their presenters was centred on television personalities such as Jonathan Ross, precisely because their appearance 'just-as-they-are' begged the question of 'what do they do?' (for all that money). Whilst this became a pressing question for public service broadcasting, as Graeme Turner has suggested, commercial television has particularly been associated with this manufacture of celebrity, 'using "ordinary" people, with no special abilities and achievements, as the "talent" in their programmes' (Turner, 2004: 53). Moreover, the association of television with the production of ordinary celebrity has tended to further undermine any interest or legitimacy in the political economy of the television personality system. Here, television celebrity is seen as part of the machinations of the capitalist culture industries that exploit both audience and contestant. As Turner suggests, such ordinary celebrity is merely a 'profitable by-product ... but the producers have only a limited commitment to trading on it once the programme has gone to air' (Turner, 2004: 54). Former reality TV contestants are therefore cycled through a range of distribution windows – from ancillary and spin-off magazines, to talk shows and perhaps some limited television work – that furthers the interests of existing media conglomerates. Whilst counter-arguments, such as those apparent in John Hartley's work (Hartley, 1999, 2004a), argue that such production of ordinary celebrity is 'democratic', neither argument accords performance much weight. And yet, performance must be understood as a key form of labour for the television personality system.

The chapters in Part II aim to set out the value of this labour, both in terms of its economic role in the political economy of television's personality system, and in terms of the evaluative judgements we might make about such performance when we pay it closer attention. In Chapter 4 I utilise a range of industry and press sources, combined with textual analysis of programming, to set out how the television personality system has developed from the early broadcast era of television that I detailed in Chapters 2 and 3. In turn, I pay attention to both the BBC's role in shaping this political economy in the United Kingdom and the challenges that the stable economies of television, and its production of fame, face in an era of digital distribution and global formats.

In Chapter 5 I pay close attention to the television text itself, concentrating on the way televisual skill operates in relation to light entertainment and lifestyle programming, in order to provide a detailed analysis of performance in vocationally and televisually skilled personalities. Whilst past analyses of television performance have tended to focus on drama (see for example, Butler, 1991; Caughie, 2000), I suggest that it is possible to analyse the signs of performance in a range of non-fiction programming. Discussing these markers as 'televisual skill', I set out how authenticity remains a key attribute in such an analysis but, as I suggested in Chapter 1, it is something that can be understood as performed. In so doing I am not suggesting that television personalities are the sole or primary authors of their programme nor even their celebrity persona. Joshua Gamson (1994) and Graeme Turner, Frances Bonner and P. David Marshall have written on the work and labour that goes in to producing celebrities by those involved in the promotion and maintenance of a celebrity image – publicists, agents, managers, etc. (Turner *et al.*, 2000). Whilst both are excellent studies, they largely consolidate the notion that televisual fame is attributed by the work of cultural intermediaries, whereas I would argue that there is an interplay between the achievements of 'talent' and the work of these intermediaries. Television may indeed produce celebrities whose fame is almost solely the work of those intermediaries, but the development of televisual skill is crucial to the longevity and distinction of the television personality's fame.

Overall what the chapters in this section point to is the centrality of television personalities to the institutions, industries, programming and pleasures of television. As James Herring, director of Taylor Herring PR, stated of the importance of presenters:

> At the end of the day, a wonderfully made programme about the history of Aston Martin is probably not as interesting as Jeremy Clarkson dropping one out of the back of an aeroplane. Presenter culture is not everything, but certainly within prime time TV, faces count.
>
> (Herring, 2006: 60)

Chapter 4

'You don't know anyone ... '
The political economy of television fame

In the penultimate episode of *Extras* Ricky Gervais's character, Andy Millman, appears as a guest on the British late-night chat show *Friday Night with Jonathan Ross*. As across so much of the series, performance, cultural value and the role of the institutions, economics and industrial practices of television fame (what I will be discussing as the political economy of television fame) intermingle in the exchange between Millman and Ross that opens the episode. Performance here functions as a complex interplay between Gervais and Ross – both of whom 'play them self' to different degrees. Thus Gervais's celebrity persona intermixes with the character of Millman – whereby Millman confidently dead-pans answers or cackles at his own wit in the style of Gervais but, unlike Gervais, appear as an emergent celebrity – whilst Ross delivers his lines in the style of his chat show persona, beginning his questioning with a faux concern before delivering a trademark 'uncomfortable' or 'inappropriate' question for comic effect. Ross, however, must move from the carefully scripted interviews of his own (team's) writing, to those provided by Gervais. This 'play' is evident in the opening exchange, which also points to the economies of television fame:

Ross: A lot of people when they get famous they find a lot of temptation in their way, they maybe drink too much, eat too much ... weight can be a problem. You look like you've always struggled a little bit with your weight. Would I be right in that?

Millman: It's not a struggle. The more I eat the fatter I get. [cackles] [...]

Ross: What are your ambitions over and above this [*When the Whistle Blows*, Millman's successful sitcom within the *Extras* diegesis]?

Millman: I suppose I would like to do, you know, serious acting and I would like to do films.

Ross: Who would you like to meet? Who would you like to work with?

Millman: You don't know anyone ....

Figure 4.1 'You don't know anyone'. *Extras* plays with the way in which television personalities' supposedly ordinary and authentic personas trade with a devalued currency in the wider economy of celebrity (screen capture from *Extras* [BBC-HBO, 2005–2007]).

The character of Ross here is positioned as the established television personality who mediates the performance and promotion of Millman's fame; something that is confirmed by Millman's puppy dog response to the invitation from Ross to hang out backstage after the show in the following scene. The resultant friendship that the pair strike up therefore seemingly confirms Millman's success: measured in terms of fame and the celebrity doors it will open up, including the opportunity to work with the film star Robert de Niro. Although certainly an *achieved* form of celebrity, Millman's rise from his position as amongst the most predominant forms of ordinary people within which television deals, the extra, confirms the contemporary narrative of fame's extension to ordinary people – particularly by television. In turn, for Millman, television's association with this devalued currency of celebrity suggests that the fame he has so far achieved is not enough to be considered truly successful; as evidenced by his desire for 'serious acting ... to do films', and Millman's derisory description of Ross's own relative fame: 'you don't know anyone'. Ross is merely a cog in the economic machinery of the Hollywood production cycle of promotion and publicity. In P. David Marshall's terms, discussed in this book's introduction, Ross's function is merely to familiarise: his own fame being entirely dependent 'upon the proximity to and powers of explaining other celebrities' (Marshall, 1997: 148).

The performance of television fame here largely conforms to that set out by John Ellis: '[i]n some ways [television personalities] are the opposite of stars, agreeable voids rather than sites of conflicting meanings' (Ellis, 1982: 107). Of course, we are not meant to take any of these characters as serious depictions of the performers' 'authentic' selves, but this play draws our attention to, and challenges, taken-for-granted assumptions about film and television fame. Moreover, it does so by placing Ricky Gervais as the show's central performer: not only narratively (De Niro appears in the storyline out of a desire to work with *Millman*), but also within the series' political economy (De Niro also appears in *Extras* because of a desire to work with *Gervais*). Far from a 'familiarising function', television's celebrity is placed as the centre around which the celebrities from other spheres orbit. As Gervais revealed in an interview with *heat* magazine following the series' second season: '... honestly, I was at the Golden Globes and all these people came up to me – Larry Fishburne, Sly Stallone, Drew Barrymore ... Susan Sarandon came up to me and said, "Can I be in *Extras*?"'[1]

Arguably the intertextual and international circulation of Ricky Gervais's image (and to a lesser extent that of Stephen Merchant) establishes him as the star of the series, whose presence is more important than, and instrumental to, the appearance of film and rock/pop stars on the programme: after series one Gervais spoke of requests from Madonna, Brad Pitt and Tom Cruise to appear in the show.[2] In turn, the appearance of Ross and others in the programme can be understood as a reversal of the Millman–Ross relationship in the episode discussed above, whereby it is Gervais whom other celebrities want to appear with in order to raise, or confirm, their popularity. It is not my intention to suggest that television personalities have a status – in terms of economic value, cultural significance, or paradoxical image – that is equivalent to film stardom. But I start this chapter with a continuation of the discussion of *Extras* for the way in which it points to both some of the failings in our understandings of television fame as well as some of the shifts in contemporary celebrity.

Such changes, and the extension of celebrity to a more diverse array of 'ordinary people', is not experienced by television alone: film stars, pop stars, radio DJs, DIY celebrities and reality TV contestants all belong to a wider economy of celebrity who mix and intermingle in the pages of celebrity magazines, online forums and the 'Twitterverse'. As Su Holmes and I have argued, famous names from all media spaces are simply 'celebs' when they appear in such contexts 'apparently "downgraded" as they jostle for space with famous socialites or Reality TV names' (Bennett and Holmes, 2010: 4). Yet, if celebrity studies has come to understand celebrity as a '"*mode of representation*", it is difficult to see how the contestants emerging from Reality TV are *any less* celebrities than other names in the media sphere' (Turner *et al.*, quoted in ibid.). I explore this decontextualisation further in Chapter 7 in relation to the multiplatform production and distribution of fame, as in this chapter I focus on what has been understood as the specificities of television fame's political economy.

From Barry King's investigation of stars as a form of capital (King, 1985), to Janet Staiger's (1995) detailing of the role stars play in Hollywood's labour divisions through to Paul McDonald's (2000) analysis of the star's function in the turn to 'high concept' filmmaking during the 1980s, the role of film stars in the economics of cinema has been the subject of a large range of scholarship. In contrast, the political economy of television's personality system has largely been ignored; seen to function either as part of the general economies of celebrity circulation, as in Gamson's (1994) and Marshall's (1997) studies, or as part of the advertiser-supported flow of television's overall organisation (Langer, 1997; Ellis, 1992). In the following section I therefore set out some of the ways in which this political economy has been understood and the problematic nature of some of this work: based as they are on the assumptions that *Extras* challenges. In this section I set out how the traditional economies of television's personality system have functioned in the broadcast era, using the example of British television personalities Ant McPartlin and Declan Donnelly's careers to trace the relationship between schedule, genre and performance mode, before going on to detail some of the challenges to this system with the rise of multiplatform, multichannel and the global distribution of television formats. In the final part of the chapter I examine the BBC presenter-pay scandal of 2006, focusing on Jonathan Ross and his departure from the Corporation in 2010. I discuss the role of public service broadcasting in the economies of television's personality system and the notion of what we might term the 'public service personality'. Returning to the example of Ross I suggest how we can understand his role in the presenter-pay scandal usefully in terms of the relationship between performance and political economy, which I pick up again in Chapter 5.

The economic imperative: Golden handcuffs, formats and risk

> There is an economic imperative … to television's construction and maintenance of personalities …. It is less a contract than a mythology … as a *system*, like cinema's star system, the mythology has material effects: the production of more personalities in the relentless search for high viewing figures.
>
> (Lusted, 2000: 252)

As I suggested in Chapter 1, television's personality system is an economic, ideological, aesthetic and cultural one, which has profound implications for the experience, organisation and meaning of television for producers and viewers alike. In economic terms, much like the use of stars in films, television personalities have functioned to reduce the risk associated with the production of programming since the inception of television broadcasting. A string of examples could be listed from global television contexts that evidence the importance of television personalities to the economics and political economy of the industry: from relatively common place instances of 'poaching', such as Graham Norton's £5 million move from Channel 4 to the BBC in 2004, through to the use of personalities such as Anne Robinson, Jeremy Clarkson or Simon Cowell to sell *The Weakest Link*, *Top Gear* (BBC, 1978–ongoing) and *X Factor* formats overseas, through to Oprah Winfrey's exploitation of her own brand power to launch an entirely new channel in 2010. Traditionally the economic import of a television personality has been recognised in the form of 'golden handcuff' deals that tie a personality exclusively to one channel. Such deals are indicative of how broadcasters have traditionally used personalities not simply as presenters of programmes, but figureheads for channels and, more recently, formats. For example, in 1999 ITV poached long-time BBC personality and *Match of the Day* host Des Lynam as part of the channel's attempt to rebrand itself as the new home of English football when it successfully, and ultimately disastrously, won the rights to Premier League and Championship football. The value of Lynam to ITV was played up by the front cover of *TV Times* for an August issue in 1999 to mark the start of the football season: Lynam appeared bound and gagged to a chair, with his hands cuffed in front of him under the header '... And they won't let him go!'. As Frances Bonner has noted, the fact a personality may be the highest cost attached to a programme 'is justified not so much because of the internal cohesion produced through the presenter's continuity nor even through any direct drawing of faithful viewers, but because of the presenter's role in promotion' (Bonner, 2003: 71). The intertextual and *performed* (as I discuss in Chapter 5) televisual image of personalities can therefore be understood as a key commodity in the economies of television broadcasting.

If, as I suggested in the chapters in Part I, we can locate the origins of television's personality system in the 1950s then it is true that its economic structures developed during the periods John Ellis describes as 'availability' and 'plenty'– a periodisation that approximates the delineation of TVII and TVIII in US network television – but have become less certain as we move from 'plenty' to a post-broadcast landscape (Lotz, 2007). The example given in Chapter 2 of the BBC's attempt to secure Benny Hill on a 'golden handcuffs' contract was, as I suggested there, the first of a number of attempts by the BBC to tie talent to the Corporation exclusively. Other examples included Richard Dimbleby, Gilbert Harding and, in a reversal of this move, the Corporation decided not to offer McDonald Hobley further work once he had signed for ITV. Such deals have become de rigueur in television's industrial practices for top named talent. The BBC Trust's report into 'on-screen and on-air talent' following the BBC presenter-pay scandal of 2006, suggested that the top thirty to forty names 'can earn more than £1 million a year from initial appearance and contribution fees', with a number of these who are deemed to 'add value to a channel as a whole ... contracted centrally with either a number of named programmes against their name, or in some cases a

combination of known commissions and commissions yet to be decided'
(Oliver & Ohlbaum Associates, 2008: 63). Whilst the report suggested that
the number of such contracts has dwindled in recent years, as discussed below,
each channel is understood to focus on making a number of golden handcuff
deals tied to the channel's brand identity. Thus, 'Channel 4 tends to directly
contract lifestyle/cookery hosts, while ITV tends to contract leading entertainment and drama talent. The BBC tends to directly contract entertainment
and lifestyle show hosts, taking a more strand-by-strand approach to drama'
(ibid.).

The nature of the television personality's economic value has generally been
understood in relation to their power to attract advertisers to a channel – and
this is certainly a key function of their place in broadcasting's economies of
'flow'. This is perhaps best described by Marshall's work, which has argued
that the commodity form of television personalities involves the association of
their image with the semiotic clutter of the television system and, more specifically, 'the obvious and omnipresent advertising function of television'. As
a result, he suggests that:

> the celebrity who arises from television programming is associated more
> directly than the film celebrity with the industrial nature of entertain-
> ment. In contrast to the film star, the television personality is surrounded
> by other messages that are unconnected to the narrative focus of his or
> her program.
>
> (Marshall, 1997: 121)

Similarly, Graeme Turner has argued that television personalities 'operate
within a different semiotic economy' than film stars. For Turner, whilst stars
'seem to be able to continually accrue meanings through successive appearances', television personalities 'are in danger of exhausting the meanings they
generate by continually drawing upon them in order to perform at all'
(Turner, 2004: 15). Like Marshall, Turner's analysis concludes that television
personalities essentially function in a manner akin to what Richard deCordova
has discussed as the 'picture personality' phase in the historical evolution of
film stardom. DeCordova demonstrates that film performers were understood
in terms of the continuousness of their persona whereby actors and personality were conflated: much as the television personality has been understood.
The picture personality therefore essentially functioned to promote further
cinema going rather than the 'star' as a valuable commodity in his/her own
right. It was only once a discourse of acting emerged, which 'worked to
legitimise film through reference to the acting of the stage', that film stardom
was invented (extracted in Evans and Hesmondhalgh, 2005: 32). The failure
to develop a discourse on non-fiction, presentational, televisual performance
is something I address in the following chapter. But the implication of this
failure for the television personality system's political economy has been to

mire our understanding in this picture personality phase. As with the picture personality, the seamlessness of television personalities' personas is seen as integral to their economic function. Indeed, Susan Murray's work on the way Arthur Godfry, Jackie Gleeson and other early US television comedy stars functioned as spokespeople for sponsors' products corroborates such an argument (Murray, 2005).

However, Marshall's argument is based on two assumptions: first, that the US commercial model of television is *the* model for television's semiotic and economic system; and second, that audiences are unable to distinguish between personality and advertising form. The former of these assumptions is challenged by the celebrity status of BBC television personalities, which as the presenter-pay scandal of 2006 revealed, places an equally heavy value on the commodity value of the television personality without the obvious and omnipresent association with advertising. Leaving aside the naivety of the audience the latter of these assumptions presumes, the centrality of an advertiser-supported television system is increasingly challenged by two trends in contemporary television: subscription pay-per-view television, such as HBO, and what Max Dawson (2007) has termed the 'unbundling' of television programming into an itemised commodity form that circulates independently of the promotional surround. It is not insignificant that a great deal of contemporary scholarship that argues for the recognition of television stardom, such as Deborah Jermyn's (2006), focuses on HBO programming – whereby performers such as Sarah Jessica Parker and James Gandolfini have been understood to circulate with the 'aura' Marshall finds impossible to locate in televisual fame because of its ad-driven economic model. For Marshall, the 'close affinity of the celebrity with the organization and perpetuation of consumer capitalism ... [shatters the] continuity and integrity of character that takes place through the interspersal of commercials in any program' (Marshall, 1997: 121).

Marshall's argument tends to 'have it both ways': on the one hand, television personalities fail to develop a coherent and distinct off-screen self that conforms to the economies of cinema's star system. On the other, it is possible for this seemingly indelible continuousness of persona to be interrupted merely by television's economy of flow. Paying attention to what Paul Jackson (then Director of Entertainment and Comedy at ITV) has described as the 'perceived career path for [TV] talent' challenges the duality of this argument. As Jackson continues, this career path emerged during the periods of scarcity and availability, structuring progression from 'theatre or radio, then moving [sic] on to television, starting on BBC Two or Channel 4, before progressing to BBC One or ITV' (Jackson, 2006: 41). I have already detailed the way in which personalities tended to move from theatre, music hall and radio to television in the era of scarcity; and as I noted in Chapter 1 this relationship – particularly between radio and TV – persists today. I want to therefore briefly concentrate on the way the careers of Ant McPartlin and Declan Donnelly ('Ant and Dec') epitomise such a pathway in the context of availability. Whilst such a pathway clearly demonstrates television personality's commodity function to television, it is also suggestive of the coherence of, and investment in, a televisual image built over a long period: one that is not 'continually broken'. In particular, I suggest how the schedule, genre and channel map out the political economy of television's personality system before going on to detail how changes in distribution, production and economies of television in an era where both television and celebrity are multiplatform challenge the stability of these economies in the era of plenty (TVIII).

Karen Lury provides a useful overview of Ant and Dec's persona as '"lads" or "cheeky" boys' in her case study of *Ant & Dec's Saturday Night Takeaway* (Gallowgate, 2002–ongoing):

> Still relatively young, the key characteristics of Ant and Dec's personae are their strong regional identity (both come from Newcastle and retain their distinctive Geordie accents and a notional 'working-class' association) and their genuine friendship. While both are attractive, neither has matinee idol looks.
>
> (Lury, 2005: 176)

Ant and Dec's televisual images therefore conform to the discourses of ordinariness I traced in Chapter 1: eliding the distinction between on- and off-screen self (their genuine friendship), appearing down-to-earth (their connotations of working-classness) and affecting intimate connections via asserting the authenticity of their image (their status as personalities rather than 'idols').

Having started their television careers on the BBC in the children's afternoon soap opera *Byker Grove* (BBC1, 1989–2006) the pair briefly left broadcasting for a short spell as pop stars – though their personas remained tethered to their on-screen characters PJ and Duncan. Whilst clearly already trading on what has become their trademark double act (Bonner, 2009), it was only in a return to television – this time in non-fiction children's programming – that they began to develop their personas as 'Ant and Dec'. The *Ant & Dec Show* (BBC1, 1995–1996) marked a change in their place in the schedules as they hosted a series of Saturday morning children's programming, which lasted across their moves to first Channel 4 and then ITV until 2001's move to Saturday evening primetime with *Slap Bang with Ant and Dec* (Granada, 2001) (a precursor to the successful *Saturday Night Takeaway*). This shift to morning television, rather than say a spot on the children's afternoon programme *Blue Peter* that might have retained their audience from *Byker Grove*, demonstrates both the maturing of their personas, as well as the significance of the schedule in the creation of television personalities. That is, whilst it is perfectly possible for television personalities to be produced outside of primetime (Oprah Winfrey is the prime example of this), the schedule remains an important element in achieving not only the necessary exposure and appeal to a mass viewership, but also the economics of this fame.

For Ant and Dec, the move to morning television allowed the duo to perform a more manic style of comedy that was in keeping with the style of zoo television in vogue from Chris Evans's *TFI Friday* (Ginger Television, 1996–2000) during the late-1990s (see Lury, 2001). Crucially, it was also performed to the same audience: now hung over from the night before. As Declan Donnelly later reflected, this timeslot was pivotal in the development of their televisual skill: a safe space 'where we all learnt our trade and ... about live television and that's where you're allowed to make mistakes and keep doing it and doing it and get the hours under your belt'.[3] Other current television personalities, such as Lauren Laverne, Simon Anstill and Cat Deeley (the latter with Ant and Dec), have similarly emerged from this timeslot. This crossover audience has long been recognised as a valuable commodity by commercial broadcasters, and Ant and Dec's place in the schedule was retained as they moved to Channel 4 with *Ant & Dec Unzipped* (C4/Dec & Ant productions, 1997), and then ITV, with *SM:TV Live* (London Weekend Television/Dec & Ant productions, 1998–2003). This switch enabled both a further distancing of their televisual image as 'Ant n Dec' from 'PJ and Duncan', as well as the ability to more fully reap the commercial rewards of the exploitation of this image, which sits in tension with public service fame (discussed below). The commodity function of the continuousness of their persona is clear: as good-looking, but unthreatening, young men their image was 'safe' for both the children's and older viewership of this timeslot; cheeky, but never risqué; laddish, but essentially moral – as referenced by the ordinariness of their close friendship and 'honesty' to their roots.

Their move from morning television to Saturday-night primetime draws our attention to the way this 'safe' image can be harnessed for a mass, family viewership. However, it also points to the way the economics of the television personality system function in a similar fashion to those in film. Thus a range of vehicles based around the broad appeal of the game show genre were created for, and by, the duo in order to make the successful transition from children's television presenter to primetime television personality. As the pair reflected in a 2000 interview with *TV Times*, ITV had 'believed' in the pair in giving them freedom to develop *SM:TV* and the subsequent formats that would bring them to primetime.[4] Within film studies, the 'star vehicle' has come to be recognised as an important aspect in not only the construction and maintenance of the star but also the functioning of that image economically and culturally. In filmic terms, the vehicle can be understood as those productions that are:

> ... built around star images. The vehicle might provide a character of the type associated with the star (e.g. Monroe's 'dumb blonde'); a situation or setting or generic context associated with the star (e.g. Wayne in Westerns); or opportunities for the star to do her/his thing (most obviously in the case of musical stars).
>
> (Dyer, 2001: 62)

Figure 4.2 The movement of Ant and Dec from morning television programming, such as *Ant & Dec Unzipped* (top left, C4/Dec & Ant productions, 1997) ...

Figure 4.3 ... and *SM:TV Live* (bottom left, London Weekend Television/Dec & Ant productions, 1998–2003) to ...

Figure 4.4 ... *I'm a Celebrity ... Get Me Out of Here* (top right, London Weekend Television/Granada, 2002–ongoing) demonstrate both the maturing of their personas and the investment made in them by television companies ...

Figure 4.5 ... as well as the significance of the schedule in the creation of television personalities (bottom right, screen capture from *Ant & Dec's Push the Button* [Gallowgate Productions, 2010–ongoing]).

This notion of the vehicle can be seen as of fundamental importance to the television personality. As a production that enables them to 'do her/his thing', the television programme presented by television personalities acts as a showcase for the various talent(s) of both the televisually and vocationally skilled performers. For example, the creation of *Nigella Express* (BBC, 2007) – complete with the reconstruction of her kitchen on an industrial estate in London's East End for the purposes of the programme – was hung not only on Nigella Lawson's cookery skills, but her persona as an excessive and lascivious mother figure.

Equally the range of vehicles created for Ant and Dec was premised on a format that enabled them to display their televisual skill. This has included formats launched by ITV for the pair – such as 2001's unsuccessful *Slap Bang with Ant and Dec* (ITV, 2001) – as well as those created by their own production company, Gallowgate, such as *Pokerface* (2006) and the more successful

Ant & Dec's Saturday Night Takeaway. This latter programme, together with the pair's involvement with the early *Pop Idol* (19 Entertainment/Thames Television, 2001) series and *Britain's Got Talent* (Talkback Thames/Syco Television/Fremantle, 2007–ongoing), has been largely credited with the revitalisation of Saturday night television as an important economic commodity in the schedule (see Figure 4.6). The reported £30 million golden handcuff deal the pair signed in 2006 and renewed in 2009 has subsequently established them as the figureheads of ITV.[5] Whilst Marshall is therefore correct to argue that this is likely to construct personalities who are 'inoffensive to the way in which television is involved in the perpetuation of consumer capitalism' through advertising, the presence and value of such golden handcuff deals suggests that their 'aura' is not 'shattered' by television advertiser-supported flow (Marshall, 1997: 121). On the contrary, the investment in talent over years, different points on the schedules and the creation of vehicles *do* create an allegiance between audiences, producers and personalities that is not always muddied by the 'semiotic clutter' of television. The television personality here operates as a way of managing risk in the creation of new shows for the purpose of renewing and refreshing the schedule in order to retain and grow viewing figures of not just a singular programme, but an entire channel and its brand identity. Moreover, as I shall go on to detail in Chapter 6, the television personality's place in the schedule has important implications beyond television's political economy, performing important ideological functions that are not restricted to merely propping up consumer capitalism.

'The days of big pay deals are over': From on-screen talent to entrepreneur

As the BBC Trust report on presenter pay detailed, the stable economies of the broadcast era are changing the relationship between 'broadcasters, studios and recording companies' as 'new platforms fragmenting [sic] revenue and spend' (Oliver & Ohlbaum Associates, 2008: 20). Paul Jackson argues that this has resulted in 'a career path today [for talent that] is less clearly defined' (Jackson, 2006: 20). This is a trend remarked upon by a number of recent industry publications on talent, including the BBC Trust's report and the collection of industry-penned essays in Mary Collins's *Shooting Stars* (Collins, 2006). Thus Peter Bennett-Jones (Chairman of independent production company Tiger Aspect) similarly comments on the difficulty of 'establishing and maintaining on-screen [talent] ... in the multiplatform' age (Bennett-Jones, 2006: 41). As the report by Oliver & Ohlbaum Associates concludes, a range of factors relating to not only the comparative fragmentation of the market in the digital era but also the failure to invest in new talent has resulted in a television personality system dominated by older faces: the 'TV of the 1970s, 1980s and early 1990s created a stock of talent with more mass market resonance than the more recent roster of talent', due to their emergence in a period of fewer channels

Figure 4.6 The television personality operates as a way of managing risk in the creation
of new shows for the purpose of renewing and refreshing the schedule in
order to retain and grow viewing figures of not just a singular programme,
but an entire channel and its brand identity (Garfield, P. [2002] 'How Ant and
Dec conquered Primetime TV', *Observer Magazine*, May 12, 1).

and larger audiences (Oliver & Ohlbaum Associates, 2008: 56). Whereas, as
with the case of Ant and Dec, different points in the schedule might previously
have been used to 'try out', or 'grow' new talent, this function is now largely
hived off to the multichannel subsidiary ventures of the main broadcasters.
Thus Dick Emery speaks of BBC3, BBC4, ITV2, More4, E4, etc., as 'the
nursery of multi-channel to grow young talent' (Emery, 2006), whilst Paul
Jackson discusses the use of now defunct channel 'ITV Play to try out new
presenters'.[6] Although the hours of programming necessary to fill the multichannel landscape may produce more presenters and celebrities, it is also
apparent that fewer make the transition to 'television personality' as I have used
the term across this book. As the Oliver & Ohlbaum Associates analysis demonstrates, of ITV's and Channel 4's top named talent currently on television

nearly half were working on television twenty years ago, with only eight of ITV's top twenty-two names new to television in the past five years; similarly, only one of Channel 4's eight highest paid performers was not on television at the same point. We have not yet fully understood the role of personalities that developed during these periods of availability and plenty, who continue to shape much of our experience of television. And yet the economies of television's personality system are already shifting. As the BBC Director General, Mark Thompson, is reported to have announced to an assembly of television personalities in 2009: 'the days of big pay deals are over'.[7]

This is not simply due to the fragmentation of audiences in the multichannel, multiplatform digital landscape, but also because of the increasing use of formats, which 'signals not only a more global TV market [but] is also a sign that top talent is not the only way of managing the increased risks of TV in the digital age' (Oliver & Ohlbaum Associates, 2008: 20). There are two corollary implications to the increase in formats for the television personality system. On the one hand, this global distribution of television formats also opens up new windows for the exploitation of television personalities' 'televisual image' and challenges the established dogma that their fame is bound to the national (Bonner, 2003; Ellis, 1992; Langer, 1997; Tolson, 1996). The recent success of UK personalities attached to formats in America and Australia – such as Gordon Ramsey, Jamie Oliver, Anne Robinson, Simon Cowell and Jeremy Clarkson – evidence this current trend. Similarly, the failure of Ant and Dec to 'break' America with their game show, *Wanna Bet* (Gurin, 2007), demonstrates both the way in which the US market functions as a signal of international success (mirroring the economies and narratives of pop stardom), as well as the difficulty of entering this market with heavily regionally encoded personas. On the other hand however, the growth of formats also represents a significant challenge to the importance of television personalities to the economic and cultural role of television celebrity. As the BBC Trust report argued, such '[r]eality and talent contests based format shows ... also help develop new sources of celebrity and performer', who compete with existing and emerging television personalities for work and fame (Oliver & Ohlbaum Associates, 2008: 20). The presence of programming formats such as *Shop Window* (BBC, 1953–1955) and *New Faces* (Alson Productions, 1954) in the United Kingdom and USA during the 1950s, which provided a showcase for aspiring talent in much the same way to the *Britain's Got Talent* or the *Idol* formats, suggests that the attempts to manufacture a line of television celebrities through such talent formats has a much longer lineage.[8] As *TV Mirror* editor Shirley-Long lamented in 1953, 'the trouble with some radio and TV "discoveries" is that they are not discoveries at all. One appearance is followed by oblivion'.[9] The implications of ordinary and DIY celebrity for the television personality system are discussed in more detail in Chapter 7. In the remainder of this section I want to briefly explore the economic relationship between personalities and formats.

The golden handcuff deals I have discussed above can be understood as examples of what Sherwen Rosen termed 'the economics of superstars' in relation to the 'worlds of sports, arts and letters and show business' during the early 1980s (Rosen, 1981: 845). For Rosen, television was centrally responsible for the increase in 'star salaries' across all these fields because the 'performer appearing on television literally clones his performance to whomever happens to tune in', regardless of whether that performance be in the form of a sporting event, theatre, drama, film or presentational performance (ibid.: 849). Rosen suggested that the interrelationship of three economic factors – limited substitutability of top performers, low duplication/replication costs and the non-exclusivity of consumption – 'enabled a limited number of superior performers to claim large proportions of total global demand for' entertainment goods (quoted in Oliver & Ohlbaum Associates, 2008: 18). In the global marketplace of formats, the use of the same personalities, such as Jeremy Clarkson, Jo Frost, Anne Robinson, Simon Cowell and Nigel Lythgoe, is demonstrative of the limited substitutability some television personalities achieve. Moreover, the development of such formats has provided some performers with increased economic power. From the creation of formats as vehicles for the promotion of their own televisual image via their own production company, as discussed in relation to Ant and Dec above, through to the position of profit-participant in not only the show but its ancillary production of both other celebrities and merchandising as well, television personalities are no longer merely what Albert Moran and Justin Malbon have detailed as one of the first decisions made in production companies' development of new formats (Moran and Malbon, 2006: 44–45): they are increasingly imbricated in the economic fabric of the format.

Nigel Lythgoe and Simon Cowell are perhaps the pre-eminent examples of this trend. Already successful producers, of television and music respectively, each has since created formats that not only generate new celebrities that they have a future economic stake in, but also places their own televisual image as central to the format's success. In turn this structure allows them to distribute not only the format globally, but their celebrity as well. Thus when Nigel Lythgoe's and Simon Fuller's format *Pop Idol* was exported to the USA as *American Idol*, one of the key ingredients to the success of the format was the presence of a cruel and hostile judge: a role Nigel Lythgoe could export himself into through the cultivation of his image as 'Nasty Nigel' – a character that called upon widely circulated images of British actors and personalities in US film and television as the 'villain', a role Anne Robinson had previously fulfilled in the export of *The Weakest Link* to the USA, but without the same proprietary interests as Lythgoe. The importance of a nasty judge to the format is not only evident in the development of the televisual image of Simon Cowell, but also in the space it provides for rows with other judges – such as those played out with Sharon Osbourne, whereby the performances of the judges becomes a key televisual trope of the series' success. Similarly, the presence of the 'nasty' judge enables other judges to maintain and promote a caring and compassionate image – particularly the cast of female judges who have replaced Osbourne, such as Cheryl Cole.

Cowell's image itself was also first, if not created, widely circulated by the *Idol* format in the United Kingdom and the USA, where he was exported as part of the format for *American Idol*. However, the opportunities for television personalities to move beyond being mere celebrity faces for programmes and channels and act as entrepreneurs in the new global economies of format sales meant that it was possible for Cowell to leverage the currency of his celebrity to create *Britain's Got Talent* as an almost identical format – after a protracted court battle with Fuller – that he sold to ITV to run during the period the *Idol* franchise was off air. Already a judge contracted as part of ITV's roster of on-screen talent, Cowell's role in *Pop Idol* extended this to a share in the winner's future recordings through the contractual obligation for contestants to appear on his record label. With the creation of *Britain's Got Talent*, Cowell is able to profit on all three levels: as a contracted personality to ITV – reported to be worth £20 million over three years;[10] as proprietary owner of the format; and as profit participant in the success of the series' manufactured celebrities. Moreover, whilst his obligations to *American Idol* have seen his place as the 'nasty' judge taken by Piers Morgan in the *America's Got Talent* format, the announcement in early 2010 that he will quit the former to concentrate on appearing in (and developing) the proprietary format of the latter situates Cowell as a key exemplar of what may be the new economies of entrepreneurial celebrity.

As Laurie Ouellette and James Hay argue, the talent search format is 'entrepreneurial in many senses', requiring contestants to refashion themselves, under the watchful eye of the judges/proprietors, in the mould of the flexible economy where 'work' itself is the reward. As they suggest, this is in line with 'the philosophy of "excellence" that emerged ruing the 1980s and 1990s to motivate workers', which emphasises self-fulfilment as a 'substitute for material compensation, security, pension plans, and so on' (Ouellette and Hay, 2008: 127). The reward of working in the entertainment industries becomes an end in itself, whereby contestants are encouraged to cultivate an 'artistic mentality' that motivates labour beyond mere economic exchange. Contestants therefore become a source of 'unpaid labor' for exploitation by the judges and the culture industries 'who profit not only from the TV shows and related merchandise, but also from the consumer goods and services ... produced through the shows as incubators of talent' (ibid.). If the stable economies necessary for the production of television personalities detailed above and in the preceding chapters are increasingly uncertain, Cowell's career suggests how formats provide new avenues for the creation of televisual images as part of a global brand. Via an understanding of the celebrity self as not simply a performance – a televisual image to be worked at as a coherently bound entity that can attract large audiences – but an opportunity for entrepreneurial exploitation, Cowell and others such as Jeremy Clarkson have extended the role of the television personality far beyond mere 'on screen' talent. As James Herring (Director of Taylor Herring PR, whose brands include *Big Brother*) argues in relation to Sharon Osbourne, the development of formats as an effective means for controlled self-promotion – including the revelation of the 'authentic' self, as in *The Osbournes* (MTV, 2005–2007) – is part of the 'new celebrity culture', where a neatly PR-controlled image is a thing of the past (Herring, 2006: 62–65). I explore this question further in Chapter 7, but I want to turn now to how such shifts may have profound effects on the way the economies of public service broadcasting inflect the television personality system's political economy.

The BBC presenter-pay scandal: Public service broadcasting and the changing economies of television fame

I have so far described the place of television personalities within the commercial, advertiser-driven economies of television. However, as the BBC Trust's report noted, in assessing the market for television and radio talent an 'important modification of the market model is the influence of public service obligations and motivations' (Oliver & Ohlbaum Associates, 2008: 54). The UK broadcasting industries spend £580 million annually on initial appearance and contribution fees for talent. Within this economy, the BBC is by far the largest player, contributing £204 million in 2006/2007 to this direct annual investment in on-screen and on-air talent. This included £75.9 million spent on 'network TV drama, entertainment, comedy, factual and children's programming', but excluded the further £38 million estimated spent on talent through the Corporation's purchase of independent commissions (ibid.: 101). The report by Oliver & Ohlbaum Associates was commissioned by the BBC Trust following a 2006 story in the *Daily Mirror* that purported to reveal the details of Jonathan Ross's new contract with the Corporation, which would see the presenter paid £16.9 million over three years (originally reported as £18 million, with neither sum confirmed by the BBC). A string of newspapers picked up on the story and the issue widened to the question of the relationship between the licence fee and the 'value for money' presenter pay represented more generally, with a number of both radio and television personalities pay deals 'revealed'. The furore that followed immediately led to an attack on the BBC by MPs, which further connected the debate to the issue of BBC Executive pay – with Director General Mark Thompson widely criticised for his £670,000 annual salary as far in excess of the Prime Minister's – and led to an independent MP inquiry that focused on radio-presenter pay. The BBC Trust commissioned a report on both on-screen and on-air talent as part of the BBC's response to an attack from which, at the time of writing in early 2010, it is not clear the Corporation has fully recovered.

The most visible sign of the Corporation's uncertain recovery has been the resignation of Jonathan Ross in early January 2010. Ross announced that he was leaving the Corporation after thirteen years presenting a range of television and radio programmes; most notably the late-night talk show *Friday Night with Jonathan Ross*. Less than one month earlier Ross, the BBC's highest profile and highly paid personality, had offered to take a 50 per cent pay cut on his record three-year contract, which is due to expire later in 2010. It is clear that the BBC's decision not to take up Ross's offer was, as *The Guardian*'s media correspondents observed, motivated by a desire to rid itself of what had 'become one of the BBC's most toxic political issues'.[11] In this concluding section, I want to examine what this parting of ways tells us about both the economies of television's personality system, and what Su Holmes has suggested is the need to understand the 'possibilities of ... public service television fame'(Holmes, 2007a: 436).

As I set out in the chapters in Part I, drawing on the work of Jerome Bourdon, the BBC must always carefully negotiate the role of the popular in public service broadcasting. Historically there has been a popular incompatibility between BBC presenters and the commercial exploitation and reward of their televisual image. Jerome Bourdon has suggested that star salaries are just one of the key sites through which public service broadcasters must 'carefully negotiate the popular', arguing that such broadcasters have only reluctantly given 'a place to its hosts, but never fully accepted them or rewarded them in proportion to their appeal' (Bourdon, 2004: 283). In particular, a tension exists between public service personalities' televisual image and commercial reward – not only in relation to the use of the licence fee to pay personalities' salaries, but also more widely. As Holmes has argued, 'public service television fame [is] something which is in part characterized by a reluctance to exploit forms of intertextual circulation in the first place' (Holmes, 2007a: 436). For example, Jamie Oliver's 2002 switch to Channel 4 and *What Not to Wear* (BBC, 2002–2007) hosts Trinny Woodall and Susannah Constantine's 2006 move to ITV have both been linked to the restrictions placed on commercial endorsements by the BBC.

The economic logics of the public service television personality, however, may also operate in reverse – and it is in such instances where the personality's relationship between the popular, public service broadcasting and commercial reward is more easily aligned. Thus, whilst the Corporation's constant reassertion that Ross's salary was lower than those offered by commercial rivals was unable to placate those who critiqued the BBC for over-paying its stars, 'the presence of public service motivation in the talent itself can persuade them to do work that is neither revenue maximising nor fully satisfies their own creative needs' (Oliver & Ohlbaum Associates, 2008: 55). As the report concluded, 'overall it was the talent working in more heavily public service genres at the BBC who might be paid more than their commercial market value, while those in more potentially commercially orientated entertainment

programming who were paid less' (ibid.: 128). We can understand this investment as the specific economies of the public service personality, whereby
certain personalities' televisual images are deemed able to carry the institutional voice of a public service organisation through evoking Reithian edicts
of 'inform, educate and entertain' – in that order. In turn, this becomes key
to their economic value: typified by the likes of David Attenborough and
Jeremy Paxman in the contemporary television landscape. As Espen Ytreberg
has suggested, the public legitimacy of public service broadcasters is often
communicated 'through persons of authority … broadcasting is about
converting institutional legitimacy into conventions of self-presentation,
focused particularly around functions like hosting and anchoring' (Ytreberg,
2002: 759). Ann Gray and Emily Bell have demonstrated how presenters
such as Simon Schama fulfil this function in authored landmark factual television (Bell and Gray, 2007) – a function Ytrebreg describes as the 'ideal types'
of public service broadcasting, the 'paternalist' and the 'bureaucrat'
(Ytreberg, 2002). The BBC's talent report confirms the importance of these
types to public service broadcasting and the role vocational skill plays in the
creation of the public service personality, suggesting there has been an 'editorial shift towards "authorship" … especially in factual programming to
focus on individual authorship and personality when presenting subjects'
(Oliver & Ohlbaum Associates, 2008: 74). Here the credibility of a personality's vocational skill – for example, Schama's status as a Professor of history
or Paxman's career as a respected journalist – is tied inextricably to the public service values of both educating and informing programming. Similarly,
Helen Wheatley has suggested how presenters such as David Attenborough
are commensurate with 'quality' programming that justifies comparatively
high expenditure by conforming to upper-middle-class taste codes (Wheatley,
2004).

    The value of such public service personalities has a much longer history of
course; one that is particularly evident during the late 1950s as the Corporation
sought to define itself in competition to the new Independent Television service by securing key presenters on golden handcuff deals. I have detailed the
BBC's battle over the popular comedic personality Benny Hill in Chapter 2,
but a similar conflict emerged over Richard Dimbleby. Dimbleby, who is arguably paradigmatic of the public service personality, presented a range of programming that not only fits within the authored factual programming format
discussed above, such as *Around Britain* (BBC, 1953–1954) and *London Town*
(BBC, 1952–1953), but has also been largely reprised for his son's – David
Dimbleby – more contemporary programming such as *A Picture of Britain*
(BBC, 2005). Such programming positioned Richard Dimbleby, and arguably
his sons, as spokespeople for the Corporation's address to the 'national' – a fact
reinforced by Dimbleby's role as lead commentator on all national public
events, such as the Queen's coronation in 1953. As Karen Lury suggests,
Dimbleby (and his sons), became established as '"the voice of the BBC" …

cultured and clearly upper class' (Lury, 2005: 63). Described by *TV Mirror* readers as 'TV's natural gentleman', the ability of such a figure to not only speak for a channel, but also fulfil public service remits was recognised by the BBC as well as the new ITV service.[12] In early 1958 Associated Rediffusion, as part of ITV, made an approach to Richard Dimbleby to act as their 'chief commentator on all their events coverage and, of course, especially Royal events'. Having already been described as 'the daddy of commentary' and 'Mr TV' by internal BBC correspondence, his potential value to the new television service was made clear in their offer of £10,000 a year for ten years to lure him away from the BBC. Internal BBC correspondence reveals the anxiety that such an offer caused, suggesting that it would be 'dangerous not to make some kind of counter offer', although not necessarily an 'equivalent "5 figure" fee'.[13] Although Dimbleby opted to remain freelance, restricting his television work entirely to the BBC, the development of such golden handcuff deals for personalities demonstrates the way in which the market for on-screen talent is inflected by public service broadcasting.

However, the relationship between BBC television personalities and pay is never straightforward, and becomes more problematic in relation to 'popular' personalities, whose talents lie closer to the 'entertainment' spectrum of Reith's tripartite articulation of public service values. As *The Guardian*'s head of online media, Emily Bell, suggested in the aftermath of Ross's departure from the BBC: '[the] problem with the stuff about his wealth in the press is [not that] entertainers always earned a lot of money, but when it comes from the licence fee it gives you a particularly difficult relationship with your audience'.[14]

Whilst such personalities may represent the ability to attract a large audience and justify the licence fee in terms of the Corporation's 'reach', their function therefore appears largely equivalent to the commercial economics of the television personality system. Discussing such personalities as 'charismatics', Ytreberg suggests that, as 'a logical consequence of this [popularity], evidence that the charismatic appears in some institutional capacity is suppressed' (Ytreberg, 2002: 765). For many commentators, Ross's departure from the BBC was inevitable following the revelation of his salary and the subsequent spotlight it shone on his performance style, which appeared increasingly divorced from public service values. Thus questions regarding whether Ross was 'worth' £6 million per year reached their nadir following the Sachsgate affair of 2008. Ross, together with fellow comedian Russell Brand, left lewd messages on Andrew Sachs's (the actor who played Manuel in *Fawlty Towers*, 1975–1979) answering machine as part of Brand's BBC Radio 2 show, informing the veteran actor that Brand had slept with his granddaughter, Georgina Baillie. This incident had resulted in a record number of complaints about the programme, the resignation of Brand and Radio 2 controller Leslie Douglas as well as the suspension of Ross.[15] Undoubtedly, as television critic Mark Lawson observed, Ross was shorn of some of his cutting edge by being forced to pre-record his shows post-Sachsgate.[16] Moreover his style of performance, which has always been described as irreverent, was now characterised as akin to a 'dirty old man' – with jokes about 'fucking' Gwyneth Paltrow receiving a cool, if not hostile, reaction in the British press. However, the notion that his 'star' was therefore inevitably on the wane deflects us from closer scrutiny of the political economy of television fame and the role of public service broadcasting within this.

Whilst issues of taste certainly contributed to the depiction of Ross as a liability to the Corporation, arguably his problematic position as a public service personality was more largely informed by the incommensurability between television personalities, public sector pay and understandings of performance. Paul du Gay's *In Praise of Bureaucracy* suggests that bureaucracy has largely been seen as an inefficient moral danger that breeds dependency, limits growth and suppresses freedom. In contrast, neo-liberal discourses of entrepreneurialism promise to solve this problem by making governments operate more like a corporate enterprise, and by replacing the bureaucrat with the manager (and the citizen with the consumer) (as summarised in Ouellette and Hay, 2008: 23). As Ouellette and Hay's study of reality TV within this framework suggests, the entrepreneurial self and the private sector is seen as an efficient alternative to the red tape and bureaucracies of the public sector (ibid.). In the depiction of Ross as a liability to the BBC, it was his pay, rather than his behaviour, that was attacked as a highly visible example of such inefficiencies.

Moreover, in an era where fame is no longer a rarefied commodity, Ross's pay stands in contradistinction to the radical, supposedly democratic potentialities of contemporary DIY celebrity. Thus whilst Ross is castigated for his pay, Simon Cowell (a figure not unknown for unkind comments to vulnerable performers) is held up as a figure who might revitalise public debate – via a commercial television format that would 'apply his unique brand of interactive TV glamour to the world of politics'.[17] Cowell's entrepreneurialism was praised by Conservative Party leader David Cameron – who said of Cowell's proposed format that 'finding something that makes politics link more directly to people is a very good idea'.[18] Tellingly, Cameron connected Cowell's efforts 'to increase the level of people power in politics' with the 'Internet age' where, as I discuss in Chapter 7, DIY forms of celebrity are praised by mainstream and business press for their entrepreneurialism; celebrity here is achieved through tireless self-promotion and the mastering of social networking technologies that position them at the vanguard of new media economies. The desire to distinguish the BBC from the perceived inefficiencies and bureaucracies of the public sector was not only evident in the departure of Ross but also BBC Director General Mark Thompson's attempt to defend the Corporation's pay structures in its wake. Claiming 'we are not a county council, we need the best', Thompson's comments returned the debate about presenter pay to the BBC executive, and the economies of public service broadcasting itself.[19] With contemporary journalistic commentary describing a forthcoming period of 'austerity Britain', high profile arguments about the (over)pay of public sector workers, including celebrities like Ross, serve to exacerbate the neo-liberal ideologies of free markets and DIY citizenship – and celebrity – as the antidote to 'big government'.

Conclusion

Together with the rise in the global trade in formats (themselves producing celetoids) and the possibility of DIY or ordinary celebrity in the digital age, these discourses of entrepreneurialism have profound implications for the political economy of television's personality system, particularly the relationship between the BBC and presenter pay. Deals such as that with Ross are unlikely to be repeated as the BBC seeks to slash its presenter wage bill. But two significant exceptions remain that shed further light on this political economy. First, and unsurprisingly, the pay of those we might more easily align with the notion of 'public service personalities' and the ability to represent its institutional voice – such as David Attenborough or Simon Schama – have largely not come into question during these debates. Second, at the 'entertainment' end of the public service spectrum the BBC has negotiated a more complex pay deal for *Top Gear* host Jeremy Clarkson, which has largely escaped the scrutiny of the presenter-pay scandal.

As I have explored elsewhere, Clarkson's televisual image is aligned with neo-liberal ideologies that emphasis consumer choice and freedoms in a way that sits uneasily with the BBC's public service remits (see Bennett, 2009). Clarkson's deal for *Top Gear* sees the presenter not only receive an annual salary reportedly in excess of £1 million, but also take a share of the profits from spin-off commercial activity in BBC Worldwide's merchandising and marketing of the series. Moreover, in August 2008 Clarkson signed a further deal with the Corporation's commercial arm for it to take a controlling stake in his company, Bedder 6, for the exploitation of the *Top Gear* brand – including international sales of the programme.[20] Clarkson's cut in the international sales of the programme format and its spin-off merchandising makes him one of the top-paid performers on television because of his 'limited substitutability'; exported as one of the key elements of the format for global distribution. The importance of Clarkson's role becomes clear when one considers that the format for *Top Gear* both long preceded his involvement (having been part of the BBC's schedules since 1978), and that it has been formatted for local production in Australia and the USA with local presenters in the 'Clarkson role'. Whilst Clarkson was amongst those personalities summoned to the BBC for Mark Thompson's announcement on the looming cuts for presenter pay deals in 2009, this focused solely on the issue of salaries. Operating within the efficiencies of the global market for television formats, an eyelid has not been batted at this highly profitable deal for Clarkson in these recent debates.

In contrast, the attack on the BBC utilised Ross as an example of the wasteful inefficiencies of the public sector. Thus whilst Clarkson's role in revitalising the fortunes of the *Top Gear* format extended his power and value to the economies of the global market in a display of entrepreneurial skill to exploit the programme's brand power, Ross was perceived merely as over-paid on-screen talent: part of a format, not integral to it (as the immediate speculation that Graham Norton would take over his Friday night slot suggested). Indeed, the MP inquiry into BBC presenter pay, which focused on radio where Ross also featured prominently, found the pay of many of the top named presenters was questionable because it was not apparent what their 'core skill' was. That is, to return to the extract from *Extras* with which I commenced this chapter – Ross merely appears on television as 'himself', a performer who merely serves to familiarise other celebrities. Ross, like other television personalities, is perceived not to 'do' anything: he appears 'just-as-he-is'. Whilst the BBC had long recognised the televisual skill that goes into the construction of this persona, it arguably became an impossible defence to make in the context of not simply Sachsgate but the shift towards entrepreneurialism that authors such as du Gay, Hay and Ouellette have detailed. At the time of writing, an impending Conservative party election victory in 2010 combined with a period moving towards BBC Charter renewal in which the licence fee has already been mooted for possible top-slicing to support public service broadcasting obligations on other channels, suggest the BBC can ill-afford to be perceived as part of the inefficiencies of public sector bureaucracy. How this will impact on the Corporation's ability to develop, recruit and retain television personalities remains to be seen but will undoubtedly affect the political economy of the television personality system not only in the United Kingdom, but as deals such as Clarkson's and Cowell's suggest, internationally as well.

In conclusion, we can return to Lusted's argument that television's 'personality system dominantly reproduces myths of individualism', which both serves to confirm the celebrity status of television personalities and the fact that they are 'special' compared to us. Whilst such a myth serves to legitimate (to greater or lesser extent) the economic reward of the television personality system, as Lusted goes on to argue, 'this statement takes no account of the pleasures sought from or delivered by the system, nor does it allow for different, especially *social*, meanings to appear' (Lusted, 2000: 251). It is to this question of pleasure I turn to in the next chapter's examination of performance and achievement, whilst the remainder of the book addresses the question of the social meanings attached to particular television personalities.

Chapter 5

The art of 'being yourself'
Pleasure, meaning and achievement in performance

When people complain to me that panel stars, like those on *What's My Line* ... have found a wonderful short cut to easy money and easy fame, I find it simplest to change the conversation ....The kind of person who is smug enough to suggest this idea could not, in his nature, have the imagination to conceive what it is like to 'be yourself' in front of the impartial lights and cameras of TV. They bring your every gesture, from an involuntary look of disapproval, to the nervous tapping of a cigarette, into several million living-rooms. If 'poise' is now the key to success and popularity in the new medium, let them remember that it is the hardest of all attributes to learn and the hardest to sustain under fire.

(Dicky Leeman, producer of *What's My Line*, 1954)[1]

Long before reality TV and the debates that have ensued about the relative value of the fame it produces, television was associated with what Graeme Turner describes as the production of celebrity 'out of nothing' (Turner, 2004: 53). As I suggested in the introduction to this book, such an understanding is fostered by the way in which television is perceived to create an 'identification between persona and role - thus giving the impression that the TV personality is just being "themselves"' (Bennett and Holmes, 2010: 70). In contradistinction to the film star's clear demarcation between on-screen roles and off-screen 'star image', the televisual image of television personalities begs the question: if television personalities merely present themselves then 'what do they do'? The positioning of personalities as 'just-as-they-are' has largely served to erase any notion of talent, skilled performance or hard work that goes towards the construction of their on-screen persona. Yet, as the quote from Leeman above suggests, 'being oneself' has long been recognised and valued as a performance by the television industry.

It is not my intention here to provide a comprehensive typology either of performers or performance modes that are evident across the television personality system. Whilst I do take televisually skilled and vocationally skilled performers separately below this is not an immutable distinction, and I make this separation here to suggest how televisual skill might function differently in each instance. What I hope to achieve in this chapter is to set out how we can take the on-screen appearances of television personalities, their 'just-as-they-are-ness', as skilled performances. In turn, such performances might merit sustained critical attention in terms of the pleasures, and displeasures, as well as cultural, economic and ideological meanings they offer up.

The relationship between performance and such meanings is inextricable, but it is also possible to analyse performance in its own right. Thus whilst there has been an explosion of work on lifestyle television since the late 1990s, commensurate with the rise in importance of the genre itself within the schedules, much of this work has focused on the representation of, and lessons offered in, taste, class, gender, sexuality, national identity and race. For authors such as Charlotte Brunsdon, Rachel Moseley, Joanne Hollows and others, such ideological constructs are 'performed' – thus it is possible to discuss Jamie Oliver's performance of masculinity or Nigella Lawson's performance of post-femininity or Julia Childs' invocation of class (Brunsdon, 2005; Hollows, 2002, 2003a, 2003b; Miller, 2007; Moseley, 2001) – but the analysis is primarily concerned with the way the 'everyday' of domesticity, such as cookery, DIY or taste, is performed in relation to these ideological categories.[2] Helen Wood and Beverley Skeggs have suggested that the predominant concern of such programming is the dissemination of middle-class practices and values as 'the standard to be achieved regardless of the necessary resources required to achieve them' (Skeggs and Wood, 2008: 561). As Laurie Ouellette and James Hay have observed, the overarching concern of 'performing the self' in such lifestyle programming is the dissemination of lessons in self-responsibility and self-enterprise. Unpicking the ideological work of the way lifestyle is presented and performed in such programming is, rightly, the task of such criticism and I make my own contribution to these debates in the following chapter.

But for the present moment, my concerns are different: that is, to show the markers of performance in television's personality system – for it is, arguably, through offering pleasures (too often dismissed as a 'reassuring presence') that such performers become and remain popular with viewers. As Niki Strange has observed in relation to cookery programming, 'if we concentrate only on cookery we may actually miss other crucial aspects of the show' (Strange, 1998: 304). This is a point equally applicable to the vocational skill that is presented in other lifestyle programming, such as gardening, fashion or property. We watch cookery, DIY, gardening and other lifestyle programmes as much for the pleasures of the presenter's performance as for the lessons we might learn. The importance of these pleasures is perhaps more apparent in light entertainment, where the presence (or absence) of a personality may be the primary motivation for watching (or not watching) a programme – if we do not like Ant and Dec we are unlikely to watch *Saturday Night Takeaway*. Performance, therefore, is fundamental to the celebrity of the television personality; whilst television may produce a plethora of celebrity and confer ephemeral fame, it is those who master the techniques necessary to create an intimate, spontaneous, immediate performance style that may be understood as 'television personalities'.

Two important consequences follow from an understanding that 'being oneself' is a performance that has to be worked at. First, that television personalities' on-screen personas – their televisual images – are a form of labour, which goes towards both the creation and maintenance of the personality's own fame and its attendant rewards, as well as a form of labour that is part of the political economy of the industry. Second, that this performance can therefore be evaluated in terms of the pleasures it offers and the successes (or failures) it achieves. In relation to this first meaning, and away from the reality-based and lifestyle-formats of television I have discussed above, the academy's interest in television performance has predominantly concerned wider debates in celebrity studies regarding the notion of the 'self'. As Brett Mills notes, since 'Goffman "performance" has become a word with a much wider sociological meaning than its everyday use about what professional, paid actors do' (Mills, 2005: 69). These wider sociological meanings are evident in the discourses of celebrity studies, where the 'self' is often understood as a performance. Joshua Gamson's study of celebrity in contemporary America suggests, particularly with the turn to postmodernism at the end of the twentieth century, that all celebrity can be understood as a performance (Gamson, 1994). His work details how the performative nature of celebrity has been long recognised in the popular press and media industries via a discourse of irony that draws attention to the artifice of celebrities' authenticity so that, 'by the 1980s *Rolling Stone* was sardonically claiming that .... "No self-respecting modern person should be without fifteen minutes' worth of the props ... that are vital to the maintenance of fame"' (ibid.: 49). Yet, in one of the key examples Gamson details – the appearance of the celebrity on the talk show – the discussion of performance is solely focused on the guest. Thus, whilst Gamson's analysis of publicists and agents suggests 'celebrities are chosen for their ability to perform themselves amusingly', the performance of the host goes largely unnoticed (ibid.: 101–103).

This notion of performance is helpful insofar as it enables us to understand that the celebrity 'self' is always a mediated construct and a key form of value-exchange in the entertainment industries. However, it does little to illuminate our understanding of the second meaning I outlined above: the way performance functions within the television text and the pleasures it offers. As Brett Mills has argued, the 'examination of acting in media has fallen predominantly to Film Studies, and has often been related to the analysis of stars' (Mills, 2005: 71). Where there has been an analysis of acting on television it has tended to focus on drama, particularly American Quality Television and the British heritage or authored-drama texts (Cardwell, 2006; Creeber, 2004; Geraghty, 2003; Jacobs, 2001; Peacock, 2006; Walters, 2008). As James Walters' analysis suggests, this body of work is indicative of a closer attention to the television text, often aided by advances in technologies such as the VCR and DVD, which demonstrates that television is capable of sustaining such critical attention:

> ... the DVD format proved wholly apposite for freezing, slowing down and replaying the nuanced gestures, looks and movements of the characters in order to describe the meanings created in the synthesis between performance style, visual composition and thematic progression.
>
> (Walters, 2008: 69)

The performance of television personalities, however, has failed to be the subject of such close scrutiny – arguably because of its perceived 'lack' in relation to not only the study of film stardom, but also because television personalities cannot be understood as 'actorly': they are perceived to merely 'perform' themselves, and therefore merit none of the critical attention that examines acting as the achievement of a transformation into a particular role. As Richard Maltby's examination of a similar criticism levelled at Hollywood film stars during the studio era suggests, such disapproval is motivated by the low cultural status attached to the medium (Maltby, 2003: 382).

In a discussion of sitcom and comedians that could be easily applied to the television personality system, Mills notes how because 'the comedy star system ... [relies on the] conflation between actor and character ... the fact that comedy performers often play what are assumed to be extensions of themselves is the cause of much of the critical antipathy towards it' (Mills, 2005: 74). We need therefore, as James Naremore and Mills do, to distinguish between acting and performance. And, in turn, to recognise that as with cinema's star system, television's personality system rests on the assumption that particular personalities 'will give certain kinds of performance and so offer certain kinds of pleasures' (ibid: 72). First, to separate acting from performance: Naremore describes the former as 'nothing more than the transposition of everyday behaviour into a theatrical realm' (Naremore, 1988: 21). As Mills explains, here 'the quality of acting is assessed through reference to the world outside of the media text and good acting is that which we easily describe as like "real life"' (Mills, 2005: 69). In contrast, '"Performance" is different to acting as it has connotations of "mastery, skill, or inventiveness"' (Naremore, quoted in ibid.). Unlike acting's drive for realism, performance 'relies on forms of excessive display that are centred on the star performer of the text' (ibid.: 70). Naremore argues that there are broadly two 'styles of performance – the representational (film acting mostly) and the presentational (direct address)' (Naremore, 1988: 36). There may be, as Naremore suggests, a dialectic between the two, as in Shakespeare, 'where characters frequently step outside the ongoing action and become commentators' (ibid.). However, as I suggested in Chapter 1, television personalities deal exclusively in presentational modes of performance that are characterised by direct address. Thus any dialectic between both forms here is structured by the movement from presentation to representation (rather than vice versa): for example, when Ant and Dec appear as characters in a sketch during *Saturday Night Takeaway* or the 'sitcom' *Chums* as part of *SM:TV Live*.

Where work has addressed these presentational modes of television performance it has predominantly tended to focus on light entertainment because it more overtly foregrounds performance in the sense that Naremore outlines. Richard Dyer's (1973) analysis of the genre and his work elsewhere on 'entertainment and utopia' (Dyer, 1981) have become a particularly important paradigm through which to view television performance, with both David Lusted and Karen Lury offering insightful critiques of the way the concept continues to inform the function of televisual skill within the genre of variety and light entertainment. Lury's analysis of contemporary light entertainment programming notes 'how little, in its essentials, it differs from ... those discussed by Richard Dyer over 30 years ago – the promise of escapism, "harmless" entertainment, slightly bawdy but not malevolent humour, a little bit of glitter and excitement, community and participation' (Lury, 2005: 176). Performance, therefore, is central to the pleasures on offer. Her analysis of Ant and Dec's skill in *Saturday Night Takeaway* suggests that their veering between the rehearsed and unrehearsed should result in them 'stumbl[ing], corps[ing] and perform[ing], apparently, as *themselves* and not as skilled professional performers' (ibid.: 184). This, however, is both part of the performance and pleasure light entertainment offers. Utopia, she argues, is made visible by light entertainment 'despite the fact that it can be amateurish, almost *because* this means that it does not *quite* give us what we want; instead, it provides glimpses and plays with fantasy, but does so in a way that is controlled and limited quite carefully' (ibid.). Like Lusted, therefore, she argues that such programming offers 'a fantasy of community', which in Lusted's case might overcome difference and bigotry – not in actuality, but at least in fostering a belief that things could be better (Lusted, 1998).

Such values are present in the programming I discuss below, but rather than rehearse these debates here I focus on the techniques (of the body) and technologies (of production) of performance more explicitly. In the first section I pay close attention to how these elements of performance function in creating a televisual image that is at once both ordinary and authentic, but also evidently 'special'; that is, extraordinarily ordinary. In the second section I focus on the performance of vocationally skilled personalities to demonstrate both the increased emphasis on televisual skill in such programming, but also to examine the notion of achievement and appreciation in performance. Here I draw on work from film and television studies to suggest how successful performances of vocational skill can be understood in relation to the cohesion of performance style and programming aims. In particular I am concerned to engage with Jason Jacobs's direction to think 'less about "television" and more about particular genres and programmes' in order to undertake an aesthetic criticism that is sensitive to 'the different aspirations of different kinds of television' (Jacobs, 2001: 430), drawing on Walters's notion of a 'synthesis' between programme aims and performance style in order to make critical evaluations (Walters, 2008).

Before proceeding with this analysis it is first worth making a brief point about the role of the schedule in television personality performance. Scheduling profoundly shapes the style of performance both anticipated by the viewer and permitted by the genre in question. Thus whilst quiz shows or cookery programmes might pervade both the afternoon and primetime slots on the schedule, the performance required in each will differ. Scheduling therefore works as an important process for differentiating the televisual image of personalities. Thus primetime personalities are distinguished from those who appear earlier or later in the schedule. As suggested in Chapter 4, television's political economy and its essentially domestic nature means that television personalities appearing in primetime will generally be inoffensive and family orientated. Other, later-schedule television personalities are thus able to generate a differentiated persona that capitalises not only on the 'niceness' of their primetime counterparts, but also (in Britain at least) the post-nine pm watershed that enables an explicit and irreverent performance, image and address. Graham Norton, who presents both Saturday night primetime as well as a late night chat show, exemplifies how these distinctions are largely the achievement of performance style. Thus whilst his performance on *The Graham Norton Show* (So Television, 2007–ongoing) draws on his sexuality for a performance laced with innuendo and explicit gags about sex (before he moved to the BBC, dildos were a recurring motif on *So Graham Norton* [So Television, 1998–2002), the mobilisation of his sexuality in his performance on *How Do You Solve a Problem Like Maria* is more akin to fairy godmother; a similar point might be made in relation to Gok Wan's primetime performances. It is important that we understand these differences in television personality as not simply motivated by genre but also affected and constructed by the nature of the schedule and what certain time slots allow or prohibit.

Televisually skilled performers: Performing authenticity and stardom

In this section I detail how authenticity might be understood as performed and, in particular, how its association with the television personality's ordinariness is negotiated by the need to signal their 'stardom'; that is, as special from other performers on-screen, such as guest celebrities and ordinary people. To briefly recall Susan Murray's work here, early television's connection to vaudeville and music hall has posited 'the ideal television performer' as one able to best exploit television's primary 'aesthetic properties – immediacy, intimacy and spontaneity' (Murray, 2005: xiv–xv). As she suggests, these properties, together with the economic goals of broadcasting that often posited personalities as sponsors' spokespeople, meant viewers were 'encouraged to believe that they could actually locate the true personality of a television star somewhere within [their] ... performance' (ibid.: 129). Her example of Arthur Godfry's revelation of a true 'self' that was irreconcilable with his on-screen persona demonstrates how this notion of authenticity functions in terms of a continuousness of on-/off-screen self. Indeed, thinking about authenticity as a kind of 'just-as-they-are-ness' in relation to the case of a personality whose off-screen antics has threatened to disrupt the coherence and continuousness of their televisual image is particularly illuminating for the way in which it draws our attention to performance.

For example, whilst Angus Deayton's presentation of *Have I Got News for You* (Hat Trick for BBC, 1990–ongoing) was always infused with a sense of sardonic wit that was far from wholesome, his sacking by the BBC for revela-tions of the use of cocaine and prostitutes in his personal life in 2002, owed more to the Corporation's desire to protect its image as a trustworthy and responsible broadcaster. Deayton's subsequent career has been marked by an attempt to both distinguish the 'real' person from the television personality, by taking on dramatic and comedic roles in a variety of series, but also by incorporating this layer of bad-boy behaviour into his televisual image. Thus his return to the BBC the following year as host for a one-off *Comic Relief Does University Challenge* (BBC, 2007) special was marked by a self-deprecating performance, whilst his potentially more long-term return to the BBC as presenter of *Would I Lie to You* (Endemol for BBC, 2007–ongoing), a panel game show that is based on the successful telling of lies, plays explicitly with incorporating his 'real life' into the authenticity of his televisual image. Authenticity therefore relates to the idea that the audience is getting the real 'Angus Deayton' or 'Cilla Black', rather than a performance.

Yet, as I suggested in Chapter 1, the use of the term 'authenticity' has had other meanings that we should be more attentive to in understanding televis-ual performance and skill. As I discussed there, work in celebrity studies has connected authenticity to 'the perpetual attempt to lay claim to the "real self" ... organized around a desire to suggest a "separable, coherent quality, located "inside" consciousness and variously termed "the self", "the soul", "the subject"' (Dyer quoted in Holmes, 2005a: 27). Indeed, it is precisely this interplay between on-/off-screen persona that produced the dialectic of the ordinary/extraordinary paradox central to understandings of film stardom (Dyer, 1979; Ellis, 1982). However, authenticity – or the appearance of it – is also a palpable mode of performance and achievement. As Philip Auslander has observed in relation to a range of theories of acting and the 'self', 'the actorly self, is in fact, produced by the performance it supposedly grounds' (Auslander, 1997: 30). Dyer's analysis of Judy Garland's performance from a sequence in *A Star is Born* (1954) demonstrates how such authenticity is 'established or constructed in media texts by the use of markers that indicate lack of control, lack of premeditation and privacy'(Dyer, 2000: 137). In so doing, he reveals how all of these qualities are constructed in performance, in the combination of technique and technical production, yet disavow their own role in the manufacture of stardom. Thus, as Dyer concludes 'we must know that her star quality has nothing to do with [mechanical] techniques ... but is grounded in her own immediate (= not controlled), spontaneous (= unpremeditated) and essential (= private) self [and it is that which] guarantees that her stardom is not a con ...' (Dyer, 2000: 137–139).

Such a mode of performance, of both technique and technical means, is pivotal to the function and success of the television personality so that authenticity, in this second sense, is about naturalising performance. In the construction of television personality fame, such a discourse intersects with the first meaning of authenticity as the elision of on-/off-screen self in inter- textual circulation of the persona. In combination these discourses serve to render performance itself invisible, so that television personalities appear 'just-as-they-are'. The successful representation of an authentic on-screen persona on television arguably involves the deployment of televisual skill, understood as an achievement of technique and technical means (see Bennett, 2008; Lury, 1995) that must disguise the manufacture of the television personality's 'performance' by the team of writers, rehearsals and production personnel that go into making any television programme. It is in such performances that much pleasure from the television personality's performance derives.

Performance, and an associated displeasure, is therefore perhaps most clearly evident when it reveals these mechanical techniques and signs of the performance's manufacture. This is perhaps most evident in the global circu- lation of formats, where a local host must 'play' the role of one of the estab- lished hosts. But it is also evident where the dialects between presentation and representational modes of performance come into conflict. For example, when a guest celebrity hosts a panel game show such as *Have I Got News for You?* the results can lay bare the machinery of the carefully written scripts and jokes, which are presented as spontaneous and unrehearsed. Thus whilst Dominic West may have achieved numerous plaudits for his naturalistic acting in *The Wire* (HBO, 2002–2008), his hosting of *Have I Got News for You?* in early 2010 was characterised by a movement between reading the script on his desk and staring wild-eyed at the camera as he strained to read the auto- cue. Equally, one could look at Ant and Dec's attempts at naturalistic acting in *Alien Autopsy* (2006) to examine this problematic in reverse. Although largely framed as a series of set pieces that allow for them to deal in a perfor- mative mode, the dialectical movement between representational and presen- tational is reversed by the presence of a narrative – something normally absent from their texts.

Beyond telling us that there are significant differences between acting and presentational performance modes, these short examples suggest how the authenticity of a television personality's televisual image is built up over a series of appearances and continuity in programme format, genre and performance style. As Langer argues:

> Each repeated appearance, even though it may not elicit 'personal data' ... nonetheless tends to build what is perceived to be a knowable and known 'television self'. This television self, increasingly authenticated with each regular appearance, coheres into the form of a 'genuine' personality.
>
> (Langer, 1997: 169)

To explore this concept further, I want to turn now to an analysis of Cilla Black's televisual image.

For Cilla Black this continuity of style and format is found in her almost constant appearance on British television for nearly forty years, having graduated from checking coats at Liverpool's famous Cavern Club (as Priscilla Maria Veronica White) to a brief but successful pop career to British television institution. Whilst her initial appearance in *Cilla*, and to a lesser extent *Surprise, Surprise*, were principally reliant on her vocational skill as a singer, the success of the latter of these, together with *Blind Date* (London Weekend Television, 1985–2003), saw programming largely hung on her televisual skill and persona alone, with little change in her televisual image over this period. By the mid-1990s, Black was considered one of the pre eminent performers on television, described by industry magazine *Broadcast* as part of London Weekend Television's 'enviable stable of the three Bs – Barrymore, Black and Beadle'.[3]

Cilla was largely structured as a variety programme, allowing Black to sing, dance and act in comedy sketches. However, the programme's original premise was designed as a vehicle for Black's musical skill and stardom, with the Paul McCartney penned theme tune, 'Step inside love', giving Black a chart topping hit in 1968. Furthermore, the programme's centrepiece was to be its request spot, whereby Cilla would surprise people by appearing in ordinary places (such as supermarkets or petrol stations) and asking for requests to be performed on the programme that week. As Black's musical star began to wane however, her televisual image became less reliant on this part of her persona. Thus, whilst *Surprise, Surprise* still privileged her vocational singing talent by giving her a 'star turn' in singing the programme's theme song, this skill was largely irrelevant for the majority of the programme's format, which promised to fulfil ordinary members of the public's dreams. Indeed, as I demonstrate in more detail below, it is this constant contact with ordinary people that reinforces the sense that the television personality's televisual image is authentic. In particular, Black's much vaunted 'humble beginnings' as the daughter of a Liverpudlian dock-worker added to the sense that this image was 'ordinary', acting as something of an intermediary between the audience and the guest stars on *Cilla* and the dream scenarios on *Surprise, Surprise*. As Karen Lury notes, northern accents on British television retain, even if notional, connotations of working-class ordinariness and authenticity (Lury, 2005: 197). Intertextual coverage which stresses these 'ordinary' beginnings therefore serves to emphasise the continuity of persona, so that a personality's televisual image is built up as authentic over a long period of time. However, this authenticity has to be negotiated by an on-screen performance which, whilst intimate, immediate, spontaneous and palpably authentic, must also clearly construct a televisual image that positions the television personality with 'star' qualities: that is, which elevates their status from television presenter to television personality.

Whilst Black's 'star-status' in these earlier programmes was largely hung on her musical stardom, the authenticity of persona established there had to be presented consistently in later programmes. This involved a complex dislocation of the associations of her image with the extraordinariness and glamour of pop stardom whilst at the same time clearly signalling her status as the 'star of the show'. In effect, such personalities must be constructed as extraordinarily ordinary. The opening sequence of *Blind Date* is therefore principally aimed at constructing Black as the 'star' of the programme, which the rest of her performance then negotiates. The title sequence of *Blind Date* introduces the format of the programme, showing us 'snippets' from up-coming moments and speculating as to how last week's contestants fared on their date. This title sequence then opens onto shots of the studio set and audience, the stage set for Black's delayed entrance, as the audience is whipped into a state of excited anticipation by the sequence's culmination in 'our Graham's' (Graham Skidmore) voice-over: 'ladies and gentleman it's '*Blind Date*'. And here is your host, Miss Cilla Bl-a-a-a-ck'. The voice-over is presented in the style of a circus ringmaster, growing gradually louder as he reaches Black's name, which is then almost shouted in an attempt to drive (or cue) the audience into an applauding frenzy for the 'star'. As Skidmore's voice-over trails off, we cut to a more central camera angle that is focused on a spotlight at the top of the set's main stairs (Figure 5.1) into which Black steps. However, rather than walking on as a starlet of the screen or projecting a sense of extraordinariness, Black appears laughing and waving to the crowd, enjoying and appreciative of the audience's applause (and occasional wolf whistle). As she reaches her presentation spot at the bottom of the stairs, the music stops and, to the respectful silencing of the audience, Black commences her introduction.

This opening sequence signals the 'stardom' of Black to both the studio and home audience. However, the rest of her performance is largely aimed at renouncing any particular extraordinariness that may pervade her celebrity status with notions of 'star' unattainability. During the introduction and following section, Black's performance is aimed at not only (re)establishing an intimate connection with the audience, but also ensuring that she remains the focal point of the programme and the entity through which the text is centred. Indeed, her walk down the stairs at the start of the show to hit her

Figure 5.1 Black steps into a spotlight at the top of *Blind Date*'s main stairs, which signals her relative 'stardom' that the rest of her performance works to negotiate so as to emphasise her ordinariness (screen capture from *Blind Date* [London Weekend Television, 1985–2003]).

'mark' spatially positions her at the centre of action, and it is her movement that guides us (and contestants) to new areas of the set.[4] By concentrating on these elements of performance, we can understand how the televisual image is constructed. Paying attention to the subsequent section of *Blind Date* therefore, we can perceive that a form of 'delegated looking' is managed by both technique and technology, to allow Black's position to be identificatory for the viewer. Black's performance technique is embellished by technology, in the form of camera angles and editing, which ensures the appearance of the contestants in the classic television mid-close-up only occurs in a relational position to Black's presence, constructing the shot as if it were a point-of-view shot. This 'placing' of the viewer ensures that Black has the ability to organise and control the programme, and in particular, the appearances/performances of the contestants. Thus, in an episode screened in December of 2001, Black can be seen to champion the cause of Joel, whose good looks and desire to work with children she finds 'adorable', eventually leading to the contestant being chosen by the picker.

Further, Black's shifting use of direct address creates a sense of intimacy between viewer and performer, bringing her comfortably into the domestic environment. James Naremore expresses how mode of address in variety performance can change rapidly to create an interesting and engaging performance:

Figures 5.2 and 5.3 Black's address shifts constantly between studio, home audience and contestant to create an interesting and engaging performance (screen captures from *Blind Date* [London Weekend Television, 1985–2003]).

'In the chatty episodes, players cultivate a shifting gaze, aimed now at the interviewer or interviewee, now at the studio audience, now at the lens of the camera' (Naremore, 1988: 35). These shifts in address also indicate how Black can be classed as a televisually skilled performer, marking her performance with control. Black is able to shift her presentation between studio audience, contestants and home viewer in a fluid performance that ensures that she does not lose the attention, or control, of any of these audiences. Thus in a typical introduction section of the programme, Black's eye and body language will utilise a direct address to camera, for the home viewer (Figure 5.2), and then switch attention to the immediate studio audience signalled both by a shift in her eye contact, which looks away from the camera (Figure 5.3), as well as an increased use of gesture, such as slightly enlarged hand movements. Finally, her attention may be focused on the contestants, such as in the final segment, which allows contestants a hug and kiss from the show's 'star', ensuring Black's ordinariness and reachable qualities are ultimately re-emphasised to both the contestants and audiences.

Indeed, the interaction with ordinary contestants showcases Black's televisual skill as she negotiates the flirtations between contestants and the occasional overtures made to her. As Su Holmes and Garry Whannel have observed, the 'allocation of social roles in the [quiz show] ... clearly shape the ... rituals of exchange' (Holmes, 2008b: 122) so that the ordinary person is 'often encouraged to display their personalities while acting as the straight man or woman to the host' (Whannel quoted in ibid). Such moments help Black to create an image of a safely-flirtatious mother figure, as the programme allows open flirtations on primetime television, secure in the knowledge that there is always the possibility of Black's censorship. As Nevin suggests, her persona effectively sanitised the *Blind Date* format: 'London Weekend Television tried other presenters in pilots of *Blind Date* but ran into a prurience problem. Cilla was brought in as "the most sexless person on television"' (Nevin, quoted in Mann, 1991: 44).

To return to Dyer's discussion of the qualities of authenticity, the presence of ordinary people emphasises the sense of immediacy, spontaneity and revelation of the essential self in televisual performance: as an element in the production that the television personality is not entirely in control of, the ordinary person's presence connotes a lack of premeditation in the television personality's performance, but also acts as a guarantee of our access to the essential, private self of the television personality through the opportunities of physical proximity and contact afforded to such ordinary people. The presence of ordinary people allows the television personality to appear 'just-as-they-really-are' alongside ordinary people. As Karen Lury and Charlotte Brunsdon have noted in different contexts, the presence of television personalities amongst the audience is to 'reassure us that they are there in person' (Lury, 2005: 179), whilst the 'point' of such audience members use as participants 'is their ordinariness' (Brunsdon *et al.*, 2001: 51). A feeling of familiarity between audience and television personality is thus made explicitly pivotal to the success of a television personality's image. Their televisual image is not only authentic, but is also one of ordinariness: being able to be 'just-as-they-are' with ordinary members of the public. As such, the aesthetic strategies discussed above largely serve to deny the role of performance.

Television's regime of liveness undoubtedly further feeds into this performance of authenticity. I have discussed the importance of liveness in early television in Chapters 2 and 3 and, whilst little of contemporary television is relayed live, television's ontology of liveness that is structured and reinforced by its scheduled flow continues to inflect performance. Thus although the pre-recorded nature of much programming enables rehearsals by the main performers and walk throughs for the 'ordinary' contestants to take place, such preparations must be disguised in order to represent performance as spontaneous in alignment with television's ontology of liveness. Thus, as Lury points out, 'one of the most common criticisms of *Blind Date* is the unacknowledged practiced nature of the contestants' apparently spontaneous responses' (Lury, 1995: 125). However, the practiced nature of these responses also suggests that the questioning and reactions of Black in relation to the contestants are also rehearsed, discussed and fine-tuned by Black and the programme's producers. Thus if Stanley Cavell is correct to suggest that on television there is 'no sensuous distinction between the live and the repeat or replay' (quoted in Auslander, 1997: 44), then part of Black's success is that it is rarely Black herself who is criticised in such terms: televisual skill ensures her performance appears spontaneous, immediate and intimate despite rehearsal. Indeed, the fact that television personalities working in light entertainment deal in heavily formatted programming ensures that each programme effectively works to fine-tune their performance, enabling them to command the space of the set effectively and ad lib within a relatively proscribed confine. 'Cilla Black' can therefore be understood not only as a constructed character but, as with film, the television personality will have varying levels of control over this persona. As Dyer notes in his study of stars, this may range from total control, to a contribution as part of a team or, more rarely, as a disparate voice against the total control of the director/producer or channel (Dyer, 2001: 153). In this section I hope to have demonstrated how this controlled performance can produce an authenticated persona who is signalled as extraordinarily ordinary. Having pointed to some of the ways in which televisual skill can be located within the text, I want to now turn to how these may structure our understanding of pleasure and achievement in performance by focusing on the vocationally skilled performer.

Vocationally skilled performers: Pleasure and achievement in performance

The notion that a category of vocationally skilled performers exists on television is perhaps best evidenced by the BBC Trust's report on talent. Having found that in light entertainment most of the current 'top presenters' were on television five, ten or twenty years ago, found this differed markedly in lifestyle programming, which brought 'the most talent from outside TV onto viewers' screens' (Oliver & Ohlbaum Associates, 2008: 113). The number of presenters in lifestyle programming who are new to television in this time period suggests how particular presenters are picked from vocational professions in order to present some skill they hold outside of television. For such personalities the *credibility* of their vocational skill is fundamental to their appearance on television and the authenticity of their image. Credibility functions in relation to the vocational skill(s) of the performer, reassuring the viewer that the skills being presented are authentic and worthwhile investing in (in the form of copying or learning). In turn, this credibility is crucial to the circulation and success of such personalities' intertextual image, which will be linked to a series of spin-off merchandising opportunities ranging from 'how to' and recipe books, gardening and cookery equipment, through to 'signature' fashion ranges. The emphasis on the credibility of the presenters' vocational skills places such personalities' performances within a difficult tension: on the one hand, required to act as 'teachers' who demonstrate and pass on the skills and knowledge of their vocational profession to viewers; on the other hand, required to marshal a performance that can sustain audience interest. As David Bell and Joanne Hollows's overview of developments in lifestyle television suggest, such programmes are:

> caught in what we might call this 'Reithian Bargain'. They have a heritage of negotiating the 'inform, educate, entertain' mantra of the BBC's paternalistic public service origins, and their subsequent development charts that continuing negotiation; the balancing between informing, educating and entertaining – ideas themselves increasingly blurred in this age of infotainment and edutainment.
>
> (Bell and Hollows, 2005: 10)

Their analysis, together with other contributions to that collection, makes clear the increasing emphasis placed on entertainment in such programming.

In this section I focus on cookery programmes, as one of the most studied forms of lifestyle and factual television, and the relationship between vocational skill and performance. As they suggest, 'developments such as pro-celebrity game shows about cooking, docusoaps following the travails of growers ... cooking-cum-dating contests, etc' have 'stretched and warped the categories' Niki Strange proposed in relation to cookery programming in the late 1990s 'almost beyond their elastic limits'. In her piece, 'Perform, educate, entertain', Strange proposed a typology of cookery programming that demonstrated the different emphases on performance and personality across the genre – from the 'cook-ed', which focused on education, to the personality-based show, which foregrounded the performance of the host (Strange, 1998: 304). Bell and Hollows's analysis suggests that as the genre has mutated, there is an increasing emphasis on the entertainment value of the personality and programme in general. As I suggested in Chapter 1, this can be found across a range of genres, where this has been a longer term shift away from the use of vocational performers as experts whose knowledge is framed by the presentation of a televisually skilled performer. Ann Gray and Erin Bell's study of television history programming, presenters and producers demonstrates an increasing emphasis on 'the ability to entertain and engage, to demonstrate a certain element of showmanship and, above all, "charisma for the camera"' (quoting Janice Hadlow, Bell and Gray, 2007: 147).

This stress on entertainment has resulted in a corollary weight placed on the presenters' performance. As Strange's examination of Keith Floyd's performances demonstrates, a television personality's performance and televisual image can disrupt and supersede the educative discourses of the cookery programme. Whilst Floyd's performances are hugely enjoyable, the question of a successful performance in such programming arguably turns on the question of balancing the Reithian bargain. Returning to Jacobs's direction to pay attention to the aspirations of particular kinds of television, I would suggest we can judge achievement of performance as 'the synthesis between performance style, visual composition and thematic progression' (Walters, 2008: 69). The performance of Jamie Oliver, often considered a 'natural', in the first episode of *The Naked Chef* (BBC, 1999–2001) and a consideration of its relationship to his subsequent performances, provides a useful short example here of the way in which vocationally skilled performers both develop their televisual skill, as well as how the deployment of this skill can result in the achievement of a performance that marries the educative, informative and performative discourses of lifestyle television.

Oliver's performance style is largely based on the ability to present cookery expertise as something fun, simple and do-able as part of everyday life. This is achieved by a range of factors, including the narrative structure of the series that not only introduces us to him at work in a restaurant, providing his vocational skill with credibility, but also sees his cooking fit around the rhymes and rhythms of the everyday: work, birthdays, child-minding, etc. In terms of performance, his widely discussed aural presentation mode of 'mockney' and English 'lad' (see Hollows, 2003a; Moseley, 2001) – signified by his catchphrases of 'pukka' and playful references to 'buns in the oven' – similarly serves to emphasise the ease and fun of cooking: ingredients are 'bashed' or 'chucked'. But this aural delivery is complemented by a visual mode of performance that emphasises movement in terms of both technique and technology. Jamie is seemingly constantly in and out of the fridge or oven, moving around the kitchen or bashing saucepans or ingredients across the work surface. Performance becomes a pleasure of the programme because of the apparent energy, and fun, with which cooking is demonstrated – a far cry from the staid delivery of Delia Smith or Fanny Craddock. Movement is, however, largely stressed via the handheld camera which, rather than cut to close-ups that might emphasise the cookery techniques involved, zooms in and out of the action, frames and reframes Oliver as he points to ingredients and moves around the kitchen. The use of relatively tight framing throughout the sequences set in the kitchen, together with the deployment of very mobile handheld camera framing, creates a kinetic performance style that is consistent with the notion of a youthful, fun and easy approach to cookery: performance might therefore be privileged over education, but in such a way that pleasure comes from the way performance teaches us not solely about a particular recipe but a particular lifestyle project.

In these early programmes, technique and technology combine to maximise the impact of Oliver's relatively inexperienced performance in front of camera. Oliver's kinetic aesthetic is a performance style that can be seen to be nurtured during the first two series of *The Naked Chef*. Oliver is regularly, but gently, prompted and cued by the off-screen director (Patricia Llewellyn), who asks questions about ingredients, techniques or events in his life. However, this conceit functions beyond merely aiding Oliver's development of televisual skill, as it enables his performance to be directed at somebody other than the home audience, keeping direct address to a minimum and emphasising the notion that we are watching him 'just-as-he-really-is', at home: cooking for narrative purposes, rather than solely for what Strange calls the instructional discourses of 'cook-ed' (Figure 5.4). In contrast, in later series the director role has disappeared and Oliver's use of direct address is more assured and whilst, particularly in his more recent *Jamie at Home* (Fresh One for Channel 4, 2007–2008), there is a greater use of cutting to close-ups to show technique, there is also greater use of the mid-close-up in static framing that requires Oliver's physical performance to embody his kinetic aesthetic; for example, by locating ingredients away from where he is cooking, his movement constantly fills the frame with energy (see Figure 5.5).

Performance of technique here is in synthesis with the technologies of production in such a way as to suggest it might conform to Andrew Klevan's analysis of achievement in performance, so that the pleasures on offer are in the cohesion between performance, technology and the diegetic world of the film or programme. As Klevan argues in relation to all the performances he scrutinises in his book *Film Performance* '[t]heir achievement is to devote themselves to the film's world' in such a way as to reward 'concentration because the acuity of their attentiveness is belied by the ease of their integration' (Klevan, 2005: 104–105). Similarly, Oliver's performance works as part of a world in which cookery is fun, relatively fast, easy and, as Rachel Moseley explains, emphasises 'family and togetherness ... selling a whole lifestyle ... a way to be through clothes, looks, domestic space and ways of being a man' (Moseley, 2001: 39). Whilst his mockney persona has been criticised as inauthentic, its signification of 'down-to-earth' ordinariness is congruent with what, as I set out above, remains the overarching aims of lifestyle television as a middle-class project. In contrast, as I turn to now, whilst other vocational performers may exhibit more complex forms of televisual skill, their achievement is of a lesser nature because it is inconsistent with the nature of the programme.

An immediate and direct contrast is apparent in the performances of Delia Smith who, as Niki Strange details, performs almost entirely in a presentational and staid mode, where movement is kept to a minimum and direct address is only focused to the camera (as opposed to co-hosts, guests or a studio audience). Moreover, the use of editing and post-production voice-over allows for the recital of carefully rehearsed or tele-prompted

Figure 5.4 In his early appearances on the *Naked Chef,* Oliver eschews direct address with his performance style nurtured by regular prompts and cues from the off-screen director (screen capture from *The Naked Chef* [BBC, 1999–2001]).

Figure 5.5 In Oliver's later appearances the producer role has disappeared and there is greater use of the mid-close-up in static framing that requires Oliver's physical performance to embody his kinetic aesthetic (screen capture from *Jamie at Home* [Fresh One for Channel 4, 2007–2008]).

instructional speeches that undermine any sense of spontaneity, immediacy or pleasure in the performance in and of itself. Whilst her televisual image is nevertheless one that is performed, performance itself is evacuated as an evaluative criterion by which we might enjoy the programme. In contrast, a programme such as *Ready, Steady, Cook* (Endemol for BBC, 1994–ongoing) heavily emphasises the role of performance in the pleasures it seeks to offer.

Ready, Steady, Cook is a long-running BBC afternoon cookery-competition format in which the host, Ainsley Harriott (formerly Fern Britton), mediates between two teams of chefs and contestants (who may or may not be celebrities) who must compete against the clock to invent and cook dishes using ingredients brought in by the contestant in front of a live studio audience. This time-based element is premised on the programme's didactic aims of creating easy and simple meals that contestants and audiences can learn in twenty minutes. Such a format is clearly in stark contrast to that of Oliver's programming discussed above. Indeed, it is because of this contrast that I suggest it is useful, as a detailed analysis allows us to move beyond the uncritically evaluative ('he's annoying'), to a more nuanced understanding of the role of (over)performance. Equally, I would suggest, it would be possible to undertake such an analysis in relation to Nigella Lawson's and Gordon Ramsay's recent programming. For example, one could profitably mine the disjuncture between Lawson's over-the-top performance in *Nigella Express* and the programme's narrative conceit that she 'whips up' these dishes amongst her 'busy' life: the inclusion of a regular format point that sees Lawson regularly return to the fridge at the end of the programme for one last taste of her recipe, as if it were a midnight snack which the camera crew were luckily still on hand to film, provides one such short-hand example.

Returning to *Ready, Steady, Cook*, the fact that it takes place in front of a live studio audience and is filmed using a traditional three camera set-up most commonly associated with light entertainment, serves to emphasis the role of performance in the format. In a similar way to Cilla Black's presentation discussed above, Harriott's performance must therefore be addressed to fellow performers and participants, home and studio audience. Harriott's use of direct address functions as a signal of his televisually skilled performance. As I suggested in Chapters 2 and 3, direct address is one of the key markers of televisual skill that creates a hierarchical arrangement within broadcasting, differentiating between those who have control within the regime (those with an immediate and seemingly unmediated/unfettered access to direct address) and those who do not (those at the bottom of the hierarchy who are not permitted to look at the camera) (Tolson, 1996: 63). The use of direct address within *Ready, Steady, Cook* exemplifies this hierarchy and the place of the television personality at its summit. For example, despite the increasing celebrity status of the (fellow) chefs appearing on the programme – in particular, Gino D'Acampo who has hosted a range of other cookery programmes and won the 2009 series of *I'm a Celebrity … Get Me Out of Here* (2004–ongoing) – only Ainsley Harriott is able to address the camera(s), and in turn, the home viewer.

Whilst the other celebrity chefs are able to address the studio audience, Harriott controls when and how this happens: for example, with the aid of the production team, studio audience members are selected by Harriott for dialogue and instruction by the chefs, during which Harriott will take over cooking duties to allow interaction. However, the chefs will always be called back

Figure 5.6 Harriott's use of direct address functions as a signal of his televisually skilled performance (screen captures from *Ready, Steady, Cook* [Endemol for BBC, 1994–ongoing]).

Figure 5.7 Arguably Harriott's expressive performance mode fulfils the aesthetics of spectacle and spontaneity...

to the fray at the ringmaster's behest. Figure 5.6 represents one of the many format points in the show in which guests, chefs and Harriott all fill the screen. Despite a similar spatial relationship to the camera, and an absence of (cooking) action, between Harriott and his two 'guest' chefs, only he is able to utilise direct address as a performance mode. However, despite the evident skill in Harriott's appearances in commanding the attention and roles of the programme's various audiences and participants, his performance remains unsatisfying; and arguably the fact that he remains a fixture in the afternoon

Figure 5.8 ...but it does so in such a way as to distract from other elements of the programme, dominating all spheres of action on the set and fails to marry that spectacle with the qualities of intimacy and immediacy necessary for successful performance...

Figure 5.9 ...so that the very performativity of Harriott's use of gesture and display works against the apparent coherence of the programme (screen captures from *Ready, Steady, Cook* [Endemol for BBC, 1994-ongoing]).

schedules attests to the failure of his performance mode to find widespread approval. (In contrast, the programme's previous host Fern Britton has moved across a range of primetime and prestigious morning programming.) The disjuncture between performance and the coherence of the programme again rests on the question of balancing the aims of a cookery programme with producing an engaging performance.

As an afternoon programme incorporating elements of the game show, a higher level of performance is necessarily evident than in Jamie's primetime 'cook-ed' series. However, Harriott continually dominates the action through his use of direct address and gesture regardless of other activities going on around him and shot composition. Thus in Figures 5.7–5.9 we can see Harriott continuing to directly address the camera from behind the cookery action and, via the use of expansive gestures, turn his attention to motivate the studio audience in counting down to the show's climax. Arguably such a performance mode fulfils the aesthetics of spectacle and spontaneity, but it does so in such a way as to distract from other elements of the programme: it cries 'look at me', dominating all spheres of action on the set and fails to marry that spectacle with the qualities of intimacy and immediacy Murray associates with successful performance. The use of expansive gestures, whilst effective in marshalling the attention and involvement of the studio audience, works against the inclusion of the home audience with his movements appearing out of scale with the domestic and small screen viewing situation of the home. Indeed, in Figure 5.9 Harriott's excessive movement is such that he is caught between cameras: continuing his direct address to the home viewer despite his performance being out of scale with shot composition and visual style. Moreover, the very performativity of Harriott's use of gesture and display work against the apparent coherence of the programme, in which the teams must compete in a pressurised situation against the clock. As he moves in and out of frame, editing is made apparent whilst, as Karen Lury suggests, the use of post-production is used to create a 'deliberate audio-hierarchy' so that Harriott's (incessant) chatting is privileged over any dramas of the contestants and game show elements themselves. As with Lury's analysis, this undermines the notion of a 'visual "democracy" (the "man in the street", the crowd, the marchers) is seen on screen, but actually very few "ordinary" people are able to speak, and those that do are controlled audibly, even if they are unruly visually' (Lury, 2005: 64–65). The failure here is to accord any due weight to other elements in the programme – instruction, pressure and even spontaneity are all subservient to Harriott's performance.

What I have suggested in the discussion of vocationally skilled performers is that there is an increased emphasis on televisual skill and, in turn, that we can understand achievement in such performance as the balancing of the didactic with the entertaining. I have concentrated here solely on lifestyle and cookery television as a genre that most readily lends itself to such discussion. However, the holding of some vocational skill is also a prerequisite for other performers to appear on television. Much as I have detailed above in relation to Oliver, other such performers may make the transition to television personality via the development of televisual skill. Sport provides a particularly compelling example, with the use of ex-players as pundits, or in the 'colour man' role for commentaries – such as John Madden's long-held position on Fox Television in the USA – through to the use of former sports stars as host of such programming. Often this host role is fulfilled by a presenter who is solely televisual skilled in order to maintain a slick movement between pundits, commentators and the producer's directions as to cuts to pitch-side reporters, team-news, pre-recorded videotape, etc. The importance of this role is evidenced by Des Lynam's golden handcuffs deal discussed in Chapter 4, but it is also apparent that some vocationally skilled performers can grow into these roles: for example, Gary Lineker on the BBC in the United Kingdom, or Paul 'fatty' Vautin on Channel 9 in Australia. Such examples are suggestive of the increased emphasis placed on performance in the presentation of vocational skill across a range of genres, so that the presence of designated experts is no longer predicated on the presence of a televisually skilled performer to mediate their appearance: vocational experts are increasingly capable of managing a professional performance. Equally, an understanding and appreciation of the role and markers of performance is increasingly widespread, as evidenced by the example of reality TV discussed in relation to *Extras* in the introduction to Part II. The achievement of successful and pleasurable performances, however, remains a matter of both attunement to the specificities of the genre and the schedule, and the attainment of television personality fame.

Conclusion

Performance is a particularly difficult area for analysis when considering television personalities. The emphasis in production, intertextual circulation of personalities' images and indeed the political economy of the television personality system all serve to disavow or naturalise performance. Yet its very invisibility is both testament to the televisual skill of the performer, as well as both its economic and aesthetic value. As a result, nearly all performance from the television personality is a matter of under-performance. In Ellis's more detailed study of performance and acting in relation to the film star, one finds a useful critique of this mode of performance that could be extended to the television personality system. There he usefully suggests that the actor may choose to over-perform, in order to emphasise the work of acting, or under-perform, which 'is not a question of restraint or lack of histrionics. It is a question of producing the effect of behaving rather than *performing*' (Ellis, 1992: 104, emphasis mine). As Ellis goes on to outline, this is always a case of comparison and suggests that the over- or under-performance of a film star is best recognised by their relationship to the supporting cast. These supporting performers, much like the role of the 'ordinary person' in the programming I have discussed in this chapter, have to work to emphasise their lines, gestures and expressions 'simply in order to signify the required meanings'. In contrast, the personality 'has the attention of the audience and is a recognised figure, with a recognised voice, face and figure' (ibid.). Most importantly, like Ellis's description of the film star, they have both the camera's attention and in the case of the television personality's appearances, the format's attention. Having such attention, anything the television personality does can be construed as significant – hence through their continual presence in the schedules, the very repetitiveness of their performances, television personalities are permitted, indeed required, to under-act in order to produce the effect that they are simply *behaving* rather than *performing*. As the opening quote from Leeman at the head of this chapter suggests, every gesture is under scrutiny in the television personality's performance

To return to the example of *Extras* with which I opened Part II, it is the over-performance of personas there that I suggested helped draw our attention to the notion of performance in relation to television personalities. Whilst this is successful in the narrative world of the fiction, I have suggested that such over-performance is generally incommensurate with the notion of achievement we might develop in evaluating television personalities' performances. I hope to have demonstrated some of the ways we can both locate and evaluate the signs of this performance so that we can better understand the role perform-ance plays in television's personality system. Performance, we can conclude, must be understood as a key form of labour performed by television person-alities on behalf of both the television industry and their own celebrity, with the aim being the successful development of a televisual image that is coherent and continuous across programmes and intertexts. The chapters in this section have sought to demonstrate the link between political economy and perform-ance. In the remainder of the book, I turn to this ideological function in rela-tion to questions of identity and the wider role of television celebrity.

Part III

The television personality system revisited

Ordinariness and DIY fame

In a previous work on television fame, I suggested that 'more work could be done on the importance of particular personalities' televisual image in relation to historical, cultural or ideological debates and trends' as the television personality system emerged as a site of study in its own right, freed from the shadows of film theory (Bennett, 2008: 50). As Susan Murray has suggested, it is 'downright odd that television historians have not yet … followed the example of their counterparts in cinema studies' to analyse television personalities in terms of their own industrial or cultural import (Murray, 2005: xvi). I hope that the previous chapters have gone some way in addressing these concerns. In the final chapters I turn to an analysis of the television personality system 'after film theory', exploring the ideological work they perform in different contexts. In these chapters I therefore move more explicitly away from drawing on both film theory, and the way in which televisual fame has been structured by its relationship to film stardom. By turns I work to address televisual fame on its 'own terms', as directed by the opening quote in the Introduction to this book, but also as part of the wider spread of celebrity culture. But in so doing, I suggest that as we focus our attention on the contemporary televisual landscape our subject of study is already shifting. The growth of celebrity culture has seen fame itself become an increasingly ordinary commodity, with figures such as Jade Goody epitomising a significant widening of fame to 'ordinary people'. In this context, it is necessary to consider how the discourses of ordinariness, authenticity, intimacy and skill that I have suggested structure much of televisual fame function in relation to not only the specificities of the television personality system, but also converge and intersect with the ordinari-isation of celebrity. The chapters in this section therefore converge particularly around this theme of ordinariness and its interrelationship with the discourses of authenticity and skill I have suggested are the hallmarks of televisual fame.

They do so by taking different television personalities' intertextual and multiplatform personas as a site of sustained study in different contexts to suggest how ordinariness is vital to the development of what many recent scholars have argued is television's role in modernity's project of the 'self' discussed in Chapter 1. In Chapter 6 I examine lifestyle programming to set out how the television personality's ordinariness is pivotal to the way expertise – as a form of vocational knowledge or skill – is administered as part of these lifestyle projects of the self. In Chapter 7 I suggest how contemporary notions of DIY celebrity draw on television fame's forms of ordinariness which, in turn, extend this project of self-formation to the achievement of celebrity itself. Drawing predominantly on Laurie Ouellette and James Hay's work, across both chapters I argue that televisual fame is central to the way contemporary forms of television promote a 'neoliberal logic of self-entrepreneurialism and commerce' (Ouellette and Hay, 2008). Thus, building on work on reality TV, I demonstrate how the role of the television personality in both lifestyle television and the formation of DIY celebrity draws on these televisual discourses to promote 'self-management techniques in individuals' congruent with conservative ideologies (ibid.: 64–65).

Lifestyle television, and particularly the forms of makeover programming that predominate the genre, has been one of the few sites to take the television personality as a site worthy of study, although this is often implicit in such work. As I suggested in Chapter 5, the focus here tends to be on lessons offered in taste, class, gender, sexuality, national identity and race by such programming. It therefore offers an ideal location for an extended analysis of the way in which the television personality's intertextual persona can be read in terms of its ideological resonances. As Tania Lewis has argued, 'the lifestyle expert can be seen to be inextricably linked to this reflexive, do it yourself (DIY) understanding of contemporary identity' (Lewis, 2007: 287). Drawing on Gareth Palmer, she suggests how such vocationally skilled personalities 'are now playing a central role in performing and legitimating certain norms of ordinariness – norms which tend to be closely tied to middle class forms of style and taste' (ibid.: 303). As I suggested in Chapter 5, drawing on Skeggs and Wood's analysis of audiences and reality TV, lifestyle programming tends to (re)present middle-class practices as the norm (Skeggs and Wood, 2008).

However, more than a paternalist culture of 'styling tips for the aspiring petit-bourgeoisie' (Palmer, 2004: 189), Chapter 6 suggests how personalities such as Alan Titchmarsh enact particular conservative ideological manifestations of national identity. Briefly drawing on the example of Steve Irwin, I go on to utilise Melissa Gregg's work on the 'importance of being ordinary' to suggest how Titchmarsh's ordinariness sets up barriers between who is included and excluded from the national. Moreover, by concentrating on Titchmarsh's intertextual construction of ordinariness across media and the various points in the schedule his programming has appeared in, I suggest how such definitions are reinforced across the institutions of television. Paying close attention to the intertextual construction of the television personality's ordinariness, rather than merely dismissing it as a continuation of their on-screen self, is therefore essential to understanding the role of television itself in everyday social life.

If the role of the ordinary discussed in Chapter 6 suggests how viewers are encouraged to identify with a particular construction of ordinariness as part of a lifestyle project in which autonomy and freedom are ceded to the claimed expertise of the vocationally skilled television personality, in contrast Chapter 7 demonstrates how the ordinari-isation of celebrity promises fame as a reward for self-enterprise. Moreover, calling on Jean Burgess's work (Burgess, 2006b, 2011) it suggests how celebrity is represented as achievable by anyone through forms of vernacular skill, such as multiplatform self-promotion, which are increasingly 'ordinary'. As P. David Marshall has argued, 'something has shifted and is continuing to shift' in the way digital media has affected the relationship between audience and celebrity. This has had profound implications on traditional models of celebrity and stardom whereby, as Marshall has recognised, 'there is a correlated downgrade in the significance in the film celebrities produced' (Marshall, 2006: 643). Any analysis of contemporary fame must therefore do so within a context in which celebrity can be understood as radically decontextualised, operating within a wider celebrity culture in which film stars intermingle with reality TV contestants and television personalities mix with video game characters or web celebrities. This is not to suggest that we can no longer pay attention to the way particular media forms inflect celebrity. Indeed, starting with television as a multiplatform medium, I suggest that we can learn much about the way celebrity functions in a mediascape of convergence by approaching digital and celebrity culture attuned to the way media histories structure this environment. Chapter 7 undertakes such an analysis by suggesting how the projects of selfhood promoted in the lifestyle programming discussed in Chapter 6 extend to a wider emphasis on the presentation of the self. Such shifts place a renewed emphasis on the entrepreneurial self, and a culture which demands strategic self-fashioning and remaking – a subject who can adapt and respond to change at will – while at the same time requiring the maintenance of an 'inner' core that can be understood as 'ordinary'. Drawing on an established media persona – that of British multiplatform television personality Stephen Fry – and one constructed via DIY media – digg.com's Kevin Rose's multiplatform, web2.0 celebrity – Chapter 7 explores what the implications of these modifications are for the forms and functions that celebrities take on in such a shared milieu.

This is not to suggest that the attainment of celebrity through self-promotion is new or novel. Joshua Gamson's study of celebrity suggests that '[h]ype, purchase, manipulation, self-promotion, association have become central elements in celebrity discourse' (Gamson, 1994: 40). However, Gamson's study then goes on to examine the role of the cultural intermediaries that perform these functions. In contrast, I suggest that what this decontextualisation of fame is more likely to produce is forms of celebrity that are achieved solely by individual self-promotion. Moreover, whilst ordinary users might attain celebrity via displaying a traditionally recognised and valued talent – such as music, like Katy Perry or Sandy Thom – fame might simply be attained via the entrepreneurial promotion of the self. Like Marshall, I suggest that the question of 'user-subjectivity' is central to this shift, which 'now informs the production of the self that doesn't necessarily replace the way that celebrities operate ... but has begun to modify the sources of our celebrity' (Marshall, 2006: 644). Graeme Turner has suggested that this shift is best understood in terms of a culture of 'DIY celebrity', in which audiences perceive their own role in celebrity culture as no longer 'merely the end-user of celebrity [sic], they can produce it themselves' (Turner, 2004: 53).

Both Turner's and Couldry's studies of DIY celebrity in relation to 'cam-girls', who use webcams to build their own celebrity profile, suggest that one of the most important purposes to which users put their new-found, user-generated, power is the production of fame from one's own bedroom. Turner's and Couldry's assessments of this phenomenon, however, turn on the question of how this celebrity shapes users' relationship with existing media players. Thus, rather than representing a democratising trend in either fame or cultural citizenship, the interests of these girls and, in turn, the meaning of their celebrity is ultimately compromised. This is because, as Couldry argues, 'webcam producers like these have to accept that they "have only limited control over the interpretive context in which people will encounter their site"' (quoted in Turner, 2004: 68). In contrast, Chapter 7 focuses on how contemporary forms of celebrity can emerge away from the 'media centre' – or at least from the ownership structures of the television and entertainment industries. Thus in Chapter 7, I examine the persona of DIY, Internet-entrepreneur celebrity Kevin Rose to demonstrate how, in contrast to the cam-girls and reality TV contestants on which much scholarship on the ordinari-isation of celebrity has focused, it is possible for the DIY celebrity to have almost unlimited control over their image. This, however, does not result in a radical, democratised formation of either celebrity or online participatory cultures.

My concern here is therefore to connect the discourses of celebrity culture with that of digital media, in particular understandings of the latter as fostering forms of 'participatory culture'. I argue that two distinct debates about celebrity and participatory culture are not only convergent, but both miss vital aspects of each phenomenon because of this. As I have traced across the book, one of the key arguments in the study of celebrity (especially television's circulation of fame) has been whether the 'ordinari-isation' of celebrity – via its extension to an increasingly diverse array of people, or 'DIY celebrities' – is good/bad for democracy. Across the book I have been concerned to move beyond this binary; in doing so here I connect this discourse with a second debate around digital media in which theorists have questioned to what extent the participatory media forms of social media are similarly good/bad for democratic exchange, extending the parameters of political and/or rational debate to increasingly diverse and ordinary people or users. Debates about the democratic potential of participatory media forms have tended to polarise around what Mark Andrejevic describes as their potential to foster either 'the revitalization of democracy', or amount to a 'passive evisceration of publicity as spectacle', whereby an 'emerging paradigm of mass customization' exists only insofar as it is able to commodify that individuation (Andrejevic, 2002: 251). That is, interacting is only on offer insofar as it allows media conglomerates to turn that 'participation' into a commodity, via counting the audience, surveilling user-preferences and customising product offerings based on user-profiles. Drawing on scholarship from television, new media and celebrity studies, I suggest that both paradigms fail to adequately account for the achievement of fame by ordinary people in a web2.0, participatory culture as a form of 'self-empowerment' that goes towards other ends than mere corporate colonisation of 'the real' (Hearn, 2006: 631). As my discussion of Kevin Rose in Chapter 7 suggests, the formation of a celebrity persona that brings together the discourses of televisual fame and reality TV's entrepreneurial self, evidences just how troubling the implications of such DIY fame might be for arguments about the democratic potential of both ordinary celebrity and participatory culture. Building on the discussion of the projects of the self discussed in relation to lifestyle programming and television personalities in Chapter 6, I suggest how Rose's DIY fame indicates how personal freedom *and* celebrity are achieved as a form of 'governmental rationality that values self-enterprise, self-reliance and lessons to be learned in privatized experiments and games of self-constitutions and group government' (Ouellette and Hay, 2008: 224). Across both chapters, therefore, television fame's construction of the ordinary emerges as a key site of ideological struggle.

Chapter 6

Just 'an ordinary bloke'
National identity and ideology

> Steve was an ordinary bloke – he doesn't need a state funeral.
>
> (Bob Irwin, September 6, 2006)[1]

The death of television natural history adventurer Steve Irwin, and the staged public funeral, in 2006 occasioned a moment of national mourning in Australia which, like that of Jade Goody's that I opened the book with, was immediately compared with that accompanying Princess Diana's death (an estimated 300 million people tuned in to the live coverage of the event).[2] Irwin's persona was immediately worked over in the media in relation to its representation of Australian-ness. On the one hand, Irwin was celebrated as an 'ordinary Australian', whom the then Prime Minister John Howard eulogised as 'a remarkable Australian' for 'being genuine, being authentic'.[3] On the other, as celebrity academic Germaine Greer pronounced, there were those who felt that not only had nature 'had its revenge', but also that Irwin's behaviour was that of a 'real Aussie larrikin' – suggesting it was both rather stupid and rather shameful in terms of what it means to be Australian.[4] Of particular interest here is the way in which the debate about Irwin's claims to represent Australian-ness was structured in terms of ordinariness and authenticity. Jonathan Rayner's examination of Irwin's persona suggests how it stressed the ordinary in a variety of ways, so as to 'personify a recognizable national type … the larrikin, [derived] from "bushman" stereotypes' which, although pre-dating the revival period of 1970s Australian filmmaking, were largely circulated by the films of that period and popularised in the image of Crocodile Dundee during the 1980s (Rayner, 2007: 109–110). As Rayner suggests, however, this image was nevertheless authentic – Irwin was 'the Australian as archetype' (ibid.: 108).

As Melissa Gregg's work on the way Howard's conservatism claimed the meaning of 'ordinary' in Australia during the late 1990s and early 2000s suggests, his cultivation of 'an image of being an "ordinary Australian" who is therefore able to speak with authority on behalf of other "ordinary Australians"', also meant that he did so 'at the expense of large sections of the population'. In this case, Irwin's position as both 'larrikin' and 'ordinary

Australian' was posited in opposition to the 'cultural cringe' of Greer's reaction above. As Gregg suggests:

> the clearest instance of this [Howard's use of the ordinary to create oppositions between who is inside/outside 'ordinary Australia'] ... is the consistency with which the opinions of ordinary Australians are used as a corrective to the so-called intellectual 'elite' (with its attendant signified including Left-wing, intellectual, educated, media literate, member of the 'chattering classes').
>
> (Gregg, 2007: 100–101)

As Rayner's detailed analysis of Steve Irwin goes on to argue, Irwin's 'textual assurance of his authenticity and accessibility, and the confirmation that he is never performing anything other than his real self, incarnates an obvious, inevitable, consensual Australian-ness' that perpetuates an image based on 'brashness, iconoclasm, egalitarianism, outspokenness and machismo' (Rayner, 2007: 115). Beyond placing the intellectual elite, such as Greer, outside the definition of the ordinary, Howard's notion of Australian-ness is therefore linked to a regressive representation of national identity that places the mythology of white-male mateship at the heart of Australian identity and, in turn, alienates and 'others' non-white, non-male identities (Bennett, 2007; Nourry, 2005).

The claims to ordinariness of both Howard and Irwin clearly signal the importance of this category as an ideological construct. Yet the way in which Irwin is posited by Rayner as 'ordinary' is complex, positioning him as a film star via reference to his appearance in *Crocodile Hunter: Collision Course* (2002). Although Irwin predominantly worked in television, Rayner is only able to make sense of the ideological function of his persona as 'ordinary' via reference to discourses on film stardom, whereby 'national cinema stars are seen to embody a representative ordinariness' (Rayner, 2007: 109). Whilst a useful analysis of Irwin's role in perpetuating an image of Australian-ness in the terms discussed above, it is intriguing that this only seems possible through an analysis of Irwin as 'film star', a derivation Rayner himself admits is hard to sustain. Following Dyer, it has long been the domain of film studies to examine stars for the way in which they 'articulate what it is to be human in society: that is, they express the particular notion that we hold of the "individual"' (Dyer, 1986: 8). However, such a discourse has been largely absent in the analysis of television personalities. And yet, as the example of Irwin suggests, the meaning of one of the central markers of televisual fame, ordinariness, is clearly a contested ideological category.

Whilst there has been substantial work on television and the ordinary (see Bonner, 2003), the notion of treating the intertextual image of television personalities as an articulation of what that ordinariness means has largely not been taken up. In this chapter, I want to focus on that intertextual image of television personalities, to demonstrate how they function in relation to ideological categories. In particular, I am concerned to demonstrate that the role of television personalities' ordinariness across both light entertainment and lifestyle television is contested and complex, integral to the way television itself functions in relationship to the everyday. Moreover, I suggest how moving beyond present understandings of television personalities' ordinariness as merely evidence of their contrast to film stardom's regime of the extraordinary/ordinary paradox allows us to unmask the ideological work at stake. Far from 'agreeable voids', the stress on television personalities' ordinariness through references to humble beginnings, common sense, working-class roots, down-to-earth personas and other such markers reveals how television personalities are capable of representing, or reconciling value- or ideological-conflicts.

The chapter first examines the way in which authenticity, discussed as a performance in Chapter 5, is connected to the intertextual circulation of a personality's image as 'ordinary'. Briefly drawing on the example of Cilla Black, I set out how ordinariness can be understood as a contested category, whereby the intertextual televisual image of a persona can be the subject of a struggle over its ideological and political meaning. I then turn my attention to the role of vocationally skilled 'experts' in lifestyle programming. Building on a range of scholarship on the ideological and cultural work performed by lifestyle programming, I suggest how the television personality can be understood as central to the role that such programming performs in modernity's project of selfhood: both of the 'ordinary' viewer and television personality. This is followed by a detailed excavation of the way ordinariness is constructed in the intertextual persona of Alan Titchmarsh, which returns the discussion to the question of national identity with which I opened the chapter.

'Fuck Cilla Black': The importance of the ordinary in television's personality system

In early 2003, *The Guardian* readers were greeted with the above headline on the newspaper's *G2* supplement at their morning breakfast tables. Produced by Turner-prize winning artist Gillian Wearing, the front cover was, as the apology by the newspaper's feature editor Ian Katz the next day attempted to persuade readers, designed as a comment on the fact that 'nastiness was the new fashion on British TV and Cilla simply wasn't nasty enough to cut it on the new Mean TV'.[5] Black had announced her retirement from *Blind Date* 'live' on-air over the weekend and, in the face of a large reader backlash (*The Independent* reported that the Press Complaints Commission had received 200 complaints by the following morning),[6] *The Guardian* protested that the image was meant to show how Black's televisual image no longer attracted large audiences in a landscape where female television personalities' performances in particular, such as Anne Robinson on *The Weakest Link* or Trinny and

Figure 6.1 The attack on Black, together with long-running defences and appropria-
tions of her image by opposing political factions, suggests that far from
merely functioning as 'friendly' faces, television personalities perform important political and ideological functions that are best understood by paying
close attention to their intertextual televisual image (Wearing, G. [2003]
'Fuck Cilla Black', *The Guardian*, January 7).

Susannah on *What Not to Wear*, were increasingly marked by insulting or
chastising the audience. (Of course, as Medhurst's work on Gilbert Harding
suggests, such nastiness is not a new mode of performance.) Yet, as Wearing's
apology to Black suggested and Katz's apology itself went on to detail, the
large number of outraged responses to Wearing's use of the word 'fuck',
compared to the paper's publication of other recent stories 'in which fuck was
one of the milder expletives deployed', was suggestive of the fact that what lay
at the heart of the reaction was the disjuncture between this offensive word
and the inoffensive, ordinary personality of Black herself.

   As I suggested in Chapter 4, drawing on P. David Marshall's work
(Marshall, 1997), the ordinariness of television personalities has generally

been understood in relationship to the way in which they can function 'inoffensively' to attract a large audience in order to sustain broadcast television's economy of advertiser-supported flow. However, such a conception fails to recognise the different ideological functions that television personalities' ordinariness can fulfil. As David Lusted has argued in his analysis of Tommy Cooper, Diana Dors and Eric Morecambe, 'each of these personalities connect a specific range of affirmations, recognitions and identifications to specific audience formations, whilst remaining broad and/or complex enough to aggregate majority audiences' (Lusted, 2000: 253). Lusted's excellent analysis of the way Tommy Cooper's 'obsessive failure at effecting magic tricks' affirms 'class resilience' by corresponding 'to the systematic lack of fit between investment in, and rewards of, labour' demonstrates the ideological meanings available in television personalities' ordinary personas (ibid.: 255). Such ideological work, I would suggest, is achieved by the relationship between the intertextual circulation of a television personality's persona as ordinary and its on-screen performance as authentic. Yet, because the televisual image of such personalities is perceived as continuous, less attention has been paid to their intertextual coverage because it is presumed to confirm their persona as simply 'ordinary'. Indeed, where there has been attention to the intertextual image of television performers, such as Deborah Jermyn's, it has focused precisely on the instances where there is a distinction between on-screen persona and off-screen self (Jermyn, 2006). However, using Ellis's basic definition of a star, as a 'performer in a particular medium whose figure enters into subsidiary forms of circulation and then feeds back into future performances' (Ellis, 1982: 1), we can understand how intertextual coverage of a personality's image serves to construct ordinariness as an important ideological category across their appearances.

Richard Dyer's study of the intertextual circulation of star images suggests how such coverage can be separated into forms of promotion and publicity that are differentiated by the amount of control exerted by the star/studio – or in the case of television, the personality/channel – over the material (Dyer, 2001: 60-61). As Tony Bennett and Janet Woollacott's study of the James Bond franchise suggests, the former type of intertextual material is aimed at helping to promote certain readings of the primary text, whilst the latter forms the basis for an ideological system of bids and counter-bids for the meanings of that primary text, which do not necessarily produce a stable and coherent meaning of their own accord (Bennett and Woollacott, 1987). Niki Strange usefully suggests how their understanding of this phenomenon's production of a range of 'textual meteorites', which orbit the primary text, might be applied in an analysis of cookery programmes and their personalities as 'sites for the extension, disruption or transformation of the discourses within the original text' (Strange, 1998: 311–312). Taking Cilla Black's intertextual image in these terms reveals how her 'ordinariness' has been the site of such bids and counter-bids for the political and ideological capital of her persona.

One of the key sites of struggle over Black's image has been its association with working-class notions of ordinariness. The association of northern accents on British television with working-class roots detailed in Chapter 5, particularly when combined with widely circulated back-stories like Black's that emphasise hard work and the lucky break ('discovered' in Liverpool's cavern club where she checked coats), is exemplified by the public argument between Black and Ricky Tomlinson concerning how 'Scouse' (working-class Liverpudlian) each was. Tomlinson's own televisual image – based on his long-running appearance in Liverpool-based soap opera *Brookside* (Mersey Television/C4, 1982–2003) and northern working-class comedy *The Royle Family* (Granada/BBC, 1998–2001) – has dealt in the continuousness of his persona and elision of on-/off-screen self as a working-class 'rough diamond', who was involved in trade union politics for much of his life before and after *Brookside*. Dubbed the 'Battle of the Scousers' by the *Liverpool Echo*, Tomlinson claimed that Black was 'part of the professional Scouser brigade', whose televisual image was in fact disingenuous because her accent was 'put on' in order to further her career;[7] that is, as distinct from other primetime personalities, but also valued by audiences for its working-class roots. As I suggested in Chapter 1, drawing on Raymond Williams's work, ordinariness has long had associations with positive depictions of the 'common people, working people, ordinary people' as a source of potential power (Williams, 1983: 194–195), and such meanings were clearly at stake in Tomlinson's accusation. Unlike Tomlinson, Black had moved away from the north of England and her televisual image is perhaps best understood in terms of the 'respectable glamour' that I discussed in relation to early female television personalities in Chapter 3: holding together sexuality and respectability by calling on middle-class taste codes. As a *Daily Mirror* article suggested, Black's persona calls up both glamour and ordinariness: 'Cilla's back in business, all dolled up in diamonds and sequins, hoovering the floor'.[8] Similarly, in an episode of *Blind Date* screened in February 2002, Black is not baited by a contestant's derogatory remarks regarding the low-taste working-class aesthetics of Liverpool, rather she retorts ' … but I'm rich! I am!'. As *The Guardian* described her in 1990, Black represented a 'very ordinary superstar'.[9]

Whilst the debate between Black and Tomlinson did little to undermine the Scouse credentials of either performer, it does demonstrate how the intertextual circulation of a television personality's image as ordinary does more than simply authenticate their on-screen persona: it also raises important questions about how notions of ordinariness might be mobilised and by whom. Over the course of her television career, Black's image was the subject of a series of bids and counter-bids that attempted to incorporate her image into particular ideologies. In particular, and in contrast to Tomlinson's Leftist claims to ordinariness, the safely flirtatious and genteel risqué-ness of *Blind Date* and homely image of Black has consistently been claimed by populist Conservative Party movements, most recently by party leader David Cameron who invited Black to the party's annual black and white ball in 2007. Similarly, during the

1980s and 1990s, articles such as 'Tories turn on to Cilla's dating game'[10] and 'Cilla blasts TV crowd for booing at Maggie!'[11] aligned Black with the Conservatives. As Gregg's work on John Howard's appropriation of the ordinary suggests, it is clearly a valuable political commodity to conservative ideologies when it is aligned with mass popularity but – positioned as the safe 'norm' of society – deprived of the radical power that Raymond Williams apportions to the 'masses' (see Chapter 1).

To return to the 'Fuck Cilla Black' *G2* cover that I discussed at the start of this section, this textual meteorite – appearing in a left-wing paper – can be understood partly as an (unsuccessful) attack on a kind of small 'c' conservatism of middle-England represented by Black: the connotations of safety, ordinariness, politeness and respectability that are central to the appeal and success of Black's televisual image. Far from merely functioning as 'safe' or 'friendly' faces that are capable of aggregating mass audiences in order to support broadcasting's economies of advertiser-supported flow, television personalities perform important political and ideological functions that are best understood by paying close attention to their intertextual televisual image. This is the task I undertake in the remainder of this chapter's focus on the relationship between lifestyle programming, the vocational skill of the televisual expert and national identity.

'Just basic, honest, ordinary working-class values': Lifestyle television and expertise

As a genre, lifestyle programming – as part of a wider turn to 'reality TV' – has been a key site of study, and battle, over the ideological work performed by television as a whole. With the boom in lifestyle television in the late 1990s, and its movement from the afternoon schedule to primetime, such programming was depicted as both dumbing down and feminising television. Whilst alert to the feminisation of primetime television that the rise in lifestyle programming suggests, the Midlands Television Research Group's '8–9 project' more helpfully suggests how this shift represented a 'daytime-ization' of the schedule that offered different lessons in cultural citizenship (Brunsdon *et al.*, 2001). As Rachel Moseley argued, perceptions of a shift from 'hard to soft, from public to private and from quality to "dumbed-down", from citizen to consumer, make use of falsely polarized classifications' (Moseley, 2001: 33). Rather, it may be argued that the educational address of such programming can be found in the way they promote and negotiate gendered, sexual, racial or national identities. Thus, programmes such as docusoaps, makeover and cookery shows display what Moseley terms, an 'everyday aesthetic', presenting valuable information to the viewer, based on a relation to their everyday, and especially domestic, lives (Moseley, 2000).

Scholars such as John Hartley have contributed to enhancing our understanding of the way in which such programming offers lessons in cultural identity (Hartley, 1999). More recently, a range of scholars have considered the role of such programming in 'lifestyle projects' of self-improvement. Drawing on the work of Giddens and others, such as that of Nikolas Rose (1996), regarding notions of the self and postmodernism discussed in Chapter 1, such scholarship has suggested the way in which lifestyle programming helps in the formation of the 'reflexive project of the self'(Giddens, 1991: 81). Less optimistic than Moseley's or Hartley's work about the lessons in cultural identity offered by such programming, this work has demonstrated the way in which lifestyle projects function as a Foucaldian form of disciplining the self in line with neo-liberal ideologies of '"empower[ing]" ourselves as enterprising citizens'. Lifestyle programming can therefore be understood to circulate 'informal "guidelines for living"' (Ouellette and Hay, 2008: 2).

Central to this function is the figure of the expert, whom we can generally understand as 'vocationally skilled' television personalities. As Tania Lewis suggests, the figure of the lifestyle expert is neither specific to television nor directly attributable to the rise in such programming during the 1990s, with:

> precursors of the lifestyle specialist [to] be found in daytime television on talk shows and magazine-style advice programs and in the 'Agony Aunt' advice columns of women's magazines. While in the past some of these experts have attained a degree of celebrity status within women's culture, their mundane knowledge tended to be marginalized (and often denigrated) within broader mainstream culture. What is new about today's lifestyle specialist or style guru, however, is that, like the makeover culture of which they are an integral component, they have shifted from the relative margins of mainstream popular culture to center stage.
>
> (Lewis, 2007: 290)

Lewis goes on to demonstrate how television has played a central role in this movement of lifestyle experts from the margin to the centre as part of this 'daytime-ization' of primetime television (Brunsdon, *et al.*, 2001). As I have suggested, such a shift has also brought about an increased emphasis on the televisual skill of vocationally skilled experts, so that they are capable of managing an engaging and professional performance: as evidenced by the movement of Alan Titchmarsh from staple of the afternoon schedule through to primetime personality discussed below. In turn, as Lewis notes, the lifestyle projects of self-enterprise are 'increasingly reliant on the figure of the lifestyle expert and associated forms of "everyday" expertise' (Lewis, 2007: 287).

The relationship between the vocationally skilled performer, as 'expert' in their chosen field, and ordinariness is, however, never straightforward (discussed further in Chapter 7). As Bonner's study of ordinary television argues, whilst experts are used across a range of programming there 'are certain programmes ... where experts are not so highly rated' (Bonner, 2003: 87). Going on to detail a study by Peter Lunt and Sonia Livingstone regarding the British talk show presenter Robert Kilroy-Silk, Bonner describes how their study found a tension between 'expertise and a laity validated in populist terms', so that Kilroy-Silk would often dismiss experts in preference to 'the opinions of "real people" who have experienced whatever it is that is under discussion' (Livingstone and Lunt, summarised in ibid.). It is important, therefore, for the vocationally skilled performer making the transition to popular television personality that they appear 'real' – as in authentic – but also ordinary – as in 'down-to-earth'. As Lisa Taylor describes, this involves the attempt to 'ordinari-ise' their knowledge (Taylor, 2002). As Ouellette and Hay's study of reality TV more generally suggests, experts are more apt to characterise themselves as '"self-made" authorities trading in applied forms of business, lifestyle, and therapeutic knowledge' (Ouellette and Hay, 2008: 3). For example, Jo Littler has demonstrated how *The Apprentice*'s Sir Alan Sugar's 'persona articulates the ... very contemporary neoliberal parable of entrepreneurial meritocracy', having enacted the 'working class made good' parable in his business successes and the promotion of *The Apprentice* as 'giving something back' (Littler, 2007: 232). As I discuss in relation to Alan Titchmarsh below, vocational skill is therefore often presented as 'ordinary' or 'common knowledge' so to reduce the distance between expert and viewer.

As Ouellette and Hay go on to argue, such programming relies on a paradox, 'in that they often resort to authoritarian governing techniques, such as "home visits" ... surveillance, pedantic lecturing ... in an effort to produce self-sufficient citizens who are "free" because they do not rely on the State or any other institution for discipline, care or sustenance' (Ouellette and Hay, 2008: 65). Similarly, McRobbie speaks of a 'double entanglement' that is evoked by the project of the entrepreneurial self, whereby 'processes of liberalisation in regard to choice and diversity in domestic, sexual and kinship relations' are directed at achieving neo-liberal values of self-enterprise as well as conservative ideologies of 'gender, sexuality and family life' (quoted in ibid.). These aims, I would argue, are largely achieved by the presence of the charismatic television personality who represents, or reconciles value- or ideological-conflicts. Most importantly it is the role of ordinariness that facilitates both the lifestyle projects of selfhood promoted in these programmes as well as these wider ideological meanings. In this section I concentrate on the relationship between Titchmarsh's ordinariness and his gardening programming before going on to suggest how this intertextual image functions in the promotion of a particular version of British national identity in the following section.

As discussed in Chapter 5, the construction and function of authenticity and ordinariness of the television personality's image differ according to whether we understand them as a televisually or vocationally skilled performer. With the latter, authenticity is complemented and reinforced by the concept of credibility. Credibility functions in relation to the vocational skill(s) of the performer, reassuring the viewer that the skills being presented are authentic and worthwhile investing in (in the form of copying or learning).

Because vocationally skilled performers generally appear in factual or lifestyle genres, it is important that their skills appear to be not only real, but also that the performer is actually 'good' at their vocational skill, rather than simply a friendly face on the television. How their expertise in this skill is negotiated is crucial to their position as a television personality.

Like Cilla Black, Alan Titchmarsh has a long and successful history on British television. Having first appeared as horticultural expert on *Nationwide* during the early 1980s, he has since become a central fixture of the television schedules, having successfully fronted the re-launch of the popular gardening programme *Pebble Mill at One* in 1991 (BBC, 1973–1986; 1991–1996 as *Pebble Mill*). Titchmarsh has become, not simply as Lisa Taylor has noted, the 'most prominent British media garden expert' on UK television, but also a fully fledged television personality (Taylor, 2002: 493). The story of *Ground Force*, a gardening makeover programme that was commissioned following the success of *Pebble Mill*, is worth briefly recounting in this context. According to the series' producer, John Thornicroft, *Ground Force* was com- missioned when 'the BBC said they wanted a programme that was a bit like *Changing Rooms*, but it had to be in the garden, [pause] with Alan Titchmarsh'. Thornicroft, on the best of *Ground Force* DVD (of which inter- estingly there are two – one a simple compilation, the other a celebration of 'The Titchmarsh years', released to coincide with his departure), goes on to explain that having two families labouring on completing a garden in a day proved too difficult. Thornicroft suggests that the programme 'only really came alive when Alan got down off that umpire's chair and started rushing around madly helping everyone. Then we felt like we were on to something'. Thornicroft's comments suggest that *Ground Force* was commissioned not only as a vehicle for Titchmarsh, but also that it was his televisual skill as much as his vocational skill that was pivotal to the success of the programme.

Titchmarsh has since left team-based programmes, such as *Ground Force*, to front increasingly individual projects, such as *How to Be a Gardener*, which ran for two series and spawned the fastest selling gardening book of all time in the United Kingdom. More importantly, his departure from these pro- grammes was to facilitate his appearance in a series of programmes away from gardening that suggest both his increased popularity, beyond simply a garden- ing expert to a television personality, and the development of his televisual presentational skills, to the extent that programmes are no longer hung on his vocational skill, but on his televisual image alone. As Jane Root, then Controller of BBC2, said in 2002: 'Alan has played a central role in *Gardeners' World*'s enduring popularity, but he is terrifically versatile and we are keen to work on more projects with him'.[12] Thus, in 2004 Titchmarsh became the lead presenter of the BBC's annual coverage of the Proms (2004–2005) and took up a contract worth a reported £1.5 million over three years to front programmes such as *British Isles: A Natural History* (BBC, 2005), a pro- gramme to which he adds his name as a by-line and is produced with the

Figures 6.2, 6.3 and 6.4 The title sequence of *How to Be a Gardener* suggest that gardening is Titchmarsh's life, investing his televisual image with credibility but constructing that knowledge as 'ordinary', 'self-made' and his persona as 'down-to-earth' (screen captures from *How to Be a Gardener* [BBC, 2002–2003]).

BBC's renowned natural history unit, pulling in over five million viewers per episode (over 20 per cent of the available audience). Indeed, despite leaving the BBC's television roster in 2007 to host an afternoon chat show on ITV (*The Alan Titchmarsh Show*) Titchmarsh was still named as amongst the 'highly valued' tier of talent by the BBC in a 2009 leaked memo that purported to detail a hierarchical ranking of television personalities at the Corporation.[13] In 2010, Titchmarsh began presenting a Friday night reality TV competition, *Popstar to Operastar* (Globe Productions for ITV, 2010), which regularly attracts over four million viewers, confirming his status as a bankable television personality.

However, before going on to look at these non-gardening programmes, it is first important to examine how Titchmarsh's televisual image is authenticated in a manner which stresses both his ordinariness and his skills as credible. *How to Be a Gardener*'s title sequence is exemplary here as it constructs Titchmarsh as someone who the audience can believe, trust and rely on for credible, expert gardening advice. The title sequence presents a mini-narrative of Titchmarsh's life that authenticates his gardening knowledge. A series of stylised images, calling up a home-cinema aesthetic, depict a young Alan not simply playing in the reconstructed garden of his youth, but rather taking pleasure in investigating it, nurturing it and developing his gardening skills as he transforms into the personality we know and trust (Figures 6.2, 6.3 and 6.4). It endows Titchmarsh with expert gardening skills – suggesting that gardening is, in fact, his life – but it also helps to anchor and remind viewers that his presentation style is one that is often described as full of 'boyish enthusiasm'.

In turn, such sequences go towards creating his image as an ordinary gardener, someone who simply enjoys 'mucking in', and about, in the garden. This image of Titchmarsh owes much to the continuity of his performance style and intertextual televisual image, particularly through *Ground Force*. The development of this programme's format, having 'stumbled' upon Titchmarsh's televisual skill, involved the addition of a supporting cast of gardeners and builders. The casting of Tommy Walsh and Charlie Dimmock as helpers in the gardening makeovers created a sense of camaraderie, whereby all performers pitched in, particularly against the British weather, to get the task done. The presence of Walsh and Dimmock allowed the programme to recreate the image of a stereotypical building site as friendly and fun (although still extremely sexist as Walsh, Titchmarsh and the programme-makers endlessly concentrated on Dimmock's breasts and her failure to wear a bra): ordinary mates having a laugh and goofing around, exemplified by the inclusion of mistakes in the programme and an extensive bloopers reel on the *Best of Ground Force* DVD. In turn, the format not only authenticated Titchmarsh's skills as credible, able to muck in with the lads and lasses, but also helped to emphasise his televisual image as a down-to-earth, ordinary, working-class bloke. As he suggested in an interview with *The Telegraph* in 2001, he was raised with 'just basic, honest, ordinary working-class values'.[14]

Frances Bonner discusses Australian gardening television personality Don Burke in similar terms, suggesting he is the archetypal 'ordinary bloke, a little on the short side ... able to turn his hand to most things and at ease with all types of people' (Bonner, 2003: 206). Yet as Bonner notes, such ordinariness also evidences the fact that 'Burke is one of the most skilled exponents of televisual sincerity that Australia has produced': 'His ability to convey both sincerity and trustworthiness is key to his place as the person who has been the longest-lasting of those persuading viewers about the desirability of this week's lifestyle suggestions' (ibid.: 207).

As Bonner's analysis goes on to suggest, the way in which this televisual skill functions is to confirm Burke's image, and the programme, as 'ordinary'. In turn, such an image helps to promote the lifestyle offered by Burke as one of collective Australian-ness that has strong connotations of the 'bush mythology' discussed at the outset of this chapter. Here, 'Australian self image is a romantic one of rural roots and outdoor competence' that has strong links to an ethos of egalitarianism. As Bonner suggests, this has been mobilised to serve a range of ideological functions: from the notion of 'democratized home ownership' through to the granting of Aboriginal land rights (ibid.: 201–202).

Similarly, Titchmarsh's performance of authenticity and ordinariness speak to a collective identity. Most importantly, this involves cultivating an investment in the lifestyle project of gardening as a form of self- and collective-improvement. Thus his performance across programmes like *How to Be a Gardener* addresses the viewer as 'we' to make gardening a collective project, whilst his performance is filled with anecdotes, jokes and observations on life and gardening's pleasures all delivered in the soft Northern accent of his Yorkshire lilt, which is often described as 'safe' and 'cosy'.[15] Such a mode of performance works towards diminishing any 'expert' status (that is, an intelligence or insight that would distinguish him as extraordinary from his audience in any way), within his televisual image. This is balanced, in his lifestyle programming, by the confluence of performance technique and technology, which work towards making his skills seem credible, ordinary, fun, do-able and worth doing in what Lisa Taylor has described as the ordinari-isation of lifestyle aesthetics and knowledges (Taylor, 2002). Titchmarsh's performance, like those of other lifestyle experts, attempts to instil a DIY ethos in the citizen-consumer that suggests these skills are readily picked up and able to be applied by the viewer in their own lifestyle projects of self-transformation. One of the most obvious techniques used in such programming to emphasis both the credibility of the vocational skill of the presenter as well as potential ease and pleasure of the viewer's investment in these skills, is the intercutting of realist aesthetic strategies and performance styles with montages of the beautiful transformations achieved to the accompaniment of a soft pop soundtrack.[16] The use of instructional post-production voice-overs is therefore kept to a minimum, replaced instead by a fun and relaxed soundtrack, whilst the didactic aims of the programme are communicated whilst he is actually 'doing' the work. Thus, the viewer will hear Alan puff and pant while digging a hole, walking up a hill, etc., rather than have a clean studio voice-over pasted on in post-production that would formalise the didactic elements of his address. As such the combination of Titchmarsh, the soundtrack and editing serve to create a relaxed aesthetic that seeks to promote the English country garden as an idealised lifestyle project; a project which, via the authenticity and credibility of Titchmarsh's persona, is delivered in a manner that seems easy and do-able for 'ordinary' viewers (i.e. non-experts). In particular, Titchmarsh's address to the ordinary is evident in the delivery of these lifestyle lessons in a matter-of-fact manner, imbued with a 'common sense' that attempts to close down challenges to his knowledge – not just of gardening but, as I now want to turn to, his other ideals of Britishness.

National identity and ideology: 'It's not jingoism, it's not xenophobia, it's just honest-to-goodness national pride and fun'

In understanding the ideological function that Titchmarsh's intertextual televisual image fulfils, it is helpful to follow the trajectory of that image from gardening personality to television personality; from daytime to primetime. I therefore want to commence by expanding on work on lifestyle programming and the role they play in the project of self-formation. Whilst Charlotte Brunsdon has provided an excellent analysis of the relationship between gardening programming and Britishness (Brunsdon, 2003), Lisa Taylor's work explicitly addresses the role that gardening programmes play in lifestyle projects of self-transformation (Taylor, 2002). Drawing on David Chaney's analysis of the way expert knowledge is ordinari-ised in modernity, Taylor suggests that gardening programming urges ordinary people to invest in gardening as a lifestyle project. On the one hand, Taylor's work argues that such ordinari-isation tends to prop up a consumer culture as well as largely reinforce dominant ideologies. On the other hand, like Moseley, she also suggests that the 'job of the personality-interpreter is to make elite artistic design knowledge readable for the ordinary would-be gardener' and, in so doing, the programmes 'might also offer people the opportunity, within the context of the commonplace routines of their everyday lives, to mould the strategies and sites of lifestyle in ways which help them to navigate their own relationship to social change' (ibid.: 488–491). This 'DIY ethos', therefore, plays an important role in the modern project of self- and identity-formation. As Chaney and Taylor suggest, changes in society have meant that lifestyles 'offer a set of expectations which act as a form of ordered control' in the face of uncertainties wrought by modernity (Chaney quoted in ibid.: 482). Titchmarsh's intertextual appearances beyond gardening programming arguably extend this project to his other performances and, in turn, these appearances complicate the meanings of his gardening programmes. By focusing on the television personality as a site of meaning, we can build on Taylor's work to think about how Titchmarsh's image and programming do not simply ordinari-ise elite knowledge or encourage investment in lifestyles, but can be read as actively promoting particular conservative ideologies and attitudes towards British national identity.

Titchmarsh's initial appearance in primetime programming took the form of *British Isles: A Natural History*. The programme opens with an aerial shot, climbing rapidly over the mountains of Scotland to the strains of a score that swells with emotional grandeur as the camera picks out the hiking figure of Titchmarsh, who introduces the viewer to a series that will celebrate Britain's natural beauty: 'just look at it' he implores, as we return to sweeping aerial shots of rising peaks and the renewed pronouncement of the score as the audience is then treated to a montage of stunning shots from across the British Isles. There is a feeling of pride established by the series' approach to Britain's natural history, which is largely framed by Titchmarsh's mode of presentation. In his opening monologue, Titchmarsh calls up his televisual image from gardening programmes, opining that:

> maybe it is a life spent working outside, tending the earth that makes me so passionate about the British Isles and proud to call this place home … on a fine day, even the most hardened cynic would have to admit that Britain is one of the most beautiful and diverse countries in the world.

This voice-over is accompanied by a series of dramatic shots of British wildlife, such as dolphins playing, a kingfisher catching its prey, and more sweeping aerial shots of stunning landscapes. Having reminded the viewer of the credibility (if not authority) and 'down-to-earth' ordinariness of his televisual image, Titchmarsh's monologue is able to assert the 'common sense' point that everyone should admit that Britain is one of the most beautiful and diverse countries in the world.

The series is full of these 'common sense' observations, which allow Titchmarsh to proclaim Britain has more bluebells than anybody else or more rocks than the Dutch. Helen Wheatley's work on natural history programming has suggested how visual pleasure in natural history programming can be read as promoting a particular middle-class taste aesthetic that is largely devoid of political meaning (Wheatley, 2004). However, in this context of bombastic nationalism and Titchmarsh's persona, visual splendour and natural history are here continually associated with a celebratory view of Britain's social history. Thus, it is not simply enough for Titchmarsh to proclaim that Britain has 'lots of coal' (hard statistics are difficult to reconcile with his common sense knowledge), which he describes as a 'super rock'. Rather he nostalgically reminisces, over shots of an old steam-engine traversing beautiful countryside that 'the empire we once had was built upon it'. Titchmarsh's description of this 'super rock' is structured so that its identity as coal is 'revealed' to the audience as the programme cuts to a wide-shot of Titchmarsh, dressed in fluorescent flak jacket and standing in front of heavy machinery, who with boyish glee throws his arms wide open and exclaims 'it's Coal!'. Glossing over the difficulties that this mineral has caused the country, particularly those inflicted on working-class communities through the destruction of the mining industry in the 1980s under the Thatcher government but also coal's status as an environmentally unsound fossil fuel, he goes on to assert that: 'It was because we had so much coal that we became a world leader, something we're still living off today'. This information is presented in the 'matter-of-fact' performance style of Titchmarsh's gardening programming. As such, it ordinari-ises a very particular view of British history; the 'down-to-earth' nature of his televisual image, combined with the cheeky 'knowingness' of his boyish enthusiasm, arguably closes down any challenges to the common-sense view presented (as fact).

This is achieved through inscribing the programme with a 'Boy's Own' aesthetic, arguably connected to ideals of the British Empire. By structuring the series as an exciting journey – zooming about in helicopters and fighter jets, blowing things up and an aesthetic of exploration and expedition – Titchmarsh's boyish enthusiasm, as enlisted by *British Isles: A Natural History*, recalls the adventures of *The Boy's Own Paper* which, formed by a religious and moral group at the end of the nineteenth century to promote a gentleman-explorer sensibility in young boys (away from the prurience of the 'penny-dreadfuls'), was heavily laden with morality, sense of empire and jingoism. Thus at the start of the series, Titchmarsh proclaims, 'I'm going on a journey … to find out what's shaped the country we know and love'. This is then immediately followed by a shot of Titchmarsh, dressed in a hard-hat and with an impish grin, detonating dynamite (Figure 6.5), the sound of the explosion launching the programme into a fast-paced montage of Titchmarsh 'travelling the length and breadth of the country by all manner of means'. Most notably, this includes him climbing aboard an RAF fighter jet which, over a shot of Titchmarsh in a locker room strapping up his military-issued boots, he declares is 'every schoolboy's dream'. Framed in close-up, Titchmarsh winks to the camera and the action cuts to a shot of him in the plane, the roar of its engines reverberating with that of the dynamite in the previous shots. The association of Titchmarsh with this 'Boy's Own' tradition, reinforces the sense that this programme is meant to be fun and educative, but also coheres with a view that celebrates a backward- and inward-looking nation.

Overall, the programme takes Titchmarsh's performance style and ordinari-ises a particular form of knowledge about Britain's social and natural past. The framing of the series as a journey is not simply one about the natural forces that shaped the land, but as Titchmarsh explicitly articulates, is an adventure in finding out what 'made Britain great'. This greatness is defined in terms such as empire, industrial revolution and a celebration of a relatively

Figure 6.5 British Isles: A Natural History presents an exciting journey, which, together with Titchmarsh's performance style and intertextual image, ordinari-ises a particular form of knowledge about Britain's social and natural past (screen capture from British Isles: A Natural History [BBC, 2005]).

backward-looking view of Britain's 'green and pleasant land'. By building on his televisual image from gardening programming as safe, cosy and a bit of fun, there is an attempt to subvert these meanings. Arguably in the face of the fast-paced changes Chaney and Taylor discuss, Titchmarsh's image works to reconcile such a middle-England viewpoint with the aims and purposes of the BBC at a period where it must be perceived to be both modern and forward-looking, 'building digital Britain', but also engaging all viewers. Most recently, in the renewal of the BBC's Charter licence in 2006, the Corporation's charge of universalism was articulated as: 'Making us aware of different cultures and alternative viewpoints through content that *reflects the lives of other people and other communities within the UK*' (Department for Culture, Media and Sport, 2006: 18, emphasis mine).

The language here is problematic, suggesting that there is a central, possibly homogenous, culture within the United Kingdom to which 'other people and other communities' might be appended. Programming such as Titchmarsh's helps to sustain this distinction between 'us' and 'them', between a unified cultural identity of Britain and its relationship to 'other communities' the United Kingdom might contain, i.e. those excluded from the national on grounds of race, faith, etc.

I want to conclude my discussion of Alan Titchmarsh by suggesting how this understanding of Britishness promoted by Titchmarsh's intertextual televisual image can then be read back into his gardening programmes, and in turn, his more recent primetime programming. In such a light, Titchmarsh's performances arguably promote gardening as a lifestyle project for middle-England and suburbia; they provide a means of dealing with the social change caused by the mass movements of globalisation – immigration, refugee and asylum seekers, more permeable borders – by retreating to suburbia, behind the walled, well-ordered gardens of Titchmarsh's design. There is plenty of evidence for such a reading from these programmes themselves, which often display xenophobia or jingoism by giving Titchmarsh space to ridicule co-star Charlie Dimmock's interest in Feng Shui or impose a British suburban garden on foreign climes, such as that for an Indian orphanage whose focal point is a water feature that is uninterested in the pressures on water supply in the subcontinent. In one notable episode, the *Ground Force* team visited the Falklands, where Titchmarsh ruminated: 'There's a new prosperity based on managing the island's fishing grounds and a lasting gratitude to all those who secured the future of these islands'. This voice-over was placed over pictures of Pioneer row, British-style bungalows and a lingering shot of Thatcher Avenue, clearly celebrating both Britain's empire and a conservative political stance. Read in this light, the lifestyle project of his gardening programme is as much about building a secure enclave – fences, paving, gates, the great British lawn, etc. – against the changes of the modern world, which threaten these values and ideals, as it is about horticultural techniques.

Whilst one could argue that it is the programme-makers, rather than Titchmarsh himself, who generate such associations, I would suggest that Titchmarsh's televisual-image is central in this reading. Such a view of Titchmarsh is reinforced by his 2004–2005 presentation of the BBC's coverage of *The Last Night of the Proms*. The choice of Titchmarsh by the BBC was part of a similar project to ordinari-ise elite artistic knowledge, as was perceived by *The Daily Telegraph*, who voiced fears that this might be 'taking cultural relativism a step too far'.[17] However, I would argue that his presence largely served to reinforce the middle-England jingoism of the event, his voice-over proclaiming that 'it's not jingoism, it's not xenophobia, it's just honest-to-goodness national pride and fun', over the top of a shot of a jubilant crowd waving Union Jacks and St George's crosses singing the traditional closing night rendition of Elgar's *Land of Hope and Glory*. This is not the only interpretation of the song or the Proms, but Titchmarsh's intertextual televisual image promotes this as the text's preferred meaning.

This suggests a problematic fit with the BBC's own role of defining an inclusive and forward-looking Britain and, whilst the use of Jeremy Clarkson to promote the BBC's new digital services suggests that the Corporation has not necessarily jettisoned such associations, Titchmarsh himself has been cast off from its television schedules, for the time being at least. Nevertheless this seems to be an image of Britain, and of Titchmarsh, that ITV *are* comfortable with – having signed Titchmarsh to a two-year deal in 2007 that was extended in 2009 as *The Alan Titchmarsh Show* was promoted to an early evening slot

Figure 6.6 Titchmarsh's connotations of Britishness permeate his televisual image across his programming appearances (screen capture from *The Alan Titchmarsh Show* [Spun Gold TV for ITV1, 2007–ongoing]).

on the schedule. Titchmarsh has described the show as 'the best conversation you could imagine having over a cup of tea'.[18] Titchmarsh's costume in Figure 6.6, which represents a regular format point of the show where Titchmarsh join a celebrity chef in the studio kitchen, suggests how the 'intertextual relay' (Neale, 1990) of Titchmarsh's connotations of Britishness permeate his tele visual image in the new programme. The Britain of this show is one in which 'hoodies' and hoodlums are to blame for tax increases on alcohol (which can be safely enjoyed by the taste palates of the middle-classes, represented here by the regular wine, spirit and beer tasting segments on the programme); a local council's investment in a modern art installation is deemed 'so stupid'; and old-fashioned decency wins out when faced with a sexist guest – such as when Titchmarsh, in arguably a stage-managed event, threw well-known misogynist John McCririck[19] off the '*AT Show*', as Titchmarsh now likes it to be known.

The appeal of Titchmarsh to a conservative, middle-England is further reinforced by the circulation of his image as an unlikely sex symbol. His ever-so-slightly racy romance novels, which are strongly coded with the sanctity of heterosexual love and agrarian back-to-the-land fantasies, combined with his association with the earth and gardening serve to construct him as a Lady Chatterley's lover, reincarnated as safe, cuddly and cosy for the flux of modernity. In a poll conducted by *Elle* magazine and widely reported by the conservative *Daily Telegraph*, Titchmarsh was voted the second sexiest man on television, beaten by George Clooney to top place, in 2000.[20] Whilst left-leaning media like *The Observer* and Channel 4, whose viewers rated Titchmarsh the sixty-second worst Briton of all time, have found this title hard to take seriously, his 'sex in a pullover [sweater]' televisual image have made him a favourite of more conservative press establishments.[21] This is best epitomised here by the interview conducted for Saga's in-house, customer magazine, *Saga Magazine* (a company whose insurance arm specialises in offering products only to customers over 50). The interviewer boasts over having made Titchmarsh blush, before gushing over the ageing sex symbol's good looks: 'It's not just that he has a thick thatch of hair, a fresh face and a flat stomach, there is something Peter Pannish about Titchmarsh's demeanour'.[22] The article goes on to recognise the love/hate divide in people's perceptions of Titchmarsh; tongue-in-cheek it cites the pro camp as containing 'the shameless women who made him "the most groped waxwork in Madame Tussauds"'. The article focuses on Titchmarsh's mild-mannered temperament, 'born of a humble working-class up-bringing', which stressed the importance of polite etiquette, before concluding that unlike other television personalities, Titchmarsh is 'old fashioned, a walking embodiment of the Fifties values with which he was brought up with …. What Titchmarsh has is deeply unfashionable but it has taken him to the top of his tree: straightforward decency.'[23]

Such an image is congruent not only with the needs of primetime television to aggregate a mass audience by creating an 'inoffensive' televisual image, but more importantly is one that works at the ideological level of naturalising what 'ordinary Britain' might mean.

Conclusion: 'Titchmarsh's Britain – where women bake fruitcakes and men grow giant vegetables'

The success of Titchmarsh's televisual image demonstrates that we can ill afford to dismiss television personalities' function in such simple terms as previous studies have understood them. Indeed, the description in *The Times* of his chat show as a celebration of 'the achievements of ordinary Britons',[24] suggests that who claims to speak for and how the ordinary is represented by television personalities is of profound importance to studies of television and celebrity. In particular, it is through a close reading of the intertextual personas of personalities that we can understand the relationships between ordinariness, national identity and the projects of the self, and self-enterprise of lifestyle programming that I have attempted to trace in this chapter.

These are tied together in Titchmarsh's image, which offers itself as 'safe' and 'cosy' in order to claim 'ordinary Britain' as a place of community, but at the same time champion the rights of the individual: in railing against the 'nanny state' in his afternoon programming or in encouraging a DIY ethos in lifestyle projects. The implications of this televisual image are perhaps most apparent in his recent incarnation as host of Friday night light entertainment programme *Popstar to Operastar*. Thus whilst a former 'gardening expert' might seem an incongruous choice for host of a reality TV 'talent search' format, Titchmarsh's televisual image is invoked precisely because it is able to reconcile such tensions between community and individualism, the 'establishment' or 'elitist' traditions of opera with pop music, and a format that promises celebrity as a reward for a process of self-enterprise that is simultaneously guided by 'experts'. Titchmarsh's 'ordinary Britain' is a deeply conservative (in both small and capital letters) ideological project which, returning to Gregg's work on the ordinary, enlists the ordinary as a binary marker to establish who lies inside or outside its 'cosy' confines. As *Guardian* television critic Sam Wollaston suggested in relation to another of Titchmarsh's programmes, Alan Titchmarsh's Britain is 'where women bake fruitcakes and men grow giant vegetables .... I imagine [Prince] Charles approves of Titchmarsh's Britain. The sun shines, the people laugh, Alan's co-host Angelica Bell stands out for not being white'.[25]

As television's personality system is increasingly suffused with the 'DIY' fame of 'ordinary people', closer attention to unpicking the varied meanings of ordinariness and authenticity, not simply as hallmarks of televisual fame but as ideological categories, is needed. This intersection of such 'ordinary' fame, ideology and self-enterprise is the subject of the book's final chapter.

Chapter 7

'Get Internet famous! (Even if you're nobody)'

Multiplatform fame and the television personality system in the digital era

Get Internet famous! (Even if you're nobody).

(*Wired* cover story, August, 2008)

Ok. This is now mad. I am stuck in a lift on the 26th floor of Centre Point. Hell's teeth. We could be here for hours. Arse, poo and widdle.

(Stephen Fry Tweet, 2:47 PM February 3, 2009).[1]

In February 2009 television personality and self-confessed digital geek Stephen Fry sent the above 'tweet' from his mobile phone to 113,068 followers.[2] However, due to blanket coverage of this 'media event' in the traditional press in the United Kingdom – leading newspapers from the *Daily Mail* to *The Guardian*, *The Sun* and *The Independent* all carried the story prominently – Fry's near escape with boredom and bodily fluids was heard by many millions more. Together with the media coverage of the use of Twitter by ordinary people, bloggers and tourists during the Mumbai terrorist attacks a few months earlier, the attention of news outlets to the platform suggested that, as one user of social news networking site digg.com argued, Fry's actions had 'FINALLY [brought] Twitter into [the] British mainstream'.[3] The place of social media in each event – the Mumbai terrorist attacks, the role of Twitter in mainstream media and its production of celebrity through coverage of the everyday – suggests that we are increasingly aware of the elision of the boundaries between the media world of professional journalists, media insiders and celebrities, and the ordinary world of users, bloggers, citizens and consumers.[4]

Indeed, selecting a posting to digg.com is not a wholly arbitrary marker of this shift in the role of DIY media. Described by *The New York Times* as the 'news site with the nerve to substitute the votes of the unwashed, unpaid masses for the refined talent of professional editors', digg exemplifies the audience's changing role in the economies of both news and celebrity. Started in founder Kevin Rose's bedroom with US$1000, digg.com had amassed US$40million of funding by late 2008 on the strength of its 30 million unique users visiting the site each month (despite remaining unprofitable).[5]

Figure 7.1 Social media forms promise the possibility of celebrity through self-promotion as well as an increased intimacy between celebrity and audience, facilitated by interactive communication with the celebrity's 'authentic' persona (image from Stephen Fry *Twitter* stream, February 3, 2009).

Digg allows users to determine the shape and priorities with which news is delivered: readers 'digg' a story read elsewhere on the web – from traditional news outlets to blogs, with major news outlets from the BBC to *The Wall Street Journal* now featuring 'digg' buttons – which provides other digg users with a link to that story. The community of digg users then decide on the story's worth, either by linking to it themselves, or rating the story from the digg site using the simple thumbs up or down motif familiar from TiVo. The front page of digg.com is therefore made up of the 'most dug' stories. Linked to the site is the hugely successful Internet television show, *DiggNation* (Revision3, 2005–ongoing), which reviews news stories submitted to digg. com and amasses over 300,000 downloads per episode and is hosted by digg. com founder Kevin Rose. The popularity of the show, in concert with Rose's association with digg.com and his exploitation of digital media platforms like Twitter have made Rose 'The most famous man on the Internet', according to business magazine *Inc.*[6] Together with co-host of *DiggNation*, Alex Albrecht (who now fronts Dell commercials in the USA), Rose has become part of what *The Guardian* in the United Kingdom and *The LA Times, The New York Times* and other mainstream US media have termed the web's first 'native' celebrities, a group of 'widely known web stars', largely coalescing as a 'stable of web personalities' at Revision3's Internet television studios. Indeed, whilst Fry might have been the most high profile UK celebrity to use

Twitter at the time (having since been eclipsed by Lilly Allen), Kevin Rose far outstripped his fame on the platform: up until August 2008 when Barack Obama's team used Twitter to such an extent that most other tweets were reduced to a mere chirp during the US elections, Rose consistently had the largest number of followers since the site launched.[7]

Beyond *DiggNation* and Twitter, however, Rose's fame is built across multiple platforms, with his emerging celebrity status being as much to do with his self-enterprise and role in digital forms of participatory culture as it is to do with fronting an online TV show. In late 2008, *Business Week* named Rose as one of the twenty-five most influential people on the web, describing him as 'the poster boy' of a list dominated by media moguls, such as Rupert Murdoch, Jerry Yang and Steve Jobs, venture capitalists and entrepreneurs.[8] Indeed, it is the symbiosis of this movement – from user to celebrity *and* Internet entrepreneur – that makes Rose particularly compelling in terms of understanding the production of celebrity in television's convergence with digital media. On the one hand, coverage of Rose in business magazines such as *Inc* and *Business Week* emphasises his entrepreneurial success as a form of vocational skill, whilst on the other his status as a digital television personality of *DiggNation* vaunts his televisual skill as central to his celebrity. Thus *The Guardian* described the filming of a live episode of *DiggNation* in London at the start of 2008 as 'mayhem', with 'more than 1,000 baying teenagers … yelling and laughing – it's part rock concert, part pantomime', with such live episodes regularly attracting over 2,000 fans.[9] Finally, through the use of web2.0 technologies for self-promotion, Rose's fame can be understood as built on a vernacular skill, ostensibly available to all, which depicts his celebrity as ordinary and achievable through a form of self-enterprise: as *Wired* declared, anyone can get Internet famous; provided they know how to deploy social networking platforms correctly. Indeed, although he has since dropped down to number 150 on the twitterholic list since Twitter entered the mainstream, accompanied by a 'digital land rush' of celebrities and media corporations keen to be associated with the 'latest thing', in late 2009 he was still placed ahead of Fry with 1,159,960 followers compared to Fry's 1,069,472.

My concern in this chapter is not, however, to compare and contrast Fry and Rose's relative fame or merit to it. Rather, I examine some of the changing contours of television personality fame and its meaning in relation to the digitalisation of television and its convergence with digital media forms. Of course the intertextual circulation of a television personality's persona is nothing new: indeed, as I suggested in Chapter 1, it is a prerequisite for the television personality system. In this regard Twitter's and other social media platforms' intertextual circulation of a personality's image, such as blogs, LastFM, MySpace and Facebook, only differs insofar as it promises the revelation of the 'authentic' self via a more immediate, intimate connection with audiences than other forms of intertextual coverage, such as the controlled PR interview or even the uncontrolled scandal press story. That is, fans might be able to elicit a response from the celebrity on their blog, Twitter stream or other interactive platform. Importantly, therefore, both this revelation of the authentic self as well as the use of such platforms for the extension and confirmation of the personality's fame is premised on interactivity as a form of self-promotion.[10] In turn, the celebrity is brought into closer proximity with not only fans but also a host of other voices hoping to be heard above the chatter and to 'make it' as DIY celebrities themselves (see Hills, 2006: 106).

In this chapter I argue that the successful creation of a DIY celebrity persona largely rests on the ability to transfer what have been some of the key discourses of televisual fame to digital media platforms, allowing followers access to their intimate, ordinary, authentic selves – but, as I shall go on to demonstrate, in a way that is demonstrative of *vernacular* skill. Attention to these televisual discourses and notions of achievement allow us to position such DIY fame at what Henry Jenkins has suggested is the intersection of grassroots convergence, 'a bottom up process', with the 'top down push of corporate convergence' (Jenkins, 2006a: 151). Such an approach moves us beyond considering whether the celebrity produced is either a democratised or devalued form of fame. Moreover, rather than producing the extension of media conglomerates' power or providing opportunities for greater democratic inclusiveness, this chapter suggests the way in which grassroots convergence culture, via its intersection with fame, can lead to the commodification of participatory culture *from within*. Paying attention to the labour and skill invested in the production of a celebrity persona in this context allows us to understand the way in which these function as part of wider discourses of the entrepreneurial self discussed in Chapters 4 and 6. However, away from the corporate structures of reality TV that various theorists have persuasively argued serve to colonise the resultant fame produced for contestants, these discourses of entrepreneurialism appear to promise greater freedoms and control in the spaces of digital media. Thus for theorists such as Jenkins (2006a, 2006b) and John Hartley (2004b) an era of DIY media, exemplified by platforms such as Twitter and blogging, allows for personal and social empowerment through the freedom to play with the construction of cultural identities. As Ouellette and Hay point out, Hartley's and Jenkins's arguments tend to take self-creation, freedom and self-governance as a form of democracy that has self-evident value. However, in line with Ouellette and Hay's arguments, I suggest that the outcome of DIY forms of media and the construction of the self they offer are perhaps better understood not as promising liberation, but freedoms that act as a form of governmentality. DIY fame, therefore, forms part of a turn towards neo-liberal strategies of public-private partnerships that 'involves not only making private agencies more responsible for public assistance ... but also transforming individuals into more responsible, accountable, and enterprising managers of themselves' (Ouellette and Hay, 2008: 24).

In what follows I first map out the correlations between DIY fame and the television personality system that I have set out in this book, looking at Rose's use of social media platforms and the Internet television programme *DiggNation* to discuss both televisual and vernacular skill. I then go on to examine how the achievement of this fame has simultaneously exploited and conferred a vocational skill, which embraces the 'entrepreneur' of the self through self-promotion. This self-enterprise is not only valued by traditional media and business paradigms – functioning to legitimate Rose's DIY, ordinary celebrity – but also embeds that fame at the centre of the architectures of participation that structure online communities (Bennett, 2011). In turn, his fame can be understood as part of what Ouellette and Hay have suggested are a matrix of techniques of the self aimed at 'governing at a distance' (Ouellette and Hay, 2008), which in Rose's case promotes celebrity as an empowering form of self-enterprise congruent with neo-liberal discourses of privatisation, personal responsibility and consumer choice.

Interacting with the authentic self: 'a bit ... boring ... (sorry Stephen)'

Various scholars have noted that the boundaries between celebrity, fan and ordinary user are being elided in the contemporary mediascape (see Holmes, various; Hills, 2006; Marshall, 2006; Turner, 2004). However, whilst most debate that follows on from this observation engages with the relative cultural value of contemporary celebrity, it is perhaps an overlooked point that what is radically decontextualised about such fame is not so much its merit, but its connection to specific media platforms. Stephen Fry's lift incident did not so much amount to a subsidiary intertextual circulation of his image that fed back into future performances – as per my discussion of intertextuality in Chapter 6 – but rather served to confirm his celebrity as a multiplatform entity. Similarly, Susan Boyle's fame has been constructed as much by the circulation of her *I Dreamed a Dream* performance on YouTube as it has by her appearance on the UK version of *The X Factor*, with the YouTube clip of her performance attracting millions more viewers than ITV's broadcast programme. Such examples suggest that we increasingly encounter celebrity in a form that is decontextualised from 'primary' texts.[11]

In such a media landscape, the contours of fame are changing; we expect, as Sean Redmond has observed, 'intimate fame everywhere' (Redmond, 2006: 27). Recalling arguments about television's ability to destabilise the image of film's 'auratic stars', Marshall has argued that in such a context 'the film star's aura of distance and distinction is breaking down': in an era of digital media that proliferates both celebrity, and information about celebrities, there is 'less possibility for industry control' (Marshall, 2006: 643).[12] In turn our understanding of what it means, what skill and work it takes, and who can become famous is challenged. Such a breakdown arguably places renewed emphasis on the presentational self. Established celebrities, from television personalities to film stars, must now compete to be heard and seen in a culture of pervasive celebrity. Marshall's discussion of Tom Cruise's manic behaviour in 2005 – including the infamous couch incident on the *Oprah Winfrey Show* (Harpo, 1986–2009) and his proposal to Katie Holmes on top of the Eiffel Tower – as a form of calculated self-promotion evidences one potential response to this crisis (ibid.). More widely, however, the increased emphasis on the presentational self as a form of self-promotion has been tied to the discourses and aesthetics we have taken for granted in television fame: ordinariness, authenticity and intimacy.

For example, Ashton Kutcher's celebrity persona has become largely decontextualised from his film stardom, with the visibility of his fame managed predominantly through his use of Twitter. Whilst widely circulated examples of his Twitter feed in the mainstream press most obviously function as a form of calculated self-promotion, such as posting pictures of his wife's bottom (ooops, did I just share Demi Moore's bottom with 4 million followers – I wonder if anyone will notice?), his tweets are largely premised on the intimate sharing of his ordinary life. Indeed, Moore's Twitter response to Kutcher's insisted on the domestic, everyday-ness of this incident: 'He is such a sneak and while I was steaming his suit too!'[13] Whilst the ordinariness of this interaction might have been largely orchestrated, over the 4,000 response messages on Kutcher's Twitter stream the emphasis is predominantly on the everyday. Thus responses to his posting ranged from those that understood it as a stunt ('#punkd #fake', NeroTunes 21/03/09); to those who perceived it as a site of privileged access ('Seriously can not believe you posted this! LOL', geekyjenn 23/03/09); to those who saw it as part of the banality of everyday life shared on his stream ('I am in LOVE with that couch!!!', aronado, 21/03/09).

Within this milieu, there is far less contradistinction between television personality, film star and wider forms of celebrity. Thus Stephen Fry's Twitter stream similarly consistently positions him as 'ordinary': as much a part of the Twitter community as the 'media world' of celebrity (Couldry, 2002). For example, Fry declares his fandom of various other 'acts' or people on Twitter, describing himself 'hooked' on Sunrise Sunset's songs or awed by meeting other celebrities such as Annie Lennox.[14] Of course, he also clearly occupies an elevated position as a celebrity, which I shall return to below, but this persona is presented as 'ordinary'. Indeed, his tweets were seen as so ordinary by one follower as to be 'a bit... boring... (sorry Stephen)', prompting Fry to threaten to quit Twitter proclaiming himself 'obviously not good enough'. The incident, which was widely reported in the British press, served to suggest a paradoxical image I traced in the discussion of performance in Part II: on the one hand, the self presented here was something that had to be worked at – so that it could be criticised as a performance, 'not good enough' to merit further attention. On the other, the self was also confirmed as authentic via a process of interaction, whereby Fry answered and apologised to his critic for the subsequent abuse he received on Twitter – 'Pls accept my apols ... I feel more sheepish than a sheep'. Similar to the way Kutcher and other celebrities do in fact respond and interact with fans and ordinary users on such platforms, the exchange suggested Fry interacts on Twitter 'just-as-he-really-is', so that following a celebrity on Twitter promised the chance to know the celebrity no longer as separated in the media world, but as an everyday, ordinary and *familiar* persona.

Indeed, whilst Twitter certainly serves as a publicity machine for any form of celebrity, including DIY celebrities, it is intriguing to note that the list of most followers is dominated by television personalities – Oprah Winfrey, Ellen de Generes, Ryan Seacrest – whilst its highest profile users in the United Kingdom are largely television personalities, including Jonathan Ross and Fry, which suggest the *skill* and *work* in creating a cohesive, intimate on-off-screen persona in television functions effectively in the digital economy of celebrity.[15] Arguably, intimacy and authenticity have already been placed as key hallmarks of Twitter's celebrity function. As Jack Schofield, *The Guardian*'s technology correspondent, suggested:

> [A] Twitter stream needs to be more than pumping out PR via an RSS feed, or getting your staff to do it for you – the technique adopted by Barack Obama and Britney Spears. Celebs whose follower lists have rocketed from zero to 50,000 may one day see them tumbling down, as disillusioned fans leave them – and, perhaps, Twitter – behind.[16]

Being ordinary, authentic and affecting intimate connections is therefore increasingly recognised as a form of work and skill in celebrity culture. Indeed, as Ernest Sternberg has argued, 'at every economic level, the ability to present oneself has become a critical economic asset' (Sternberg, 2006: 420). Moreover, understood in these terms, fame is rarely simply attributed in Rojek's terms (Rojek, 2001): in the clamour of voices in the blogosphere and self-promotion of the net, some users within a community are able to master the techniques and technologies of self-publicity in order to stand out from all those people who turn the webcam, blog, Twitter, MySpace and a myriad of other social networking tools on themselves.

Kevin Rose's DIY fame exemplifies the way such mastery functions at the intersections of not only discourses of televisual fame and performance, but also the entrepreneurial self. In the remainder of this section I concentrate on Rose to explore this issue of performing the self in DIY media forms and its connection to the television personality system. Whilst the interest in Kutcher's and Fry's tweets is undoubtedly premised on the access they promise to a pre-existing celebrity persona, the techniques of self-presentation are increasingly shared. As Sternberg argues, we are consistently asked to realise our 'value' by 'calculated self-presentation, using techniques originally meant for the making of celebrities' (Sternberg, 2006: 420). Thus, I want to first set out the way in which the performance tropes of televisual skill that I have set out across the book are also apparent in DIY formations of celebrity, before turning to the way use of social media technologies in the multiplatform presentation and promotion of the self can be understood as a form of vernacular skill that is increasingly ordinary. This notion of vernacular skill draws on Jean Burgess's work on vernacular creativity to describe the ordinary, everyday practices of user-generated-content production (Burgess, 2006b). Such a study enables us to better understand the ideological function that such DIY forms of celebrity fulfil, which I turn to in the final section of this chapter.

In order to achieve this, I concentrate on the podcast *DiggNation* and its status as a text of both television and of digital participatory culture. As a podcast released by 'Internet television' studio Revision3, *DiggNation* clearly calls our attention to its status as 'like TV': performance tropes of direct address, the mise-en-scène of a cheap chat show complete with 'guest' couch – which has featured *Late Night with* ... host Jimmy Fallon and Ashton Kutcher (see Figure 7.2) – combine with technologies of simple front-lighting, auto-cues (in the form of laptops) and title sequences. As a text of participatory culture, it draws our attention to its membership of an online community and fandom: the first episode opened without a title sequence, but rather a clip from *The Family Guy* (20th Century Fox Television/Hands Down Entertainment, 1999–ongoing) that affirmed the show's and its creators' interest in shared fan culture.[17] Moreover, despite the moniker 'Internet television', production values are very low, with *The New York Times* describing Revision3's programming aesthetic as 'a hybrid of the polished shows created for the networks and the amateur videos that populate sites like YouTube'.[18] The stress on the production of the show as a form of vernacular creativity that anyone might undertake is made apparent in subsequent publicity's attempts to explain the success of the show: as co-host Albrecht makes clear, 'We just did it for ourselves. The fact that people actually watched it shocked us – it's blown up beyond all recognition. Really, it's the Wild West';[19] whilst Rose claims that he and Albrecht are simply doing what a 'lot of geeks do ... but don't have a camera'.[20]

As host of *DiggNation*, Rose performs the role of television presenter – indeed he had previously held guest and small host spots on the San Francisco local cable channel 'TechTV'. However, this role is carefully balanced with the programme's claims to be part of the wider user-generated-content ephemera that circulates amongst its audience of Internet geeks. Most importantly, as I shall return to in the final section, Rose's ownership of digg.com and Revision3 studios is both constantly downplayed or depicted as something anyone in the user community of Internet geeks might achieve: a small Internet start-up built from his bedroom. As Jim Louderback (chief executive of Revision3) suggests, the web has increased the sense of proximity and friendship between personality and audience: 'In the US, we [once] had television icons; people you put on a pedestal; gods. ... [on the web] the hosts come out of those communities and they're just like them.'[21]

Figure 7.2 *DiggNation* clearly calls our attention to its status as 'like TV': performance tropes of direct address, the mise-en-scène of a cheap chat show complete with 'guest' couch, combine with technologies of simple front-lighting and autocues (in the form of laptops) (screen capture from *DiggNation* [Revision 3, 2005–ongoing]).

This is complimented by a performance mode reminiscent of those discussed in relation to early television in Part I. In a similar way to the parallels drawn between vaudeville, music hall and the performance modes of early television set out there, Henry Jenkins has suggested that certain elements of vaudevillian performance tropes can be found in the early performance modes of amateur video on YouTube. One of the tropes Jenkins focuses on is the 'interrupted act', whereby a performer 'courts a sense of the amateurish which also places a high emphasis on spontaneity – many videos are carefully staged so as to look unrehearsed. There is not necessarily a push towards liveness, but there is a push towards "realness"' (Jenkins, 2006c).

In terms of *DiggNation*, aside from the occasional 'live specials' filmed in front of an audience, any sense of 'liveness' is seemingly removed by the programme's status as a podcast, with audiences either downloading the show and transferring it to their iPods or portable media devices or watching on an online, on-demand video-player. In *DiggNation* spontaneity is most obviously marked by the retention of the kinds of disruption Jenkins discusses in relation to vaudeville and by the continual 'corpsing' of Rose and Albrecht – elements that might otherwise be edited out by the pre-recorded nature of the show, such as Rose throwing up on Albrecht's couch or the constant spillage of beer bottles on equipment. Karen Lury suggests that corpsing, 'whereby people forget lines, giggle or in other ways break the frame of performance … manifests itself as the inability to sustain the look of the camera, or the other performer' (Lury, 1995: 127). However, in so doing, these instances of corpsing engender a moment where the performer 'reveals his or herself as truly live, uncontrolled and expressive', which confirms the authenticity of their image to the audience (ibid.). This lack of control also signals a diminished difference between self and performance – most notably marked by the irregular length of podcasts, which can be between thirty minutes and an hour, depending on the performance of the hosts (often linked to the amount of beer consumed during filming).

In many ways the on-demand nature of the podcast actually underscores the relationship of authenticity and intimacy that are the hallmarks of early television fame. For example, just as the adoption of direct address as a performance mode by television personalities from the music hall and vaudeville served to create an intimate relationship between viewer and personality, so it serves a similar function in *DiggNation*. However, the status of the programme as on-demand podcast means that it will often be watched on a handheld media device or laptop: as viewers lean forward into the screen or hold it up close to see the details of stories or expressions, a greater sense of intimacy is therefore created between viewer and host. As Louderbeck argues:

> When you watch TV, you're seven feet away and sitting back. But when you watch on your iPod or your laptop, it's only inches away or you're holding it in your hands. I wonder whether the intimacy of our handheld devices and computers creates more of a sense of intimacy and sharedness and companionship than just sitting back and watching TV.[22]

Intimacy here, therefore, feeds back into authenticating Rose's image as part of the community: a companion for the commuter run. Most importantly, Rose downplays his own celebrity status in a move that both asserts his membership of the ordinary community as well as confirms his status as celebrity by recalling the star mythology that Holmes details, whereby media coverage of celebrities tends to express 'approving attitudes towards celebrities who appear to be fundamentally *unchanged* by wealth and fame' (Holmes, 2005a: 31). Thus the form of televisual skill displayed by Rose places an emphasis on intimate connections with an authentic self which, as I want to turn to now, is further heightened by his vernacular skill in the deployment of social media tools.

As I suggested in Chapter 1, the revelation of the 'real' or authentic self has remained a privileged site even in the construction of ordinary celebrity. Annette Hill's oft-quoted study of *Big Brother* audiences suggests that viewers look for the moments of truth, which might be glimpsed through the improvised performance of *Big Brother* contestants, as a key site of pleasure and evaluation of the text, particularly the contestant's relative merits to fame (Hill, 2002). Hill's study points to the importance of surveillance as the key aesthetic trope in reality TV and its construction of ordinary celebrity. As I suggested in the discussion of *Extras* in Part II, the familiarity of this aesthetic has made contestants more adept at managing a performance under such surveillance. However, this process of surveillance has been extended beyond the confines of the *Big Brother* house: to 'seem natural' when people are filmed for programmes without their knowledge (Couldry, 2004: 57–74), or as part of the 'value-generating labor' (Andrejevic, 2002: 262) exchange that underpins e-commerce's targeted marketing (such as Amazon's 'Customers who bought this item also bought'). Couldry's and Andrejevic's arguments ultimately return to reality TV in order to assess how contestants' (willing) submission to surveillance works as a form of validating and exposing the 'real' self in the construction of a devalued form of celebrity; one that is controlled by existing media conglomerates. For Andrejevic, the democratising promise of participatory mediums therefore offers 'publicity as celebrity': a hybrid combination of what different camps perceive as the net's potential to foster either the 'passive evisceration of publicity as spectacle' or 'the revitalization of democracy' (ibid.).

However, in the case of Rose, his role on Internet television is not one of contestant but host, and his submission to surveillance *is* away from television. Surveillance takes the form of exposure to, and control of, web2.0 platforms that track his every move: from Twittering his current activities – 'having a glass of wine with @kurtsmom' – to blog entries, updating his MySpace profile, documenting his life on Flickr to sharing his bookmarking, music and news interests via LastFM, del.ic.ious and, of course, digg.com. What is therefore missing from Andrejevic's equation of DIY celebrity with mere publicity is the question of both *control* and *achievement*. That is, extrapolating from the role of reality TV, Andrejevic and Couldry place the control and power over the celebrity images created as belonging to the existing media industries – with the fame attributed to contestants illusory or fleeting. However, if Rose's celebrity simply exemplifies Andrejevic's argument that reality TV and digital media mean that 'the private life of … of anyone who trains the webcam on him- or herself' is opened to scrutiny and possible fame, then this negates the fact that Rose has had to work to achieve his celebrity. In particular, he has deployed a level of vernacular skill to master social networking platforms so as to ensure people are watching and listening to him amongst the 'chatter' of the web: an image that he himself has controlled, edited, tagged and filtered (rather than those produced in a media conglomerate's editing suite).

As with Andrejevic, digital culture theorist Clay Shirky has suggested that in the self-promotion of the net, 'fame happens' (Shirky, 2008: 93): some users within a community are able to master the techniques and technologies of self-publicity in order to stand out from all those who turn the spotlight of web2.0 tools on themselves. If these tools and techniques of self-promotion are increasingly ordinary, then one requires a degree of 'vernacular skill', to master them to become famous. *Wired*'s proclamation at the head of this chapter that anyone can get 'Internet famous' seemingly corroborates the hollowness of the 'democratic' fame made possible by the net's 'interactivity', declaring Julia Allison to be 'the latest, and perhaps purest, iteration of the Warholian ideal: someone who is famous for being famous'. Allison's, rather limited, fame is apparently divorced from any talent or achievement, having become well-known simply through self-promotion. However, such a description belies the skill of self-promotion that has gone into achieving this celebrity status, with the article going on to not only detail Allison's mastery of a myriad of social networking tools that have made her famous over a nineteen-page special – from endless Twitter updates to publicity stunts aimed at being seen in the right company at the right venue, through to endless blog and comment posts – but also offering tips on 'how to promote yourself', 'be the hero', or 'boost your geek cred'. The discourse here affirms the possibility of DIY celebrity, such as that explored by Graeme Turner's (2004), Catherine Lumby's (2007) and Nick Couldry's (2002) discussions of webcam girls, whereby the ordinary person feels empowered by the potential to make themselves famous: as Allison asserts, this 'technology gives us direct power over our own brand'.[23] The seemingly never-ending line of wannabe celebrities that queue up for talent show auditions, or post 'quirky' videos on YouTube or their blogs, suggests that this brand needs to be worked at constantly in order to stand out from the crowd. That is, not only is the desire, but also the tools with which to become famous, increasingly ordinary.

The achievement of fame via the cultivating of a following across these web2.0 platforms results in a persona that is no less mediated, nor less surveilled, than those discussed by critics of reality TV. However, here users have greater control over the image presented and constructed – because this fame resides largely on presentation of the self as publicity, users can detail their every move or, more importantly, editorialise to construct a mediated self that is as exciting and interesting as possible. A familiar dichotomy between private and public self therefore continues to persist in web2.0 fame – as Rose himself admits:

> There's two different sides to what we do. When I do *DiggNation*, I'm partying with the fans. It's just us being geeks and going crazy, and when I'm here at work, it's a very different environment. I spend most of my nights going to the rock-climbing gym and drinking tea. And then once a month, I go to a party, and pictures get taken, and it paints a different picture.[24]

However, because the construction of this image is a constant and interactive process – fans of Rose can post, comment or read messages on his blog or MySpace page, know his exact whereabouts via Twitter, or share his taste in music via LastFM – this self-surveillance promises an intimacy and authenticity that is distinct from television and film.

As with Fry and Kutcher, Rose will by no means be able to interact with all of his audience. But he can, and must, interact with at least some of the audience in order to sustain his profile – the mediated self constructed is a constantly interacting one, inviting the audience to feel part of his community: at any point they could solicit a response from him, or meet him for a beer. Arguably this is a step beyond what Bonner describes as the way in which television presenters constantly make viewers feel 'let in' on their relationships and everyday lives; indeed the availability and authenticity of his image seemingly blurs the boundaries between 'media' and 'ordinary' world (Bonner, 2003: 52). Importantly therefore, the authentic image maintained across these sites is one that is constantly open: happy to share ideas, thoughts and criticisms on new technologies, gadgets, games and, via such interactions, assert his position as part of the user community – describing his fame as 'not celebrity: it's internet celebrity'.[25] The question regarding the democratic nature of this fame therefore turns not necessarily on Rose's achievement of fame, but how this structures his relationship with fans and the online community at digg.com. And it is here that I suggest we can understand such fame intersecting with discourses of the entrepreneurial self that serve as a form of governmentality in order to encourage self- and collective-regulation as a form of empowerment.

Fame as entrepreneurial self-governance

How this kid made $60 million in 18 months.
(*Business Week* cover story, August 14, 2006)

In a 2006 issue of *Business Week* Kevin Rose appears on the front cover dressed in T-shirt, beanie and headphones, posed with two thumbs up and a cheesy grin: a caricature of the cool Internet geek. As I suggested at the beginning of this chapter, the vernacular and televisual skill of Rose discussed above converges with his vocational skill as an Internet entrepreneur, so that there is a symbiosis of his movement from ordinary user to both celebrity and entrepreneur, with each mutually reinforcing and confirming the status of the other. *Business Week*'s cover story of Rose's Internet, entrepreneurial success is but one of a number of high profile instances of approving coverage of Rose's celebrity in the business press – others have included coverage of 'get togethers' with Bill Gates, Richard Branson and Steve Jobs through to his inclusion on CNN's top 100 'people who matter' list and *Business Week*'s applauding of CEOs who use Twitter.[26] As part of the display of his vocational skill (that simultaneously serves as a form of self-promotion via his vernacular skill), Rose positions himself as happy to be solicited for advice by fellow users on a range of platforms on their potential new ventures or on how to boost their profile. For example, during the credit crunch of 2008 that perpetuated an Internet hype mooting a shift from web2.0 towards web3.0, Rose posted a blog entry on how to 'Start something during Web 2.5'.[27] Uploaded using Seismic's vlogging tool, his post circulated across a number of platforms that generated a visible (and visual) dialogue between Rose and would-be entrepreneurs that provided feedback and help develop some 'really exciting' ideas on how to 'start your own start-up'. In a similar vein, in January of 2009 Rose wrote for the well-respected Tech-crunch website on '10 ways to increase your Twitter followers' as a means of accruing cultural capital.[28] Most importantly, the vocational skill he offers as business advice is premised on aligning himself with more broadly held philosophies of participatory culture, such as by promoting DRM-free music, open-source software, or championing Pirate Bay's move to 'encrypt the Internet'. Like Titchmarsh's vocational skill discussed in Chapter 6, Rose's knowledge is 'common sense' in the ordinary cultures of online geek communities.

However, the role of celebrity online is far from clear cut and is often understood as antithetical to participatory culture and community. As Clay Shirky has argued, the increasing popularity of blogging – and particular bloggers – results in a corresponding diminishment of its interactive, communal and participatory value. Thus, as a particular blog's popularity increases:

> no matter how assiduously someone wants to interact with their readers, the growing audience will ultimately defeat that possibility ... [the blogger has] to start choosing who to respond to and who to ignore, and over time, ignore becomes the default choice. They have, in a word, become famous.
>
> (Shirky, 2008: 93)

Far from the radical, democratising potential of DIY celebrity or citizenship promised by such interactive technologies, Shirky reminds us that as the Internet or blogosphere becomes a mass medium this 'is what "interactivity" looks like ... no interactivity at all with almost all the audience' (ibid.).

Yet the authenticity of Rose's persona established above (he is an ordinary geek too), together with the credibility of his vocational skill, allows for this apparent contradiction between fame and participatory culture to be negotiated. Matt Hills has argued that such forms of fame can be understood as a kind of 'sub-cultural' celebrity that evidences a discernible hierarchy in fan networks, which is particularly apparent when 'textual poachers [turn] textual gatekeepers', as they gain access to the media world and become celebrities themselves (Hills, 2006: 116). Leaving aside the problematic example of Russell T. Davies with which Hills chooses to illustrate his argument, whereby Davies was already a media insider before his status as fan of *Dr Who* came into play, Hills's argument appears too simplistic because it depicts the construction of such celebrity as a form of cultural resistance, 'not just another powerless elite' (ibid.). In this perspective fans therefore have power to write or change storylines, bring back or save programmes or even 'make it' as media insiders, such as Davies. But, to a large extent, these activities fulfil corporate profiteering as much as act as forms of resistance; indeed, as John Caldwell's work on crowd-sourcing has suggested, even making it as a 'media insider' is part of media conglomerates' strategies of exploiting free labour in the flexible economies of digital media (see Caldwell, 2008; 2011). Nevertheless, the elucidation of fandom's production of 'its own subcultural stratifications' remains useful, particularly with respect to the way Hills argues that such 'subcultural celebrity is necessarily linked to subculturally-valorized *achievements*', such as writing fan-fiction (Hills, 2006: 115–116, emphasis mine). However, rather than see this subcultural celebrity in opposition to the 'manufactured' mass-mediated celebrities of the culture industries' capitalist exploitation of consumers, as Hills does, I suggest that Rose's fame demonstrates how the achievement of DIY fame may actually be congruent with neo-liberal discourses of capitalist enterprise.

To understand this connection we need to return to the way Rose's fame is built via vernacular and vocational skill, whereby both discourses serve to position him as a successful 'entrepreneur of the self'. Rose's ability to 'start your own start-up' via labour conducted not solely in the workplace, but in its convergence with the commercialised leisure sphere – where blogging and other forms of social networking meet – is demonstrative of what du Gay and McRobbie have argued is the entrepreneurial self's necessary response, and exploitation, of the flexible economy promoted by neo-liberal government. This emphasis on what McRobbie describes as positioning 'self-fashioning as a requirement of work' (McRobbie, quoted in Ouellette and Hay, 2008: 103–104) is part of a wider cultural turn in capitalism that seeks to 'harness interpersonal relationships, cultural bonds alongside informality, emotion and "creativity" in order to produce economic success' (Littler, 2007: 235). As Jo Littler has demonstrated, this turn to 'soft capitalism' has created a paradox whereby the promotion of 'the virtues of decentralisation … and bottom-up mechanisms, [has] also treated CEOs as superheroes' (Surowiecki quoted in ibid.). Littler goes on to suggest, using Alan Sugar and Dov Charney as exemplars, that 'many celebrity CEOs seem to offer a means of reconciling this paradox, by intertwining the twin imperatives of being a "corporate superhero" with the bottom-up mechanisms symptomatic of the cultural turn' (ibid: 236). Importantly, drawing on Lowenthal's account of celebrity as idols of mass consumption, Littler demonstrates how business celebrities are established in contradistinction to the 'distracting figures of mass entertainment; they are somehow not the "real" celebrity, not the real false idols', their celebrity status is '*allowed* and *respectable*' (ibid.: 232, emphasis original). As founder of digg.com Rose occupies a similar position but, more problematically, one that extends the discourses of entrepreneurial meritocracy to the self-enterprise connected with DIY celebrity, understood as a bottom-up process. In turn, like the paradox of modern capitalism, his celebrity introduces a hierarchical architecture of participation into the self-organising communities of digital culture.

His ownership of the digg.com site therefore raises important questions about the relationship of celebrity and participatory culture. Graeme Turner's work on the 'demotic' nature of the ordinari-isation of celebrity suggests that the demotic, if not merely generating diversity for its own sake, might otherwise prove so unruly and anarchic as to be 'capable of instigating but not easily organising or managing social and cultural change' (Turner, 2006). However I would suggest that, where meritocratic understandings of DIY fame can be accommodated, the entrepreneurial self is capable of not only managing social and cultural change, but deriving profit from it: not in the name of existing media conglomerates, but in the services of its own celebrity. This social change is therefore not radical, but rather one that is congruent with neo-liberal discourses that value self-enterprise and the privatised facilitation of civic and community obligations. Whilst such a position is seemingly incompatible with the open nature of online participatory communities, Rose's position as 'one of' these communities enables this tension to be reconciled around what Henry Jenkins terms the 'moral economy of information' that emerges with participatory culture. Jenkins describes this as 'a sense of mutual obligations and shared expectations about what constitutes good citizenship within a knowledge community' (Jenkins, 2006a: 255). Digg.com, as a social news site, arguably epitomises such a knowledge community chiming well with Jenkins's use of Pierre Levy's notion of collective intelligence; providing for a 'deterritorialisation of knowledge, brought about by the ability of the net and the Web to facilitate rapid many-to-many communication [to] enable broader participation in decision making, new modes of citizenship and community' (Jenkins, 2006b: 136). In allowing for the collective shaping of news values and sharing of information, digg.com provides for a flow of ideas between users in a space designed to promote comment and exchange. However, whilst such communal activity might produce collective intelligence that is democratically beneficial, as Axel Bruns's discussion of issues around copyright, reward, authorship and communal ownership sets out, it also produces a tension: the question of financial reward for collective effort. Bruns draws on Pesce to set out the fundamental problem: 'If the host of the community takes the content generated by that community and realizes profit from that content, the creators of that content will immediately be afflicted with a number of conflicting feelings' (Pesce quoted in Bruns, 2008: 283).

The dilemma for Bruns and Pesce is clear: in order to encourage participation, all users within a community must feel valued, whilst this may not necessarily mean a direct call for status as a 'profit participant', it does involve ensuring that no one appears to 'cash in on the produsage' of the community (ibid.: 267). What makes this a particularly compelling area for investigation in terms of Kevin Rose as ordinary user, owner of digg.com and star of *DiggNation* – as vernacularly, vocationally and televisually skilled – is that all three of these 'iterations' of Rose's persona espouse the kind of open-source, collective intelligence ethos and fan activity that Bruns, Jenkins and others perceive as the hallmark of participatory culture. Although digg.com users do not actively 'create content' on the digg site, linking to and commenting on news stories elsewhere on the web, their activity can be understood as precisely the kinds of value-generating labour that Andrejevic suggests is the hallmark of the online economy's reliance on surveillance (Andrejevic, 2002). There is, however, a necessary corollary to Pesce's and Bruns's question of collective ownership that I shall return to in my conclusion: not simply who gets paid and how, but who takes responsibility and liability when the community is found to infringe – in terms such as piracy, privacy or decency that have framed attempts to regulate the web.

Clearly in the above quotation from Pesce the reference to hosting is of websites, which involves the economic and labour costs of site maintenance, storage, design, etc. However it also draws our attention to its other media-related meaning: Rose's role as host of *DiggNation*. Here the differentials between Rose's status as ordinary user, digg.com owner and celebrity, become more apparent. For example, *DiggNation* opens with a series of sponsorship messages that are indicative of a more closed structure than that promoted on digg.com. What is particularly interesting about this shift is the way in which it trades on the authenticity and ordinariness of Rose's persona to recall the relationship between star and sponsor detailed in Murray's study of early US television stardom. Spontaneity there was aligned with a performance mode that had to 'exude an honesty or "naturalness" that would engender trust in the audience', which was established via the authenticity of persona, in order to successfully pitch products (Murray, 2005: 117). For Rose, speaking honestly and openly about sponsors' products and reviewing others involves a similar negotiation built on the authenticity of his persona established through web2.0 communities, but sold back to these audiences through television, marketed under the interactive hyperbole of 'podcasting', 'Internet television' and Revision3's positioning of itself as the 'first media company that gets it, born from the Internet, on-demand generation … [and hosted not] from Hollywood … [but] from the same passionate fan base as our audience'.[29] This enables Rose to sell and promote a range of products, from video games and web-hosting services through to beer sponsorship deals and, more impressively, the creation of an online version of some episodes with a 'clickable interface', whereby anything and everything in view is on sale: from Rose's Mac Powerbook to his sweater (Figure 7.3). I do not want to moralise over what might be perceived as Rose 'fleecing' his audience by continually selling sponsors' products to them – certainly his tech-savvy audience is one that is not likely to be easily exploited in terms of financial capital or media literacy. However, more problematically, Rose's role as salesman extends to his position as host of digg.com, indeed in episode one of *DiggNation* such an exploitation of his authentic image allows Rose to feel able to talk 'openly and honestly' about digg.com as if it were somebody else's site entirely. In fact although knowledge of Rose's ownership of the site circulates widely intertextually, it is never openly acknowledged on the show.

Figure 7.3 The authenticated persona of Kevin Rose as host allows him to act as salesman, speaking 'honestly and openly' about products, or simply acting as a clickable interface to consumer products (screen capture from videoclix.tv).

Whilst *Business Week*'s interview with Rose summarises his philosophy about Digg's business model as 'community first, ads later', arguably it is the authenticity of his persona as an ordinary Internet geek that enables Rose to negotiate the facilitation of the community and collective intelligence of digg whilst simultaneously commercially exploiting it. Describing the experience of attending a live *DiggNation* episode as akin to being in a mosh pit, *The Guardian*'s Zoe Margolis set out the importance of the user community to both digg's success and the celebrity of its hosts: 'Digg is not just another tech site. Because they [the users] themselves contribute to it with links and stories that they recommend to others, it's theirs'.[30] As the headline quote from the article makes clear – 'The democratic approach is a very valuable thing' – Rose underscores both the democratic and commercial potential of digg as a web2.0 social media site. The 'value' of democracy is therefore something sellable – as Rose goes on to suggest, for digg this means the site 'will serve as a means of gathering metrics for third party websites, providing them insights into who's digging their content, who they are spreading it to'.[31] This business model has made digg.com estimated to be worth over US$60 million – with Rose and co-founder Jay Adelson the only profit-participants. Surveillance therefore returns to the equation, again within the control of Rose and digg.com, but this time in the form of commercially exploiting the user preferences, activities and interactions of the community that he has developed.

Such a problematic directs us to the arguments of Andrejevic and others discussed earlier in the chapter regarding the way surveillance promises inter-active democracy, but largely only functions to underpin the value-generating labour exchange of the interactive economy, reducing democracy to 'publicity as celebrity'. However, as Ouellette and Hay argue, the kinds of participation that Andrejevic is sceptical of in the enactments of 'democracy' by reality TV and digital media, whereby the citizen-consumer is always a commodity to be counted, 'do not necessarily mark a withering away of government (ceding the work of state institutions to commercial TV), but rather an extension of government – even as this extension in another respect makes government more reliant upon privatized, commercial resources' (Ouellette and Hay, 2008: 218). Like Caldwell's (2011) work on the way media conglomerates exploit user-generated-content, Ouellette and Hay describe this as a kind of 'outsourcing', suggesting that through a number of devices reality TV con-stantly 'invokes modes of citizenship, cultural commerce and philanthropy that 'do not involve "entitlements" and models of civic participation that do not "depend" on the Welfare State' (Ouellette and Hay, 2008: 6). Rose's celebrity extends this model to DIY forms of media: the persona I have sketched out here promises that those who are able to harness the enterprising self, via skills that are vernacularly available, may be able to practice a form of celebrity and cultural commerce that invokes such a model of citizenship. Personal freedom *and* celebrity are achieved as a form of 'governmental rationality that values self-enterprise, self-reliance and lessons to be learned in privatized experiments and games of self-constitutions and group govern-ment' (ibid.: 224).

Conclusion: Digg this?

One might object to my analysis above that Rose's celebrity is hardly relevant to his relationship to the millions of users on digg.com. Given the 30 million or more user base of that site compared to the 300,000 or so downloads of the *Digg Nation* podcast or Rose's one million followers on Twitter, as Rose himself notes above, his 'Internet celebrity' is not all that pervasive compared to traditional forms of celebrity. However, in achieving the kinds of freedoms discussed above through enterprising techniques of the self, Rose's celebrity is clearly valued by traditional media outlets. This is particularly evident in the business press I have drawn on throughout this article, where Rose's Internet, entrepreneurial celebrity is positioned at the vanguard of forming new media economies as old business models have increasingly been disrupted and undermined. Thus whilst studies of ordinary users, audiences and fans have always suggested such groups are powerful, Rose's power extends far beyond the ability to change storylines or save a show. Rather, it might also include the ability to affect media economies of new start-ups and, possibly, the tra-ditional television industry itself: under the title 'More trouble for Hollywood', the *Los Angeles Times* reported on Rose's decision to 'ditch cable [and TiVo for] Internet and Netflix' as a major challenge to broadcasting business models; a proclamation happily coinciding with the agreement of Netflix's long-term sponsorship deal with *DiggNation*.[32] Elsewhere the *Los Angeles Times* had suggested that the cohort to which Rose belonged, the '*Twitter* titans', 'wield substantial influence. With a few keystrokes, they can put a new website on the map – or they can take one off'.[33]

As a leader of that community, how Rose conducts himself and runs digg. com – as both celebrity 'poster boy' of web2.0 and Internet entrepreneur – in relationship to the 'moral economy' of participatory culture is profoundly important. Whilst Rose certainly benefits from selling his user base to advertisers, as I suggested above, this has been achieved partly through his negotiation of the moral economy of digg.com: in early 2007 users began posting and linking to stories on digg.com about the encryption key for unlocking DVDs, which would enable users to rip and burn copies of HD and Blu-ray DVDs. The story was one of those 'most dugg' by users, consistently appearing on the front page of digg. Here the privatised form of civic culture that Rose had facilitated threatened to cut both ways: fearing litigation, and aware of his own *individual* liability in a site that traded on collective intelligence, Rose instructed digg administrators to systematically remove any such postings. However, digg's actions were perceived as censorship by its community of users and not in line with the ethos of the site which, after all, gave users the right to determine the shape of the news and what is important to the community.[34] Rose therefore responded on his blog:

> … after seeing hundreds of stories and reading thousands of comments, you've made it clear. You'd rather see Digg go down fighting than bow down to a bigger company. We hear you, and effective immediately we won't delete stories or comments containing the code …. If we lose, then what the hell, at least we died tryin.[35]

Clay Shirky interprets this move by users as an instance of 'civil disobedience', with digg's response recognising the 'implicit bargain that his users assumed they had with Digg and, by extension, him'. As a result, Shirky argues that this demonstrates the way that the social networking tools of web2.0 are marking 'progress from coordination into governance, as groups gain enough power and support to be able to demand that they be deferred to' (Shirky, 2008: 291–292). Whilst I have sympathy for such a view, ultimately this distracts us from the entrepreneurial moves that Rose has made; most notably, this has included the continual manoeuvring of the business in order to be sold to Google – the masters of maximising value-generating labour through surveillance in the online economy.[36] Indeed, when Rose sold off the social networking start-up, Pownce, he created in 2008 to media firm Six Apart, he was heavily criticised for failing to promote the service in the same way as he uses Twitter to promote his own brand. Similarly, whilst Rose has displayed some ambivalence towards the selling of/to the digg.com audience by delegating the task of advertising sales to Microsoft, sponsorship has continued to increase on *DiggNation* – for example, the beer sponsorship deal noted above took the form of a six-week 'drink-a-long'. Moreover, the relationship between digg.com and *DiggNation* has become more pivotal, with digg.com promoting 'digg meet ups' to now coincide with live episodes of *DiggNation* that serve as media events to confirm Rose's and Albrecht's celebrity. Meanwhile Revision3 has laid off a large number of its staff and shows as a result of the 2008 'credit crunch', focusing the brand's identity almost solely on the affiliation of the studio with digg.com via *DiggNation*.[37] Digg's 'democratic approach', therefore, is only valuable insofar as it is compatible with Rose's project of celebrity and self-enterprise. The lessons in group governance offered by Rose's success as entrepreneur of digg.com appear less about promoting a radical new form of democracy, nor its evisceration or dumbing down, but more in line with neo-liberal discourses that promote privatisation of public functions and the transformation of individuals into 'more responsible, accountable, and enterprising managers of themselves' (Ouellette and Hay, 2008: 24).

Nevertheless, Rose's and digg.com's trajectory still eschews a narrative that can easily be described as the co-option of participatory culture by media conglomerates. Henry Jenkins argues that social media forms like blogging represent a form of 'grassroots convergence' which, as a 'bottom up' process, intersect with the 'top down push of corporate convergence'. Jenkins is careful to balance the more optimistic claims of Levy regarding the way in which such cultural forms will enable the 'new proletariat [to] … free itself by uniting, by decategorizing itself, by forming alliances …'. Instead, in noting the intersection of corporate and grassroots convergence, Jenkins observes that the participatory culture of online cultures may be co-opted by commodity culture 'but can also increase the diversity of media culture, providing opportunities for greater inclusiveness' (Jenkins, 2006b: 151). Such rhetoric is clearly aligned with the arguments that understand the extension of celebrity to 'ordinary people' as democratic that I have discussed throughout this book, but their intersection produces troubling questions. In particular, what the example of Kevin Rose and digg suggests is a willingness to turn both the self – via entrepreneurial acts of transformation into a celebrity – and the user community – via selling the user base to advertisers, etc. – into commodity culture from *within*. Similar to the celebrity CEOs that are positioned as reconciling 'bottom-up' mechanisms with 'superhero' status, Rose's construction of his ordinary celebrity and its connection to the collective intelligence of digg.com promises 'emancipation whilst perpetuating inequalities' (Holmes-Smith quoted in Littler, 2007: 239).

This is not simply because of Rose's ownership of the site. Rather, the reward of celebrity itself, in exchange for the endeavours of self-enterprise and self-promotion, serves to act as a form of self-governance that is congruent with neo-liberal discourses of privatisation, personal responsibility and consumer choice. That is, Rose's persona – and digg.com itself – espouse a DIY ethos to not only celebrity, but also democracy: the site effectively 'empowers' the users of digg to determine what news is important in structuring the community's 'public sphere', wresting control from established media conglomerates and placing it in the hands of the community. However, in facilitating a consumer choice of which 'public spheres' to participate in, we must also be aware that any ensuing debates on these platforms occur on *private* property. As Jean Burgess has argued in relation to YouTube, such platforms are not 'really public at all, but a private enterprise generating public value as a side-effect of the active participation of consumer-citizens'. They therefore 'enable participation and engagement to flourish, while at the same time deriving value from them' (Burgess, 2011: forthcoming).

For digg and Kevin Rose the success of the site simultaneously serves to confirm Rose's celebrity as 'worth having' because, in the discourses of stardom, it brings attendant financial reward, social mobility and power. Rose's persona negotiates the paradoxes here of bottom-up, 'grassroots' convergence with top-down control by insisting on his 'ordinary' celebrity; all the while promoting what du Gay has suggested is the need for citizen-consumers to become '"entrepreneurs of the self" within a deregulated capitalist economy that devalues organized labor and job security' (quoted in Ouellette and Hay, 2008: 103). As with Ouellette and Hay's arguments, such an understanding of the entrepreneurial self involved in the formation of DIY celebrity suggests that if 'anything Jenkins' argument – like Hartley's – does not press hard enough at the paradoxes of freedom and control, of self-actualization through learning or of the practice of entering into forms of self-government as self-discipline' (ibid.: 224). Most importantly, for my purposes here, such an understanding is possible only via tracing the discourses of televisual fame – ordinariness, authenticity, intimacy and skill – into what many have argued are new, radically decontextualised forms of ordinary celebrity. The study of celebrity in all its various contexts, therefore, has much to learn from paying greater attention to the specificities of television fame.

Conclusion

Stardom and the small screen

A number of impetuses have been responsible for examining the television personality in such depth. First, a desire to revise and unpick the reasons for the apparent reluctance of film, television, media and celebrity studies to consider the television personality as worthy of extended attention; in particular to address the failure to examine television personalities as a site of cultural, economic, ideological and economic meaning in their own right. Arguably, this has been due to a positioning of the television personality as an ordinary and subservient form of fame compared to film stardom, whilst at the same time the expansion of fame to an increasingly diverse and 'ordinary' group of celebrities has tended to overlook the specificity of television's personality system. As Holmes has suggested, the proliferation of mass celebrity has led to 'something of a crisis in terminology when it comes to discussing fame in the contemporary media landscape' (Holmes, 2005b: 9)

In speaking to the specificity of televisual fame a second impetus, therefore, has been to address the often baffling, contradictory and unexplained use of the term 'television personality' within television, film, celebrity and media studies, whereby the term was used as a catch-all for every type of celebrity who appeared on television. I have argued that it is not only possible, but also *necessary*, to reserve particular terms within the general field of celebrity for specific kinds of performers in order to better understand celebrity culture, as well as television's role within this and society more widely. Even in an era of media convergence, where the boundaries between television and other digital media forms are increasingly less discrete, this book has suggested that television does produce its own distinct forms of fame. As chapters on early and digital television personalities in this book have demonstrated, televisual fame is a complex, hybrid formation whereby the television personality system intersects and intermingles with wider formations of celebrity culture: whether that is music hall, radio, Twitter or podcasting. Yet, despite these connections, what I hope is also clear from such a study is that it is not helpful to term all of television's most prominent performers merely as 'celebrities' or 'television personalities'. Moreover, taking televisual fame seriously and as a site worthy of study does not require us to subsume such fame within the rhetoric of stardom, nor simply treat it as part of a more pervasive celebrity culture. There are fundamental differences between the star and the television personality, the personality and presenter, actor or contestant and each has a different relationship to the status and culture of 'celebrity'. These differences have influenced my use of the term 'television personality' rather than, say, merely terming those discussed in this book as 'television stars' or 'television celebrities'.

Third, in turn, I have argued that we must move beyond film theory and an understanding of the term 'television personality' as signifying a 'lack' in relation to film stardom. Judging television personalities' fame by television standards, as the opening quote to this book directed us, allows us to understand their fame as achieved via skilled performances, their ordinariness and authenticity constructed and their ideological functions complex. Such a study demonstrates how the television personality is differentiated from other forms of celebrity, who may not have the same cultural, ideological, semiotic significance; most particularly because they may not always achieve the same longevity in their fame. Furthermore, I have suggested that the very fact that television personalities function in relation to notions of ordinariness, authenticity and intimacy, makes unpicking the ideological meanings of such performers and fame more pressing. Television personalities must be understood as actively involved in the promotion, and maintenance, of particular meanings about what it means to be 'ordinary' across a range of identity formations: from national identity to race, sexuality to gender. Television personalities are central to the way television teaches us about the projects of self-formation that circulate around not only a range of genres, but also in the creation and meaning of contemporary celebrity itself.

As part of this concern I have been interested to locate how later conceptual understandings of television fame might be better informed by an examination of their historical roots. Unearthing the archive of televisual fame is a task far beyond the scope of one book, let alone the two chapters that specifically address that issue here, but I hope to have pointed to the way in which UK broadcast history challenges taken-for-granted assumptions about television personalities – their ordinariness, intimacy, authenticity and performance modes – and has demonstrated these qualities are the result of particular historical, institutional, national and economic conjunctures. Tracing these discourses across a range of historical instances suggests how their meanings have changed over time, but also inflected wider formations and understanding of celebrity. Thus, a further interest has been to examine the way in which a closer analysis of televisual fame can help us better examine and understand emergent, DIY, forms of contemporary celebrity. The discourses of ordinariness, intimacy, skill and authenticity that I have demonstrated are central to television's formation of celebrity are likely to become more important in a digital, DIY, media landscape.

The book's discussion of the changing nature of celebrity and television points to my final concern to engage with fundamental debates in celebrity studies regarding the relative value and worth of contemporary fame. As I have suggested, this is a debate primarily structured around two binary positions that sees the extension of celebrity to more 'ordinary' people as either good or bad for democracy and society. I have attempted to move beyond these binaries and point to the way in which these debates, regardless of the position adopted, have tended to place television at the forefront of this extension of celebrity and, in so doing, have failed to accord due weight to the specificities and varieties of televisual fame. Of course, the chapters here make only one small contribution to the study of television personalities as important and distinct in their own right. The everydayness of television and the sheer volume of its flow, together with the proliferation of multiplatform programming, means not only that television's production of celebrity moves swiftly on but also that pinning down the intertextual persona of individual personalities becomes a difficult task. The examples chosen across the book predominantly focus on the United Kingdom, but do include a number of personalities who are perhaps no longer as important in the schedules as they once were (Cilla Black, for example). There is often a pressure in television studies, and one detects it in the emergent field of celebrity studies, for currency and the provision of up-to-date (almost totalising) accounts of programming, genres, economics or personalities. To some extent the endless flow of television itself creates this pressure. But as Jason Jacobs aptly described it in relation to the study of television aesthetics, this is an 'infantile disorder', and we would do well to learn from the confidence of our colleagues in film studies on this point (Jacobs, 2006).[1] However, whatever the national-specificity and the currency of the performers discussed in this book, my emphasis is on the conceptual mapping of television's personality system and, moreover, a discussion of those that we can truly deem television personalities as I have sought to define this category here.

Across these areas of analysis, it is worth noting that the role of the audience has been largely absent. Whilst I have suggested the way in which audiences themselves might be able to produce their own forms of celebrity via self-promotion and the mastering of antecedent forms of televisual skill, more work needs to be undertaken on the precise meanings and pleasures television personalities offer to audiences and fans. An examination of audiences will undoubtedly reveal the way in which television personalities offer specific identificatory positions that can enrich our understanding of the television personality system. By considering the television personality as an important text in itself, television and celebrity studies can subsequently consider what is the significance of the 'types' represented by current, past and failed television personalities. For example, whilst I have suggested that the domesticity of television does not necessarily produce personalities who can solely be understood in terms of their ability to amass large audiences via an 'inoffensive' televisual image, it is also true that the domestic nature of television and its links to the familial and feminine has led to a system that inherently produces more high profile female performers than its cinematic counterpart. Within the current British television landscape, Nigella Lawson, Davina McCall, Cat Deeley, Delia Smith and Judy Finnegan (with Richard Madeley, of course) may all be considered bankable television personalities who producers can 'safely' create vehicles for. Although a far cry from the sheer numbers and range of male televisual counterparts, in contrast to cinema, where Julia Roberts, Angelina Jolie and Sandra Bullock represent the almost singular presence of women as Hollywood blockbuster stars, femininity and televisual fame appear more easily reconciled (arguably making the ideological meanings pervaded a more important site of study: television personalities represent norms, rather than the exceptional). Equally, however, we may note the large absence of non-white faces on British television: of the personalities discussed, only Ainsley Harriott, Gok Wan and Ian Wright are Black-British, and with the disappearance of Sanjeev Bhasker and *The Kumars at No. 42* (Hat Trick, 2001–2006) from the schedules there are no British-Asian high profile personalities on contemporary UK television.

Finally, in the changing television landscape, where digital television and its multiplatform nature suggest a significant shift in broadcasting to narrowcasting, television personalities may become increasingly important. As channels utilise them as a branding device, television personalities are more likely to be recognised as markers of quality, differentiation and identificatory figures for viewers. Arguably, as specialisation occurs in the form of narrowcasting and new delivery platforms emerge, the ideological functioning of the television personality may become more apparent and an increased variety of television personality types may develop. A better understanding of television personalities has much to tell us about 'stardom and the small screen', not only in relation to television but also celebrity and digital culture more widely.

Notes

Introduction

1   Anon. (1956) *TV Mirror Annual*, London: Amalgamated Press.
2   Gallacher, I., *et al.* (2009) 'Goodbye Jade: Thousands turn out for Princess Diana-style funeral', *Daily Mail*, April 6. Available HTTP: www.dailymail. co.uk/tvshowbiz/article-1166725/Goodbye-Jade-Thousands-turn-Princess-Diana-style-funeral.html.
3   Hughes, D. (2009) 'Jack Straw climbs aboard the Jade Goody bandwagon', *The Telegraph*, February 20. Available HTTP: http://blogs.telegraph.co.uk/news/davidhughes/8660197/Jack_Straw_climbs_aboard_the_Jade_Goody_bandwagon/.
4   McVeigh, T. (2009) 'Why Jade's struggle for life is a tale of our times', *The Observer*, February 8, 30. Available HTTP: www.guardian.co.uk/lifeandstyle/2009/feb/08/jade-goody-cervical-cancer-debate.
5   Sky News, October 22 2009. Available HTTP: http://news.sky.com/sky-news/Home/UK-News/Jade-Goody-Credited-With-Large-Increase-In-Cervical-Cancer-Screening-In-Last-Year/Article/200910415411610?f=rss.
6   As *The Times* reported, Oprah Winfrey gave 'Barack Obama the ultimate celebrity endorsement' by declaring 'he is the one'. Oprah Winfrey, quoted in Reid, T. (2007) 'First lady of television, Oprah Winfrey, gives Barack Obama the ultimate celebrity endorsement', *The Times*, December 10. Available HTTP: www.timesonline.co.uk/tol/news/world/us_and_americas/us_elections/article3026893.ece.

1 The television personality system

1   See, for example, the 'starring race' special comment and debate section of *Feminist Media Studies*, 7(4): 455–469.
2   In relation to newscasters, see, for example, John Langer's essay on the 'Television's personality system' (Langer, 1997) and Margaret Morse's essay on the news personality (Morse, 1986). Of course, just as television actor and television personality may cross over positions, the newscaster may occasionally cross over into the position of television personality, as in the case of Natasha Kaplinsky who, besides presenting morning news programming, has appeared in *Strictly Come Dancing* (BBC, 2004–ongoing). In relation to

television comedians see Susan Murray's *Hitch Your Antenna to the Stars* (Murray, 2005), Brett Mills's study of sitcom (Mills, 2005) or Frank Krutnik and Steve Neale's examination of film and television comedy (Krutnik and Neale, 1990).

3   Indeed, drawing on Lury's arguments about television memory, Bonner suggests that Cilla's persona as a pop-singer is only available to older audiences: 'for younger viewers of *Blind Date*, she has only ever been "mumsie"' (Lury cited in Bonner, 2003: 74).

4   Indeed, comedy is one of the most difficult distinctions to make in terms of its 'vocational' or 'televisual' origin. I have opted to place performers like Graham Norton and Jonathan Ross on the side of the latter because of their programmes' reliance on the chat show format and the ability of such performers to marshal the attention of the cameras, studio audiences, celebrity guests and ordinary contestants. In addition, it is television that provides their main income and the monetary value to those who employ them.

5   Of course, I am conscious here that such televisual skills may be closely linked to those of radio performance and I discuss the relationship between radio and television further in Chapter 2. Similarities and differences in terms of qualities of voice, notions of intimacy and modes of address between both media is a larger discussion than I can have here. I therefore wish only to note that it would seem rather facile to exclude performers whose career spans both television and radio from consideration as television personalities. Such an approach would be analogous to negating the star status of those film stars who also perform on the theatre stage.

6   Lawson, M. (2001) 'On the box: who are these people?', *The Guardian*, November 20, G8. Available HTTP: www.guardian.co.uk/media/2001/nov/20/broadcasting.g23.

7   Ronald Waldman to 'All L.E. Producers', November 29 1954, T16/91/2 (BBC Written Archives Centre [BBC WAC hereafter]).

8   Saade, J., and Borgenicht, J. (2004) *The Reality TV Handbook: An Insider's Guide*, San Francisco, CA: Quirk Productions, 53–57.

Part I 'TV must train its own stars'

1   Payne, J. (1953) 'TV must train its own stars', *TV Mirror*, November 21, 1(13): 21.

2 An 'irreconcilable opposition'

1   Ronald Waldman to 'L.E. Producers', April 6 1951, T16/91/1 (BBC WAC).

2   Anon. (1958) 'Comedians find television can be no joke', *The Times*, November 5, n.p. Accessed via *Times Archive* 04/06/09.

3   Quoted in Williams, B. (1954) 'Will TV "kill" the music hall?', *TV Mirror*, July 10, 3(2): 13–27.

4   Eric Maschwitz to Director of Television Broadcasting, January 18 1960, T16/91/2 (BBC WAC).

5   Dagmar Kift's history of the music hall suggests that by the late 1940s and early 1950s few regional music hall venues remained, although notable

exceptions did exist – particularly in the north of England where the links to working-class culture traditionally associated with music hall remained at their strongest (Kift, 1996: 163–184).

6   Kift suggests that average capacity of London music halls was approximately 1,500 patrons (Kift, 1996: 21).
7   Anon. (1953) 'Lucky girl', *TV Mirror*, October 3, 1(6): 22.
8   Letter to 'Your Point-of-View' (1954) *TV Mirror*, October 16, 3(16): 5.
9   Shirley-Long (1954) 'Look Out', *TV Mirror*, October 2, 3(14): 8.
10 Goss, A. (1954) 'It all costs MONEY', *TV Mirror*, January 16, 1(16): 14.
11 Anon. (1953) '"Dessie": The star TV has forgotten', *TV Mirror* August 27, 1(2): 6.
12 Challis, D. (1954) 'My gamble: Interview with Benny Hill', *TV Mirror*, September 9, 3(10): 10–11.
13 Shirley-Long (1954) 'Look Out', *TV Mirror*, April 17, 2(16): 6.
14 Goss, A. (1954) 'It all costs MONEY', *TV Mirror*, January 16, 1(16): 14.
15 Ronald Waldman to Cecil Madden, November 15 1955, T16/91/2 (BBC WAC).
16 According to *The Times* figures examining pay in summer venues during 1957. Anon. (1958) 'Gay show beside the seaside', *The Times*, September 4, n.p. Accessed via *Times Archive* 04/06/09.
17 Williams, B. (1954) 'Will TV "kill" the music hall?'.
18 See 'Look Out' columns, *TV Mirror*, 3 July to 17 July, 1954.
19 Anon. (1955) 'Light fare', *The Times*, September 19, n.p. Accessed via *Times Archive* 04/06/09.
20 Anon. (1958) 'Comedians find television can be no joke', *The Times*, November 5.
21 Ronald Waldman to 'All L.E. Producers', November 29 1954, T16/91/1 (BBC WAC).
22 Ronald Waldman to 'L.E. Producers', April 6 1951, T16/91/1 (BBC WAC).
23 Quoted in Anon. (1953) 'Waldman speaks out', *TV Mirror*, October 24, 1(9): 9.
24 Pedrick, G. (1954) 'Variety: What Arthur Askey thinks', *Radio Times*, February 7–13, 122(1578): 6.
25 Letter to 'Your Point-of-View' (1954) *TV Mirror*, December 19, 1(17): 3.
26 Ronald Waldman to Cecil Madden, November 15 1955, T16/91/2 (BBC WAC).
27 Kenneth Adam to Eric Maschwitz, July 11 1958, T16/91/2 (BBC WAC).
28 Eric Maschwitz to Director of Television Broadcasts, January 18 1960, T16/91/2 (BBC WAC).
29 The audition notes on Benny Hill's BBC file describe him as 'a young man of very pleasant appearance in a dinner jacket ... with talent and a good personality. Should prove suitable Tele'. Audition Notes, February 5 1948, BH File 1, (BBC WAC).
30 Hunt's study makes the important point that 'the pathologising of Hill won't do ... with success on this scale, "attacks" and "defences" aren't entirely the point' (Hunt, 1998: 46).

31 In an interview with Roger Sands, conducted in 1983, Hills boasts that he is on the cover of French and Spanish *TV Times* at the same time (quoted in Slide, 1996: 104).

32 *TV Mirror* front cover, March 13, 1954, 2(11): 1.
Albert Moran's entry on Hill for the *Encyclopedia of Television* concurs, suggesting that Hill was not only 'in effect created by television', but was the first television comic to have been so constructed. Whilst there were equally, or indeed more, famous television personalities during the early 1950s, Moran notes that comics such as Tony Hancock or Arthur Askey established their 'definitive comic persona in radio and then extended this to television'. See Moran: http://www.museum.tv/archives/etv/H/htmlH/hillbenny/hill-benny.htm (site accessed 21 August, 2008).

33 Shirley-Long (1954) 'Look Out', *TV Mirror*, October 10, 1(7): 7.

34 Shirley-Long (1954) 'Look Out', *TV Mirror*, February 27, 2(9): 5.

35 Anon. (1954) 'Open letter to Benny Hill', *TV Mirror*, July 17 3(3): 9.

36 Ibid.

37 Anon. (1956) 'Hooray! Now I'm back on TV', *TV Times*, September 7, 4(45): 31.

38 Anon. (1959) 'Where intimate revue falls short on television', *The Times*, January 22, n.p. Accessed via *Times Archive* 04/06/09.

39 Williams, B. (1954) 'Bransby Williams remembers', *TV Mirror*, July 3, 3(1): 10.

40 Pedrick, G. (1954) 'Variety: What Arthur Askey thinks', 5.

41 It is, however, worth noting here that Auslander's use of this notion of performance of the actorly self is extended to television, and specifically television comedy, in an analysis of Roseanne Barr later in his book. This includes an examination of the performance modes of the sitcom and stand-up comedian on television, and thus provides a useful term of reference here in understanding the discourses of authenticity and sincerity evident in the 1950s (Auslander, 1997: 116–125).

42 Challis, D. (1954) 'My gamble: Interview with Benny Hill', 11.

43 Anon. (1953) '"Pleased to meet you"… say five million viewers', *TV Mirror*, August 27, 1(2): 4.

44 'Open letter to Benny Hill', op. cit.

45 George, B. (1955) 'A great man for repartee', *Radio Times*, December 31–January 13, 5.

46 Evans, W. S. (1954) 'Viewers have made him a STAR', *TV Mirror*, March 13, 2(11): 8.

47 Ayers, R. (1955) 'Benny Hill: Television comedian', *Radio Times*, December 31–January 13, 5.

48 Letter from Ronald Waldman to Richard Stone, October 10 1955, Ref. 35/RW, BH File 1 (BBC WAC).

49 From Tom Sloane to Television Bookings Manager, June 22 1956, BH File 1 (BBC WAC).

50 Shirley-Long (1954) 'Look Out', *TV Mirror*, January 2, 2(1): 7.

51 Letter from Ronald Waldman to Richard Stone, n.d. (the letter appears between that dated June 22, 1955 and the contract agreed below in Hill's file) BH File 1 (BBC WAC).

52 BBC Contract, *Benny Hill Show*, November 7 1957, Ref: 35/BB, BH File 1 (BBC WAC).

53 Letter from Tom Sloane to Richard Stone, April 1 1960, Ref 35/TS, BH File 2 (BBC WAC).

54 This first figure comes from a letter from Tom Sloane to Eric Maschwitz, April 22 1960, BH File 2 (BBC WAC), whereas Sloane's reference to the comparative size of Hill's proposed fee refers to a counter offer by the BBC that was closer to £11,000 in a letter from Tom Sloane to Eric Maschwitz, February 18 1960, copy/cao/17.11.1960, BH File 2 (BBC WAC).

55 Letter from Eric Maschwitz to Tom Sloane, May 19 1960, Ref: 4152 TC Main, BH File 2 (BBC WAC).

56 From Cecil Madden to Ronald Waldman, June 30 1952, T16/91/1 (BBC WAC).

57 Anon. (1958) 'When the best can be popular: Banishing a heresy', *The Times*, June 9, n.p. Accessed via *Times Archive* 12/06/09.

3 'Too much glamour?'

1 Shirley-Long (1955) 'Look Out', *TV Mirror*, April 16, 4(16): 7.

2 Dyer's discussion of Lana Turner indicates how 'glamour clothes distinguish the wearer from those whose clothes have to permit labour'; for Turner, this involved 'trains, folds in the skirt and off-the-shoulder dresses' (Dyer, 1991: 233).

3 Thomas, E. (1954) 'Thank you Ally Pally', *Radio Times*, March 12, 122(1583): 6.

4 Ibid.

5 BBC TV Policy General 1934–1939, 'Announcements', September 5 1935, T16/78 (BBC WAC).

6 Cecil Madden to Clive Rawes, September 8 1952, NM File 1 (BBC WAC).

7 Stanford, P. (2005) 'Bronwen Astor: Scandal and Lady Astor', *The Independent*, 17 December, 2006, n.p. Available HTTP: www.independent. co.uk/news/people/profiles/bronwen-astor-scandal-amp-lady-astor-428761.html (site accessed 12 March, 2009).

8 Anon. (1956) 'It's over to ITV for Mac Hobley', *TV Times*, May 4, 3(27): n.p.

9 Anon. 'Girl of the week', *TV Mirror*, December 11, 3(24): 9.

10 See Jeffery Sconce's work (2000) on haunted media for the way in which early television technical problems were often understood in terms of 'other-worldly' visitations.

11 Purser, P. (2001) 'Obituary: Peter Haigh', *The Guardian*, January 27, n.p. Available HTTP: www.guardian.co.uk/news/2001/jan/27/guardianobituaries.

12 Letters to 'Postcard competition: Invisible announcers?' (1954) *TV Mirror*, July 10, 3(2): 3.

13 Benedetta, M. (1954) 'The man for great occasions', *TV Mirror*, March 20, 2(12): 13

14 Peters, S. (1954) 'Sylvia Peters writes on what it's like being a TV announcer', *TV Mirror*, January 9, 2(2): 10.

15 BBC TV Policy General 1934–1939, 'Announcements', September 5 1935, T16/78, (BBC WAC).

16   From Ronald Waldman to Clive Rawes, January 18 1954, T16/91/1 (BBC WAC).

17   Anon. (1958) 'Great Britain: To the Queen's taste', *Time Magazine*, January 6. Available HTTP: www.time.com/time/magazine/article/0,9171,868093, 00.html.

18   Editor's response to reader letter to 'Your point-of-view' (1954) *TV Mirror*, March 27, 2(13): 3.

19   Rawes, C. (1954) 'Curtain up', *TV Mirror*, June 5, 2(23): 18.

20   Letters to 'Postcard competition: Invisible announcers?', op.cit.

21   Letter to 'Your point-of-view' (1955) *TV Mirror*, January 15, 4(3): 2.

22   Letter to 'Postcard competition: The beauties you chose' (1954) *TV Mirror*, February 6, 2(6): 3.

23   Letter to 'Your point-of-view' (1954) *TV Mirror*, March 6, 2(10): 3.

24   Peters, S., op. cit.

25   Anon. (1955) 'The stars enjoy their ... fan fair ... even though each letter may cost them a shilling', *TV Mirror*, March 12, 4(11): 23.

26   Letter to 'Your point-of-view', (1953) *TV Mirror*, October 24, 1(9): 21.

27   Peters, S., op. cit.

28   Anon. (1953) 'Sylvia Peters' new dresses', *TV Mirror*, September 19, 1(4): 17.

29   From Clive Rawes memorandum to Make-up and Wardrobe Manager, November 25 1953, NM File 1 (BBC WAC).

30   From Television Booking Manager to Head of Drama, Television, July 11 1958, NM File 1 (BBC WAC).

31   Rawes, C. (1953) 'Announcer's suite', *TV Mirror*, October 10, 1(7): 12.

32   Ibid.

33   Ackworth, M. (1954) 'This announcing business', *TV Mirror*, February 12, 2(7): 12.

34   Ibid.

35   Anon. (1954) 'Postcard competition', *TV Mirror*, February 6, 2(2): 2.

36   Ackworth, M., op. cit.

37   BBC TV Policy General 1934–1939, 'Announcements', January 1 1936, T16/78, (BBC WAC).

38   Noelle Middleton contract, December 15 1953, NM File 1 (BBC WAC).

39   Malcolm, M. (1954) 'On the back of my script', *TV Mirror*, March 27, 2(13): 13.

40   Shirley-Long (1954) 'Look Out', *TV Mirror*, September 4, 3(10): 9.

41   Anon. (1955)) 'Ad spot news', *TV Mirror*, December 17, 5(25): 25.

42   Green, J. (1956) 'Is "voice only" rule right?', *TV Times*, January 6, 2(16): 7.

43   Ibid.

44   Waldman, R. (1954) 'The variety of television variety', *Radio Times Annual 1954*, London: BBC Publishing, 52–53.

Part II 'Oooh, I'm an entertainer ... it's what I do'

1   A sitcom within the internal narrative world of the sitcom *Extras*.

2   Or, for international marketing purposes, *American Idol* on the programme's US airing.

3   See for example *Big Brother 3* contestant Alex Sibley's performance to 'That's the way I like it', characterised by mime and direct address to the camera. Available HTTP: http://video.google.com/videoplay?docid=-5953001553062667504#.

4   See Jean's comment on Harrington, S. (2007) 'The best 10 minutes of television? ... Ever?', *Flow* 5.06. Available HTTP: http://flowtv.org/?p=82.

5   Wyatt, E. (2007) 'Going out, Gervais picks bang over whimper', *The New York Times*, December 15. Available HTTP: www.nytimes.com/2007/12/15/arts/television/15gerv.html?_r=1.

6   Itzkoff, D. (2009) 'Winning Oscars and demolishing celebrities with Ricky Gervais: Part 1', *The New York Times*, March 25. Available HTTP: http://artsbeat.blogs.nytimes.com/2009/03/25/winning-oscars-and-demolishing-celebrities-with-ricky-gervais-part-1/.

4 'You don't know anyone ... '

1   Hilton, B. (2009) 'Is swearing big and clever? No, that's why it's funny: Ricky Gervais interview', *heat*, March 7–13, 68.

2   Hilton, B. (2005) 'I work out seven days a week. Incredible isn't it: Ricky Gervais interview', *heat*, July 23–29, 88.

3   Interviewed on *This Morning*, February 18, 2009, transcript. Available HTTP: www.digitalspy.co.uk/tv/news/a179092/ant--dec-smtv-is-career-highlight.html.

4   Anon. (2000) 'Crunch time for Ant and Dec', *TV Times*, n.d.: n.p.

5   Reports based on estimates as a £30million 30-month contract. See Gibson, O. (2008) 'Trust clears BBC of overpaying its top stars', *The Guardian*, June 3. Available HTTP: www.guardian.co.uk/media/2008/jun/03/bbc.television.

6   See Karen Lury's work for an excellent analysis of the role performance plays in the changing economies of post-broadcast television represented by ITV Play (Lury, 2011).

7   Brown, M., and Dowell, B. (2009) 'BBC stars are told: The days of big pay deals are over', *The Guardian*, June 10. Available HTTP: www.guardian.co.uk/media/2009/jun/10/bbc-pay-top-stars.

8   As Nigel Lythgoe, creator of *Popstars*, *Survivor* and *So You Think You Can Dance?*, admits 'Certain formats should never be forgotten, *Blind Date* for instance, because *Britain's Got Talent* is really *New Faces* or *The Gong Show*, whilst we're [*So You Think You Can Dance?*] basically *Opportunity Knocks*'. Interviewed in Armstrong, S. (2010) 'Nice work for nasty Nigel Lythgoe', *The Guardian*, January 11. Available HTTP: www.guardian.co.uk/media/2010/jan/11/nigel-lythgoe-television-dance.

9   Shirley-Long (1953) 'Lucky girl', *TV Mirror*, October 3, 1(6): 22.

10 Littlejohn, G. (2006) '£20 million Xtra for Cowell', *London Evening Standard*, December 18. Available HTTP: www.thisislondon.co.uk/music/article-23378694-20-million-xtra-for-cowell.do.

11 Plunkett, J., and Pidd, H. (2010) 'Jonathan Ross leaves the BBC', *The Guardian*, January 7. Available HTTP: www.guardian.co.uk/media/2010/jan/07/jonathan-ross-bbc-moving-on.

12   Letters to 'Postcard competition: My favourite star – and why?', (1953) *TV Mirror*, December 5, 1(15): 3.

13   From Michael Peacock (Assistant Head of Outside Broadcasts, Television) to Cecil Madden, April 29 1958, RD File 2c 1958 (BBC WAC).

14   *Media Talk* podcast episode January 7 2010. Available HTTP: www.guardian.co.uk/media/organgrinder/audio/2010/jan/07/media-talk-podcast-jonathan-ross-quits-bbc-nigel-lythgoe.

15   See Lisa Kelly's excellent analysis of the affair and the role of 'comedy' in scandal (Kelly, 2010).

16   Lawson, M. (2010) 'Jonathan Ross's downfall was of his own making', *The Guardian*, January 7. Available HTTP: www.guardian.co.uk/media/2010/jan/07/jonathan-ross-bbc-downfall.

17   Frith, N. (2009) 'The politics factor: Simon Cowell unveils plans to launch election debate show', *Daily Mail*, December 15. Available HTTP: www.dailymail.co.uk/news/article-1236002/The-Politics-Factor-Simon-Cowell-unveils-plan-launch-election-debate-show.html.

18   Ibid.

19   Robinson, J., and Jones, S. (2010) 'Mark Thompson sparks new BBC row with county council comment', *The Guardian*, January 8. Available HTTP: www.guardian.co.uk/media/2010/jan/08/mark-thompson-row-bbc-council.

20   Conlan, T., and Sweney, M. (2008) 'Jeremy Clarkson and BBC Worldwide become business partners', *The Guardian*, August 8. Available HTTP: www.guardian.co.uk/media/2008/aug/08/jeremyclarkson.bbc.

5 The art of 'being yourself'

1   Leeman, D. (1954) 'Are panel games easy money?', *TV Mirror*, October 2, 3(14): 25.

2   For example, Joanne Hollows discusses the way in which cookery functions as a 'performance of the self' for the 'bachelor' that is invested in particular lifestyle and taste codes that are in line with particular gendered and classed dispositions towards cookery and domestic labour (Hollows, 2002: 152).

3   The star terminology is interesting here, calling up the Hollywood studio era of stardom, which is further reinforced by Ken Roaft's (then Deputy Controller of London Weekend Television) comments in the same article that 'LWT has always operated a mini-star system'. Quoted in Wood, C. (1995) 'Star cheque', *Broadcast*, February 10, 22.

4   See Bill Lewis's essay on the use of space in the game show to indicate a contestant's progression (Lewis, 1986).

6 Just 'an ordinary bloke'

1   Quoted in Bhat, D. (2006) 'Steve was an ordinary bloke – he doesn't need a state funeral', *The Times*, September 6. Available HTTP: www.timesonline.co.uk/tol/news/world/article629956.ece.

2   According to a number of sources, a worldwide audience of 360 million tuned in to the event held at Australia Zoo in Queensland, where 5,000

mourners (largely dressed in Irwin's trademark khaki short and shirts) attended the ceremony. See: www.cbsnews.com/stories/2006/09/19/ entertainment/main2024587_page2.shtml?tag=contentMain;contentBody.

3 Maynard, R. (2006) 'Australia stands still for Steve Irwin's memorial', *The Guardian*, September 21. Available HTTP: www.guardian.co.uk/ world/2006/sep/21/australia.mainsection.

4 Greer, G. (2006) 'That sort of self-delusion is what it takes to be a real Aussie larrikin', *The Guardian*, September 5. Available HTTP: www.guardian. co.uk/world/2006/sep/05/australia.

5 Katz, I. (2003) 'Were we right to do this?', *The Guardian*, January 8. Available HTTP: www.guardian.co.uk/artanddesign/2003/jan/08/art. artsfeatures.

6 Lister, D. (2003) 'Artist says sorry for "insult" to Cilla Black', *The Independent*, January 8. Available HTTP: www.independent.co.uk/news/ media/artist-says--sorry-for--insult-to--cilla-black-612824.html.

7 Gunby, E., and Slater, M. (2002) 'Battle of the Scousers', *Liverpool Echo*, December 17. Available HTTP: www.liverpoolecho.co.uk/liverpool-news/ local-news/2002/12/17/battle-of-the-scousers-100252-12461176/.

8 Marshall, W. (1983) 'Cilla's back in business, all dolled up in diamonds and sequins, hoovering the floor', *Daily Mirror*, March 3, 4.

9 Mackenzie, S. (1990) 'A very ordinary superstar', *The Guardian*, October 17, 36.

10 Anon. (1989) 'Tories turn on to Cilla's dating game', *Today*, February 16, 3.

11 Davies, A. (1989) 'Cilla blasts TV crowd for booing at Maggie!', *The Sun* November 23, 4.

12 BBC Press Release, June 6 2002. Available HTTP: www.bbc.co.uk/press office/pressreleases/stories/2002/06_june/28/alan_titchmarsh.shtml.

13 Mitchell, D. (2009) 'If Delia Smith's not a star, I'm a suet pudding', *The Observer*, December 20. Available HTTP: www.guardian.co.uk/ commentisfree/2009/dec/20/david-mitchell-bbc-delia-smith.

14 Richardson, N. (2001) 'Horny-minded son of the soil', *The Telegraph*, April 9. Available HTTP: www.telegraph.co.uk/culture/4722806/Horny- minded-son-of-the-soil.html.

15 As Sam Wollaston, a regular TV critic for *The Guardian*, described it: 'If Titchmarsh's voice was a building it would be a village hall, or perhaps a tea room. If it was a musical ensemble, it would be a brass band. It's cosy and quaint, ever so slightly cheeky, but not in a way that's going to upset anyone'. Wollaston, S. (2007) 'Last night's TV', *The Guardian*, October 20. Available HTTP: http://media.guardian.co.uk/broadcast/comment/0,,2195600,00. html.

16 A recurrent aural motif in *How to Be a Gardener* is the Beta Band's *Squares*, with its lyrics, 'I fell asleep among the flowers', serving to create a relaxed aesthetic.

17 Woods, J. (2004) 'And just why shouldn't I present the Proms?', *The Daily Telegraph*, August 8. Available HTTP: www.telegraph.co.uk/arts/main. jhtml?xml=/arts/2004/07/08/bmtitc08.xml&sSheet=/arts/2004/07/10/ ixartright.html.

18 Quoted in Cook, E. (2007) 'Alan Titchmarsh: Heavenly host', *The Times*, September 8. Available HTTP: http://women.timesonline.co.uk/tol/life_and_style/women/body_and_soul/article2406250.ece.

19 McCririck is a horse-racing pundit who hosted Channel 4's long-running *At the Races* and has courted controversy throughout his television career by playing to a persona of bigotry and misogyny.

20 Barber, L. (2000) 'Gardener's question time', *The Observer*, October 22. Available HTTP: http://observer.guardian.co.uk/print/0,3858,4079811-102278,00.html.

21 Barber opens her article on Titchmarsh by proclaiming: 'Alan Titchmarsh is a sex god. Deep breath. Try again. Alan Titchmarsh is a sex god. Titchmarsh. Alan. Sex. God. Is…. Nope. It's no good – I still can't make that leap of faith' (ibid.).

22 Anon. (2006) 'A constant gardener', *Saga Magazine*, June, 2006.

23 Ibid.

24 Cook, E. (2007) 'Alan Titchmarsh: Heavenly host'.

25 Wollaston, S. (2007) 'Alan Titchmarsh's Britain – where women bake fruit-cakes and men grow giant vegetables', *The Guardian*, June 4, G2, 31.

7 'Get Internet famous! (Even if you're nobody)'

1 http://twitter.com/stephenfry/status/1174476459.

2 http://www.guardian.co.uk/media/mediamonkeyblog/2009/feb/04/stephen-fry-stuck-in-lift.

3 http://digg.com/tech_news/Stephen_Fry_FINALLY_bringing_Twitter_into_British_mainstream.

4 Jarvis, J. (2008) 'In Mumbai, witnesses are writing the news', *Media Guardian*, December 1. Available HTTP: www.guardian.co.uk/media/2008/dec/01/mumbai-terror-digital-media.

5 Stone, B. (2008) 'Digg.com digs up some more cash', *The New York Times Blog*, posted September 24. Available HTTP: http://bits.blogs.nytimes.com/2008/09/24/diggcom-digs-up-some-more-cash/.

6 The 'web stars' quote comes from Johnson, B. (2008) 'Stars in your lap', *The Guardian Weekend Magazine*, February 23. Available HTTP: www.guardian.co.uk/technology/2008/feb/23/interviews.internet; the 'web personalities' quote comes from Sarno, D. (2008) 'Revision3's Web TV runs on star power', *LA Times Web Scout Blog*, posted July 29. Available HTTP: http://latimesblogs.latimes.com/webscout/2008/07/revision3s-web.html; and the 'most famous man on the Internet' comes from Chafkin, M. (2008) 'Kevin Rose of Digg: The most famous man on the Internet', *Inc Magazine*, November. Available HTTP: www.inc.com/magazine/20081101/keeevviin_Printer_Friendly.html.

7 Schonfeld, E. (2008) 'Barack Obama overtakes Kevin Rose on Twitter – McCain is nowhere in sight', *Tech Crunch*, August 13. Available HTTP: www.techcrunch.com/2008/08/13/barack-obama-overtakes-kevin-rose-on-twitter-mccain-is-nowhere-in-sight/. *Twitter* lets users send short, 140 characters or less, messages about their current activities to their 'followers', who subscribe to a *Twitter*-feed and receive the messages in real-time, either

online or via mobile phone. See: http://twitter.com/kevinrose; and http://twitter.com/BarackObama.

8   Business Week Tech Team (2008) 'The poster boy: Kevin Rose', *Business Week*, n.d. Available HTTP: http://images.businessweek.com/ss/08/09/0929_most_influential/18.htm.

9   Johnson, B. (2008) 'Stars in your lap', *The Guardian Weekend Magazine*, February 23.

10   Platforms such as Twitter can therefore be understood as lying at the intersection of publicity and promotion discussed in Chapter 6.

11   My thanks to Sean Redmond for elucidating this point.

12   Although, in October 2009, the studios had not given up trying to exhort such control, with Disney and Dreamworks reportedly placing limitations on the use of twitter and social networking sites in stars' contracts, www.guardian.co.uk/film/2009/oct/19/hollywood-twitter.

13   http://twitter.com/mrskutcher/status/1366809329.

14   Chivers, T. (2009) 'Stephen Fry Twitter boost for schoolgirl singer Sunrise Sunset', *The Telegraph*, October 15. Available HTTP: www.telegraph.co.uk/technology/twitter/6334106/Stephen-Fry-Twitter-boost-for-schoolgirl-singer-Sunrise-Sunset.html.

15   http://twitterholic.com/top100/followers/ (site visited 30 October 2009). The list also features a number of pop music and movie stars, such as Britney Spears and Ashton Kutcher, but the list otherwise contains corporations (CNN) and politicians (Obama).

16   Schofield, J. (2009) 'Are celebrities good for the future of the Twitterverse?', *The Guardian*, February 12. Available HTTP: www.guardian.co.uk/technology/2009/feb/12/twitter-celebrity.

17   *The Family Guy*'s status as cult or fan culture is evidenced by the kind of fan activism that Roberta Pearson discusses in her work (Pearson, 2011).

18   Helft, M. (2006) 'Young Internet producers, bankrolled, are seeking act II', *The New York Times*, September 25. Available HTTP: www.nytimes.com/2006/09/25/technology/25digg.html?scp=3&sq=%22kevin%20rose%22&st=cse.

19   Albrecht quoted in Johnson, op. cit.

20   Rose quoted in Helft, op. cit.

21   Quoted in Johnson, op. cit.

22   Quoted in Johnson, op. cit.

23   Tanz, J. (2008) 'Almost famous', *Wired*, August 2008: 106–125. As the article goes on to explain, *Gawper* – along with other media gossip sites such as *Radar Online* and *Valleywag* – 'detail her every exploit'.

24   Chafkin, op. cit..

25   Ibid.

26   See for example, http://money.cnn.com/galleries/2007/biz2/0706/gallery.peoplewhomatter.biz2/72.html or http://images.businessweek.com/ss/09/05/0508_ceos_who_twitter/32.htm.

27   *kevinrose.com*, posted October 25, 2008. Available HTTP: http://kevinrose.com/blogg/2008/10/26/forget-web-2030-start-something-during-web-25.html.

28 Rose, K. (2009) '10 ways to increase your Twitter followers', *TechCrunch*, January 25, http://www.techcrunch.com/2009/01/25/kevin-rose-10-ways-to-increase-your-twitter-followers/.

29 http://revision3.com/about/.

30 Margolis, Z. (2008) 'The democratic approach is a very valuable thing', *The Guardian: Technology*, June 12, T5. Available HTTP: http://www.guardian.co.uk/technology/2008/jun/12/interviews.internet.

31 Ibid.

32 Anon. (2008) 'More trouble for Hollywood? Kevin Rose ditch cable, TiVo for Internet, Netflix', *LA Times Blogs: Technology*, posted October 28. Available HTTP: http://latimesblogs.latimes.com/technology/2008/10/more-trouble-fo.html.

33 Sarno, D. (2008) 'Revision3's Web TV Runs on Star Power', *LA Times Web Scout Blog*, posted July 29.

34 Rose quoted in Stone, B. (2007) 'In web uproar: Antipiracy codes spreads wildly', *The New York Times*, May 3. www.nytimes.com/2007/05/03/technology/03code.html?_r=1&sq=%22kevin%20rose%22&st–cse&adxnnl=1&oref=slogin&scp=3&adxnnlx=1226649791-JpU+nvZoKtGfa24C/8WLjQ.

35 Rose, K. (2007) 'Digg this: 09-f9-11—02-9d-74-e3—5b-d8-41-56-c5-63-56-88-c0', *Digg: The Blog*, posted May 1. Available HTTP: http://blog.digg.com/?p=74.

36 See: www.techcrunch.com/2008/07/22/google-in-final-negotiations-to-acquire-digg-for-around-200-million/.

37 The studio's other main commitment has been to *The Totally Rad Show*, which is fronted by Alex Albrecht.

Conclusion

1   Of course, this is not to deny film studies has pressures – indeed, in the United Kingdom, where the move to assess university's research funding in relationship to 'impact', such pressures may be felt more acutely in the predominantly Arts and Humanities based film departments. Again, this is not to suggest that Arts and Humanities disciplines cannot have social, economic and other forms of impact.

References

Andrejevic, M. (2002) 'The kinder, gentler gaze of *Big Brother*: Reality TV in the era of digital capitalism', *New Media & Society*, 4(2): 251–270.

Auslander, P. (1997) *From Acting to Performance: Essays in Modernism and Postmodernism*, London: Routledge.

—— (1999) *Liveness*, London: Routledge.

Babbington, B. (ed.) (2001) *British Stars and Stardom: From Alma Taylor to Sean Connery*, Manchester: Manchester University Press.

Bailey, K. (1950) *Here's Television*, London: Vox Mundi.

—— (1957) *The Television Annual for 1956*, London: Odhams Press Limited.

Becker, C. (2009) *It's the Pictures that Got Small: Hollywood Film Stars on 1950s Television*, Middleton, CT: Wesleyan University Press.

Bell, D., and Hollows, J. (2005) 'Making sense of ordinary lifestyles', in D. Bell and J. Hollows (eds) *Ordinary Lifestyles: Popular Media, Consumption and Taste*, Maidenhead: Open University Press, 1–18.

Bell, E., and Gray, A. (2007) 'History on television: Charisma, narrative and knowledge', in H. Wheatley (ed.) *Re-viewing Television History: Critical Issues in Television Historiography*, London: I.B. Tauris, 142–155.

Bennett, J. (2007) '*Head On*: Multicultural representations of Australian identity in 1990s national cinema', *Studies in Australasian Cinema*, 1(1): 61–78.

—— (2008) 'The television personality system: Televisual stardom revisited after film theory', *Screen*, 49(1): 32–50.

—— (2009) 'From flow to user flows: Understanding "good science" programming in the digital TV landscape', in R. Holliman *et al.* (eds), *Investigating Science Communication in the Information Age: Implications for Public Engagement and Popular Media*, Oxford: Oxford University Press, 183–204.

—— (2011) 'Architectures of participation: Fame, television and Web2.0', in J. Bennett and N. Strange (eds) *Television as Digital Media*, Durham, NC: Duke University Press, forthcoming.

Bennett, J., and Holmes, S. (2010) 'The "place" of television in celebrity studies', *Celebrity Studies Journal*, 1(1): 65–80.

Bennett, T., and Woollacott, J. (1987) *Bond and Beyond: The Political Career of a Popular Hero*, London: MacMillan Press.

Bennett-Jones, P. (2006) 'Fortune favours the brave', in M. Collins (ed.) *Shooting Stars: A Collection of Essays, Musings and Rants on Talent and TV in the Noughties and Beyond*, London: Premium Publishing, 39–47.

Berry, S. (2000) *Screen Style: Fashion and Femininity in 1930s Hollywood*, Minneapolis, MN: University of Minnesota Press.

Bignell, J. (2005a) 'Exemplarity, pedagogy and television history', *New Review of Film and Television Studies*, 3(1): 15–32.

—— (2005b) 'And the rest is history: Lew Grade, creation narratives and television historiography', in C. Johnson and R. Turnock (eds) *ITV Cultures: Independent Television Over Fifty Years*, Maidenhead: Open University Press, 57–70.

Biressi, A., and Nunn, H. (eds) (2004) *Reality TV: Realism and Relativism*, London: Wallflower Press.

Boddy, W. (2004) *New Media and Popular Imagination: Launching Radio, Television, and Digital Media in the United States*, Oxford: Oxford University Press.

Bonner, F. (2003) *Ordinary Television*, London, Sage.

—— (2009) 'Bouncing off one another: Double acts and teams in television presenting', paper presented at *Screen Studies Conference*, Glasgow University, 3–5 July, 2009.

Boorstin, D. J. (1961) *The Image: Or What Happened to the American Dream*, Harmondsworth: Penguin.

Bourdon, J. (2004) 'Old and new ghosts: Public service television and the popular – a history', *European Journal of Cultural Studies*, 7(3): 283–304.

Bratten, L. C. (2002) 'Nothin' could be Finah: *The Dinah Shore Chevy Show*', in J. Thumin (ed.) *Small Screens, Big Ideas: Television in the 1950s*, London: I.B. Tauris, 88–104.

Briggs, A. (1995) *The History of Broadcasting in the United Kingdom. Vol.4: Sound and Vision*, Oxford: Oxford University Press (original work published 1979).

Bruns, A. (2008) *Blogs, Wikipedia, Second Life, and Beyond: From Production to Produsage*, New York: Peter Lang.

Brunsdon, C. (2003) 'Lifestyling Britain: The 8–9 slot on British television', *International Journal of Cultural Studies*, 6(1): 5–23.

—— (2005) 'Feminism, post-feminism, Martha, Martha and Nigella', *Cinema Journal*, 44(2): 110–116.

Brunsdon, C., Johnson, C., Moseley, R., and Wheatley, H. (2001) 'Factual entertainment on British television: The Midlands TV Research Group's "8–9 Project"', *European Journal of Cultural Studies*, 4(1): 29–26.

Burgess, J. (2006a) 'Defining vernacular creativity', *Creativity/Machine*, posted May 10. Available HTTP: creativitymachine.net/2006/05/10/defining-vernacular-creativity/.

—— (2006b) 'Hearing ordinary voices: Cultural studies, vernacular creativity and digital storytelling', *Continuum: Journal of Media & Cultural Studies*, 20(2): 201–214.

—— (2011) 'User-created content and everyday cultural practice: Lessons from YouTube', in J. Bennett and N. Strange (eds) *Television as Digital Media*, Durham, NC: Duke University Press, forthcoming.

Butler, J. G. (1991) 'I'm not a doctor, but I play one on TV', *Cinema Journal*, 30(4): 74–89.

Caldwell, J. (2004) 'Convergence television: Aggregating form and repurposing content in the culture of conglomeration', in L. Spigel and J. Olsson (eds)

Television after TV: Essays on a Medium in Transition, Durham, NC: Duke University Press, 41–74.

—— (2008) *Production Culture: Industrial Reflexivity and Critical Practice in Film and Television*, Durham, NC: Duke University Press.

—— (2011) 'Worker blowback: User-generated, worker-generated and producer-generated content within collapsing production workflows', in J. Bennett and N. Strange (eds) *Television as Digital Media*, Durham, NC: Duke University Press, forthcoming.

Cardwell, S. (2006) '"Television aesthetics" and close analysis: Style mood and engagement in *Perfect Strangers*', in J. Gibbs and D. Pye (eds) *Style and Meaning: Studies in the Detailed Analysis of Film*, Manchester: Manchester University Press, 179–194.

Caughie, J. (2000) *Television Drama: Realism, Modernism and British Culture*, Oxford: Oxford University Press.

Collins, M. (ed.) (2006) *Shooting Stars: A Collection of Essays, Musings and Rants on Talent and TV in the Noughties and Beyond*, London: Premium Publishing.

Couldry, N. (2002) *Media Rituals: A Critical Approach*, New York: Routledge.

—— (2004) 'Teaching us to fake it: The ritualized norms of television's 'reality' games', in S. Murray and L. Ouellette (eds) *Reality TV: Remaking Television Culture*, London: New York University Press, 57–74.

Creeber, G. (2004) *Serial Television: Big Drama on the Small Screen*, London: BFI Publishing.

Creeber, G., and Hills, M. (2007) 'Editorial – TVIII: Into or towards a new television age?', *New Review of Film and Television*, 5(1): 1–4.

Crisell, A. (1994) *Understanding Radio*, 2nd edn, London: Routledge.

—— (2002) *An Introductory History of British Broadcasting*, 2nd edn, London: Routledge.

Dawson, M. (2007) 'Little players, big shows: Format, narration, and style on television's new smaller screens', *Convergence*, 13(3): 234–235.

deCordova, R. (1990) *Picture Personalities: The Emergence of the Star System in America*, Urbana, IL: University of Illinois Press.

Department for Culture, Media and Sport (2006) *White Paper – A Public Service for All: The BBC in the Digital Age*, London: HMSO.

Desjardins, M. (2002) 'Maureen O'Hara's "Confidential" life: Recycling stars through gossip and moral biography', in J. Thumin (ed.) *Small Screens, Big Ideas: Television in the 1950s*, London: I.B. Tauris, 118–130.

—— (2009) '"The elegance ... is almost overwhelming": Discursive struggles over models for early television stardom', paper presented at *Télévision : Le moment expérimental de l'invention a l'institution (1935–1955)*, International Colloquium University Paris 8/l'Institut National de l'Audiovisuel, 27–29 May, 2009.

Doty, A. (1990) 'The cabinet of Lucy Ricardo: Lucille Ball's star image', *Cinema Journal*, 29(4): 3–20.

Dyer, R. (1973) *Light Entertainment*, London: BFI.

—— (1979) *Teachers' Study Guide 1: Stars*, London: Educational Advisory Service/BFI Publishing.

—— (1981) 'Entertainment and utopia', in R. Altman (ed.) *Genre: The Musical*, London: BFI Publishing, 175–189.

—— (1986) *Heavenly Bodies: Film Stars and Society*, London: Macmillan.

—— (1991) 'Four films of Lana Turner', in J. G. Butler (ed.) *Star Texts: Image and Performance in Film and Television*, Detroit, MI: Wayne State University Press, 214–239.

—— (2000) 'A *Star is Born* and the construction of authenticity', in C. Gledhill (ed.) *Stardom: Industry of Desire*, London: Routledge, 132–140.

—— (2001) *Stars*, revised edn, London: BFI Publishing (original work published 1979).

Ellis, J. (1982) 'Star/industry/image', in *Star Signs: Papers from a Weekend Workshop*, London: BFI Publishing, 1–12.

—— (1991) 'Stars as a cinematic phenomenon' in J. G Butler (ed.) *Star Texts: Image and Performance in Film and Television*, Detroit, MI: Wayne State University Press, 300–315.

—— (1992) *Visible Fictions: Cinema, Television, Video*, London: Routledge (original work published 1982).

—— (2000) *Seeing Things: Television in the Age of Uncertainty*, London: I.B. Tauris.

Emery, D. (2006) 'Foreword', in M. Collins (ed.) *Shooting Stars: A Collection of Essays, Musings and Rants on Talent and TV in the Noughties and Beyond*, London: Premium Publishing, 7–15.

Evans, J., and Hesmondhalgh, D. (2005) *Understanding Media: Inside Celebrity*, London: Open University Press/McGraw Hill.

Gamson, J. (1994) *Claims to Fame: Celebrity in Contemporary America*, Berkeley, CA: University of California Press.

—— (2001) 'The assembly line of greatness: Celebrity in twentieth-century America', in C. L. Harrington, and D. D. Bielby (eds) *Popular Culture: Production and Consumption*, Oxford: Blackwell, 259–282.

Geraghty, C. (2000) 'Re-examining stardom: Questions of texts, bodies and performance', in C. Gledhill and L. Williams (eds) *Reinventing Film Studies*, London: Arnold, 183–201.

—— (2003) 'Aesthetics and quality in popular drama', *International Journal of Cultural Studies*, 6(1): 25–45.

Giddens, A. (1991) *Modernity and Self Identity: Self and Society in the Late Modern Age*, Palo Alto, CA: Stanford University Press.

Goddard, P. (1991) '*Hancock's Half-Hour*: A watershed in British television comedy', in J. Corner (ed.) *Popular Television in Britain: Studies in Cultural History*, London: BFI Publishing, 75–89.

Goffman, E. (1969) *The Presentation of the Self in Everyday Life*, London: Penguin.

Gregg, M. (2007) 'The importance of being ordinary', *International Journal of Cultural Studies*, 10(1): 95–104.

Grossberg, L. (1987) 'The in-difference of television', *Screen*, 28(2): 28–45.

Guignon, C. (2004) *On Being Authentic*, London: Routledge.

Gunning, T. (1986) 'The cinema of attraction: Early film, its spectators and the avant-garde', *Wide Angle*, 8(3/4): 63–70.

Hall, S. (1993) 'Culture, community, nation', *Cultural Studies*, 7(3): 349–363.

Hartley, J. (1999) *Uses of Television*, London: Routledge.

—— (2004a) '"Kiss Me Kat": Shakespeare, *Big Brother*, and the taming of the self', in S. Murray, and L. Ouellette (eds) *Reality TV: Remaking Television Culture*, New York: York University Press, 303–322.

—— (2004b) 'From republic of letters to television republic? Citizen readers in the era of broadcast television', in L. Spigel and J. Olsson. (eds) *Television after TV: Essays on a Medium in Transition*, Durham, NC: Duke University Press, 386–417.

Heap, J. (1951) *Daily Mail Television Handbook*, Stoke-on-Trent: Associated Newspapers.

Hearn, A. (2006) '"John, a 20-year-old Boston native with a great sense of humour": On the spectacularization of the "self" and the incorporation of identity in the age of reality TV', in P. D. Marshall (ed.) *The Celebrity Culture Reader*, London: Routledge, 618–633.

Herring, J. (2006) 'Nice programme, shame about the face', in M. Collins (ed.) *Shooting Stars: A Collection of Essays, Musings and Rants on Talent and TV in the Noughties and Beyond*, London: Premium Publishing, 57–67.

Hill, A. (2002) '*Big Brother*: The real audience', *Television & New Media*, 3(3): 323–341.

Hills, M. (2006) 'Not just another powerless elite? When media fans become subcultural celebrities', in S. Holmes and S. Redmond (eds) *Framing Celebrity: New Directions in Celebrity Culture*, London: Routledge, 101–118.

Holland, P. (1987) 'When a woman reads the news', in H. Baehr and G. Dyer (eds) *Boxed in: Women and Television*, London: Pandora Press, 133–150.

Hollows, J. (2002) 'The bachelor dinner: Masculinity, class and cooking in *Playboy*, 1953–61', *Continuum: Journal of Media & Cultural Studies*, 16(2): 143–155.

—— (2003a) 'Oliver's twist: Leisure, labour and domestic masculinity in *The Naked Chef*', *International Journal of Cultural Studies*, 6(2): 229–248.

—— (2003b) 'Feeling like a domestic goddess: Post-feminism and cooking', *European Journal of Cultural Studies*, 6(2): 179–202.

Holmes, S. (2001) 'As they really are, and in close-up': Film stars on 1950s British television', *Screen*, 42(2): 167–187.

—— (2004a) '"All you've got to worry about is having a cup of tea and doing a bit of sunbathing...": Approaching celebrity in *Big Brother*', in S. Holmes and D. Jermyn (eds) *Understanding Reality TV*, London: Routledge, 111–135.

—— (2004b) '"Reality goes pop!": Reality TV, popular music and narratives of stardom in *Pop Idol*', *Television & New Media*, 5(2): 147–172.

—— (2005a) '"Off guard, unkempt, unready?": Deconstructing contemporary celebrity in *heat* magazine', *Continuum: Journal of Media & Cultural Studies*, 19(1): 21–38.

—— (2005b) '"Starring ... Dyer?": Re-visiting star studies and contemporary celebrity culture', *Westminster Papers in Communication and Culture*, 2(2): 6–21.

—— (2006a) 'It's a jungle out there!: The game of fame in celebrity reality TV', in S. Holmes and S. Redmond (eds) *Framing Celebrity: New Directions in Celebrity Culture*, London: Routledge, 45–66.

—— (2006b) 'The "give-away" shows – who is really paying?: "Ordinary" people and the development of the British quiz show (1945–58)', *Journal of British Cinema and Television*, 3(2): 284–303.

—— (2007a) 'The BBC and television fame in the 1950s: Living with *The Grove Family* (1954–7) and going *Face to Face* (1959–1962) with television', *European Journal of Cultural Studies*, 10(4): 427–445.

—— (2007b) '"A friendly style of presentation which the BBC had always found elusive"? The 1950s cinema programme and the construction of British television history', in H. Wheatley (ed.) *Re-viewing Television History: Critical Issues in Television Historiography*, London: I.B. Tauris, 67–81.

—— (2008a) '"The viewers have ... taken over the airwaves"? Participation, reality TV and approaching the audience-in-the-text', *Screen*, 49(1): 13–31.

—— (2008b) *The Quiz Show*, Edinburgh: Edinburgh University Press.

—— (2010) '"Whoever heard of anyone being a screaming success for doing nothing?": "Sabrina", the BBC and television fame in the 1950s', *Media History*, forthcoming.

Hood, S. (1983) *On Television*, London: Pluto Press.

Hunt, L. (1998) *British Low Culture: From Safari Suits to Sexploitation*, London: Routledge.

Jackson, P. (2006) 'High maintenance, high performance: Talent in the UK and the US, and how to manage it', in M. Collins (ed.) *Shooting Stars: A Collection of Essays, Musings and Rants on Talent and TV in the Noughties and Beyond*, London: Premium Publishing, 17–28.

Jacobs, J. (2000) *The Intimate Screen: Early British Television Drama*, Oxford: Oxford University Press.

—— (2001) 'Issues of judgement and value in television studies', *International Journal of Cultural Studies*, 4(4): 427–447.

—— (2006) 'Television aesthetics: An infantile disorder', *Journal of British Cinema and Television*, 6(3): 19–33.

Jenkins, H. (2006a) *Convergence Culture: Where Old and New Media Collide*, New York: New York University Press.

—— (2006b) *Fans, Bloggers and Gamers: Exploring Participatory Culture*, New York: New York University Press.

—— (2006c) 'YouTube and the vaudeville aesthetic', *Confessions of an Aca/Fan*, posted November 20. Available HTTP: www.henryjenkins.org/2006/11/youtube_and_the_vaudeville_aes.html.

Jermyn, D. (2006) 'Bringing out the star in you?: SJP, Carrie Bradshaw and the evolution of television stardom?', in S. Holmes and S. Redmond (eds) *Framing Celebrity: New Directions in Celebrity Culture*, London: Routledge, 96–117.

Keane, J. (1998) *Civil Society: Old Images, New Visions*, Palo Alto, CA: Stanford University Press.

Kelly, L. (2010) 'Public personas, private lives and the power of the celebrity comedian: A consideration of the Ross and Brand "Sachsgate" affair', *Celebrity Studies Journal*, 1(1): forthcoming.

Kift, D. (1996) *The Victorian Music Hall: Culture, Class and Conflict*, trans. R. Kift, London: Cambridge University Press.

King, B. (1985) 'Articulating stardom', *Screen*, 26(5): 27–45.

Klevan, A. (2005) *Film Performance: From Achievement to Appreciation*, London: Wallflower Press.

Krutnik, F., and Neale, S. (1990) *Popular Film and Television Comedy*, London: Routledge.

Landy, M. (2001) 'The extraordinary ordinariness of Gracie Fields: The anatomy of a British film star', in B. Babbington (ed.) *British Stars and Stardom: From Alma Taylor to Sean Connery*, Manchester: Manchester University Press, 56–67.

Langer, J. (1997) 'Television's personality system', in T. O'Sullivan and Y. Jewkes (eds) *The Media Studies Reader*, London: Arnold Publishing, 164–172 (original work published 1981).

Lewis, B. (1986) 'TV games: People as performers', in L. Masterman (ed.) *TV Mythologies: Stars, Shows and Signs*, London: Comedia Publishing, 42–54.

Lewis, T. (2007) '"He needs to face his fears with these five queers!" *Queer Eye for the Straight Guy*, makeover TV, and the lifestyle expert', *Television & New Media*, 8(4): 285–31.

Littler, J. (2007) 'Celebrity CEOs and the cultural economy of tabloid intimacy', in S. Holmes and S. Redmond (eds) *Stardom and Celebrity: A Reader*, London: Sage, 230–243.

Lotz, A. (2007) *The Television Will Be Revolutionized*, New York: New York University Press.

Lumby, C. (2007) 'Doing it for themselves? Teenage girls, sexuality and fame', in S. Holmes and S. Redmond (eds) *Stardom and Celebrity: A Reader*, London: Sage, 326-340.

Lury, K. (1995) 'Television performance: Being acting and "corpsing"', *New Formations*, 26: 114–131.

—— (2001) *British Youth Television: Cynicism and Enchantment*, Oxford: Oxford University Press.

—— (2005) *Interpreting Television*, London: Hodder Arnold.

—— (2011) 'The "basis for mutual contempt": The loss of the contingent in digital television', in J. Bennett and N. Strange (eds) *Television as Digital Media*, Durham, NC: Duke University Press, forthcoming.

Lusted, D. (1998) 'The popular culture debate and light entertainment on television', in C. Geraghty and D. Lusted (eds) *The Television Studies Book*, London: Arnold Publishing, 175–190.

—— (2000) 'The glut of the personality', in C. Gledhill (ed.) *Stardom: Industry of Desire*, London: Routledge, 251–258.

McDonald, P. (2000) *The Star System: Hollywood's Production of Popular Identities*, London: Wallflower Press.

Maltby, R. (2003). *Hollywood Cinema*, 2nd edn., Oxford: Blackwell Publishing.

Mann, D. (1991) 'The spectacularisation of everyday life: Recycling Hollywood stars and fans in early television variety shows', in J. G. Butler (ed.) *Star Texts: Image and Performance in Film and Television*, Detroit, MI: Wayne State University Press, 333–355.

Marshall, P. David. (1997) *Celebrity and Power: Fame in Contemporary Culture*, Minneapolis, MN: University of Minnesota Press.

—— (2006) 'New media – new self: The changing power of celebrity', in P. D. Marshall (ed.) *The Celebrity Culture Reader*, London: Routledge, 634–644.

Medhurst, A. (1991) 'Every wart and pustule: Gilbert Harding and television stardom', in J. Corner (ed.) *Popular Television in Britain: Studies in Cultural History*, London: BFI Publishing, 59–75.

—— (2007) *A National Joke: Popular Comedy and English Cultural Identities*, London: Routledge.

Miller, T. (2007) 'Television food: From Brahmin Julia to working-class Emeril', in T. Miller (ed.) *Cultural Citizenship: Cosmopolitanism, Consumerism, and Television in a Neoliberal Age*, Philadelphia, PA: Temple University Press, 112–143.

Mills, B. (2005) *Television Sitcom*, London: BFI Publishing.

Moran, A., and Malbon, J. (2006) *Understanding the Global TV Format*, Chicago, IL: Chicago University Press.

Morley, D. (2005) 'Mass', in T. Bennett, L. Grossberg and M. Morris (eds) *New Keywords: A Revised Vocabulary of Culture and Society*, Oxford: Blackwell Publishing, 207–209.

Morse, M. (1986) 'The television news personality and credibility: Reflections on the news in transition', in T. Modleski (ed.) *Studies in Entertainment*, Bloomington, IN: Indiana University Press, 55–79.

Moseley, R. (2000) 'Makeover takeover on British television', *Screen*, 41(3): 299–314.

—— (2001) 'Real lads do cook – but some things are still hard to talk about: The gendering of 8–9', *European Journal of Cultural Studies*, 4(1): 32–39.

—— (2002) *Growing Up with Audrey Hepburn: Text, Audience, Resonance*, Manchester: Manchester University Press.

—— (ed.) (2005) *Fashioning Film Stars: Dress, Culture, Identity*, London: BFI Publishing.

—— (2008) 'Marguerite Patten, television cookery and the construction of post-war British femininity on television', in S. Gillis and J. Hollows (eds) *Home Fires: Feminism, Domesticity and Popular Culture*, New York: Routledge, 17–32.

Mulvey, L. (1989) 'Visual pleasure and narrative cinema', in L. Mulvey (ed.) *Visual and Other Pleasures*, Basingstoke: Macmillan, 14–26.

Murray, S. (2005) *Hitch Your Antenna to the Stars: Early Television and Broadcast Fame*, New York: Routledge.

Naremore, J. (1988) *Acting in the Cinema*, Berkeley, CA: University of California Press.

Neale, S. (1990) 'Questions of genre', *Screen*, 31(1): 45–66.

Negra, D. (2002) 'Re-made for television: Hedy Lamarr's post-war star textuality', in J. Thumin (ed.) *Small Screens, Big Ideas: Television in the 1950s*, London: I.B. Tauris, 105–117.

Nourry, D. (2005) 'Body-politic (national imaginary): "Lest we forget … mateship (empire) right or wrong"', *Continuum: Journal of Media & Cultural Studies*, 19(3): 365–379.

Oliver & Ohlbaum Associates (2008) *On-Screen and On-Air Talent an Assessment of the BBC's Approach and Impact a Report for the BBC Trust by Oliver & Ohlbaum Associates*, London: BBC.

Ouellette, L., and Hay, J. (2008) *Better Living through Reality TV: Television and Post-Welfare Citizenship*, Oxford: Blackwell Publishing.

Palmer, G. (2004) '"The new you": Class and transformation in lifestyle television', in S. Holmes and D. Jermyn (eds) *Understanding Reality Television*, London: Routledge, 173–190.

Peacock, S. (2006) 'In between *Marion and Geoff*', *Journal of British Cinema and Television*, 3(1): 115–121.

Pearson, R. (2011) 'Cult television as digital television's cutting edge', in J. Bennett and N. Strange (eds) *Television as Digital Media*, Durham, NC: Duke University Press, forthcoming.

Rayner, J. (2007) 'Live and dangerous? The screen life of Steve Irwin', *Studies in Australasian Cinema*, 1(1): 107–118.

Redmond, S. (2006) 'Intimate fame everywhere', in S. Holmes and S. Redmond (eds) *Framing Celebrity: New Directions in Celebrity Culture*, London: Routledge, 27–44.

Rogers, M. C., Epstein, M., and Reeves, J. L. (2002) '*The Sopranos* as HBO brand equity: The art of commerce in the age of digital reproduction', in D. Lavery (ed.) *This Thing of Ours: Investigating The Sopranos*, London: Wallflower Press, 42–57.

Rojek, C. (2001) *Celebrity*, London: Reaktion Books.

Rose, N. (1996) 'Assembling the modern self', in R. Porter (ed.) *The History of the Self*, London: Routledge, 224–248.

Rosen, S. (1981) 'The economics of superstars', *The American Economic Review*, 71(5): 845–858.

Sandon, E. (2009) 'Experimental television at Alexandra Palace: The BBC and its Light Entertainment programming', paper presented at *Télévision: Le moment expérimental de l'invention a l'institution (1935–1955)*, International Colloquium University Paris 8/l'Institut National de l'Audiovisuel, 27–29 May 2009.

Schickel, R. (1985) *Common Fame: The Culture of Celebrity*, London: Pavilion Books.

Sconce, J. (2000) *Haunted Media*, Durham, NC: Duke University Press.

Shirky, C. (2008) *Here Comes Everybody: The Power of Organizing without Organizations*, London: Allen Lane.

Skeggs, B. (1997) *Formations of Class and Gender*, London: Sage Publications.

Skeggs, B., and Wood, H. (2008) 'The labour of transformation and circuits of value "around" reality television', *Continuum: Journal of Media & Cultural Studies*, 22(4): 559–572.

Slide, A. (1996) *Some Joe You Don't Know: An American Biographical Guide to 100 British Television Personalities*, Westport, CT: Greenwood Press.

Smith, J. (2009) 'Titans of our educational system: Early stars of American Educational Television', paper presented at *Télévision: Le moment expérimental de l'invention a l'institution (1935–1955)*, International Colloquium University Paris 8/l'Institut National de l'Audiovisuel, 27-29 May, 2009.

Spigel, L. (1992) *Make Room for TV: Television and the Family Ideal in Postwar America*, Chicago, IL: University of Chicago Press.

Stacey, J. (1994) *Star Gazing: Hollywood Cinema and Female Spectatorship*, London: Routledge.

Staiger, J. (ed.) (1995) *The Studio System*, Piscataway, NJ: Rutgers University Press.

Sternberg, E. (2006) 'Phantasmagoric labor: The new economics of self-presentation', in P. D. Marshall (ed.) *The Celebrity Culture Reader*, London: Routledge, 413–438.

Stokes, J. (1999) *On Screen Rivals: Cinema and Television in the United States and Britain*, Basingstoke: Macmillan.

Strange, N. (1998) 'Perform, educate, entertain: Ingredients of the cookery programme genre', in C. Geraghty, and D. Lusted (eds) *The Television Studies Book*, London: Arnold, 301–312.

Taylor, L. (2002) 'From ways of life to lifestyle: The "ordinary-ization" of British gardening lifestyle television', *European Journal of Communication*, 17(4): 479–493.

Thompson, G. F. (1985) 'Approaches to "performance"', *Screen*, 26(5): 77–79.

Thumin, J. (2004) *Inventing Television Culture: Men, Women, and the Box*, Oxford: Oxford University Press.

Tolson, A. (1996) *Mediations: Text and Discourses in Media Studies*, London: Arnold.

Turner, G. (2004) *Understanding Celebrity*, London: Sage.

—— (2006) 'The mass production of celebrity', *International Journal of Cultural Studies*, 9(2): 153–165.

Turner, G., Bonner, F., and Marshall, P. D. (2000) *Fame Games: The Production of Celebrity in Australia*, Cambridge: Cambridge University Press.

Walters, J. (2008) 'Repeat viewings: Television analysis in the DVD age', in J. Bennett and T. Brown (eds) *Film and Television After DVD*, London: Routledge.

Wheatley, H. (2004) 'The limits of television? Natural history programming and the transformation of public service broadcasting', *European Journal of Cultural Studies*, 7(5): 325–339.

—— (2007) 'Introduction: Re-viewing television histories', in H. Wheatley (ed.) *Re-Viewing Television History: Critical Issues in Television Historiography*, London: I.B. Tauris, 1–14.

Williams, R. (1983) *Keywords: A Vocabulary of Culture and Society*, London: Fontana.

Ytreberg, E. (2002) 'Ideal types in public service television: Paternalists and bureaucrats, charismatics and avant-gardists', *Media, Culture & Society*, 24(6): 759–774.

Index